SOUTHERN REGION ENGINE WORKINGS

The prestige train was the up and down "Golden Arrow" worked by Stewarts Lane men. BR kept two 'Britannia' class Pacifics specially for the duty. No. 70004 *William Shakespeare* slows down to take the curve to Petts Wood at Bickley on 27th July 1955. Duty No. 4 is shown on the disc.

Brian Morrison

The branch line scene with the push and pull train at Hawkhurst, shortly before closure. The train would propel from Hawkhurst with the H class 0-4-4T at the rear. Maunsell set No. 609 was a conversion from main line steam stock. The engine duty, No. 304 (Sats), is displayed on the disc and would be a late turn duty for a Tonbridge engine and men.

SOUTHERN REGION ENGINE WORKINGS

C J Gammell

OPC

Oxford Publishing Co.

Dedication

To all the roster and list clerks who laboured by day and night over many years to make sure that the job was completed 'on time', and that the time sheet was correctly filled in with the relevant 'time and a half' on the appropriate pages.

First published in 1994.

A catalogue record for this book is available from the British Library.

ISBN 0 86093 510 8

Oxford Publishing Co. is an imprint of Haynes Publishing,
Sparkford, near Yeovil, Somerset, BA22 7JJ

Printed in Great Britain by Butler & Tanner Ltd, Frome and London

Typeset in Times Roman Medium

All photographs are by the author, unless stated otherwise.

Title page: Tunbridge Wells West locomotive shed in March 1961, with H class 0-4-4Ts in steam. No. 31005 was constructed at Ashford in May 1907 and withdrawn from service in September 1963. Steam was abolished on the Central Division in 1965, but the building still stands today.

J. Smallwood

References used

A/R = assisting required
A.N.R. = assisting not required
C. shunting = carriage shunting
E = empty stock
F = freight train
F. shunting = freight shunting
M = milk train
O/R = on rear
P = passenger train
P/O = pull out
Q = conditional
S.R.E. = shunt release engine
V = vans
‖ = light engine
xx = uncertain time

DUTIES	1–499	L. East
"	501–780	C. Div
"	100–465	SW. Div

(The 24-hour timetable was adopted by BR from June 1965.)

Contents

N class 2-6-0 No. 31873 passes Worting Junction with a heavy mixed freight to Southampton Docks on 19th June 1965. The engine was transferred to the South Western Division after steam was abolished on the Central Division in 1965 and was withdrawn in 1966.

Introduction

This is a publishing first – and there are not many authors who can say that, especially those of railway books. Engine workings or diagrams are the duties of the locomotive known as the locomotive roster. This is not to be confused with the American term 'loco roster' which is a locomotive list. The duty of the locomotive has to be worked out well before a new timetable operates.

The engine diagrams are published twice yearly with the working timetable in summer and winter. Steam engines have to work trains from one point to another and then go off on to the next piece of work, but they need fuel, water, attention to the fire and lubrication. Steam engines also have to face the right way round so they have to be turned on a turntable or triangle. The engines have to be released if they are shut in at terminal points. Either the engines push the train out themselves or are released by another engine. Having worked out the duties of the locomotives, the next stage is that of the driver and fireman's duties. The engine crews have different requirements, and conditions of service have been agreed and negotiated over many years between railway management and the local drivers' union representatives. Any alterations to the existing workings have to be agreed between management and locomen through their Local Departmental Committee and regular meetings are arranged to discuss new timetables and rosters. When the fixed working has been agreed the duties are published. The list clerk then puts the drivers and firemens' names onto the duties and these are then displayed on the locomens' noticeboard. A new list is compiled every week with the engine crews changing each week.

Engine workings or diagrams, not to be confused with the diagram book (the engineer's weight restriction book), were compiled by each railway company and by each region after 1948. The system became standardised by the British Railways Board in the late sixties and was known as 'Locomotive Programmes' which were issued at regional headquarters. Shown in this book are the regional locomotive workings from the Southern Region, as printed in the Southern format inherited from the Southern Railway and its predecessors. How far back in time printed engine workings were published is uncertain but the Southern Region alone of all of BR's regions was the only part of the system to publish its workings in printed book form. The engine workings were printed by a commercial printer twice a year and published just like any ordinary book. The Southern Railway inherited the system which is thought to have originated from the South Eastern & Chatham Railway, although the London, Brighton & South Coast Railway also had printed engine duties. There have been suggestions that the Great Eastern printed its own engine duties, but I do not know of any surviving books.

The Southern Region changed several times during its existence. From 1950 all lines west of Exeter became Western Region but in 1958 the former Southern lines beyond Exeter were transferred back to the Southern until 1963 when all lines west of Salisbury went back to the Western Region.

Three sets of engine workings are shown, to represent the three divisions of the Southern Region. The South Eastern Division (London East District) was the first part of the Southern Region to be modernised and dieselisation started in 1958 with stage one of the electrification in 1959. This was followed by complete eradication of steam by 1961 with stage two of the electrification scheme. To illustrate the steam age on the South Eastern the Winter 1957 London East workings have been selected, as that was the last year of full steam working before modernisation started. On the Central Division the 1960 winter workings are detailed, as this was the last year before dieselisation started to make heavy inroads into the steam workings. For the South Western Division the Winter 1966 workings are featured, as this was the last full year of steam working before complete abolition in July 1967. All the workings included are for the weekday timetable as these show a typical day rather than the odd weekends and also covers freight working, which could be just as interesting as the prestigious express passenger workings.

On the Central Division the duty numbers commenced at 500 so as not to confuse with the two adjoining divisions. All Southern locomotives had to carry the disc route headcode on the front of the locomotive. The engine duty number would normally be placed on the disc and at busy times the train number would be on the top disc, especially on bank holidays, when an abnormal service would operate. Regrettably most photographers could only be out on the lineside at weekends and bank holidays when the abnormal type of service was operated. The engine workings evolved over the years, no presiding genius inventing them from scratch so they gradually grew up as the traffic increased and alterations were applied.

In these documents we see the steam age in full swing, the labyrinthine world of engine workings which is still unknown to the public at large and little known to the average enthusiast. Here we see the nocturnal duties of the suburban freight and the obscure branch line as well as the Pullmans. The nation's freight trundles through from obscure goods depots. Where were Ewer Street, Brockley Lane, and Camberwell Goods? What was Grand Vitesse, Hole in Wall and the Kensington Belle? All have now gone forever, a relic of when the railways were the prime mover, not only of people but the country's freight.

LONDON EAST DISTRICT

(12hr clock used in 1957 workings)
STEWARTS LANE

Duty No. 1
7P/5F BB class
summer only.

Duty No. 2
8P MN class

	Stewarts Lane Loco	8.35am	‖
8.42am	Victoria	9. 0am	P
10.40am	Dover Marine	xx	‖
xx	Loco Yard	11.40am	‖
xx	Dover Marine	11.55am	E
12.10pm	Folkestone Junction	3.50pm	E
4. 5pm	Dover Marine	xx	‖
xx	Loco Yard	5.50pm	‖
xx	Dover Marine	6.10pm	P
7.50pm	Victoria (propel)	8. 8pm	E
8.12pm	Carriage Sidings	xx	‖
xx	Stewarts Lane Loco		

Stewarts Lane men take the morning working which is the Boulogne boat train running at 9.0am during wintertime. Dover men work the up boat train being relieved at 8.5pm at Victoria by Stewarts Lane men who propel the train into the carriage sidings.

The first Bulleid Pacific, No. 35001 *Channel Packet*, built at Eastleigh in 1941, is seen passing through Chatham on 30th March 1959. The station is being rebuilt for the electrification in June 1959. The engine was rebuilt shortly afterwards in August and withdrawn by BR in November 1964.

Stewarts Lane BB class No. 34088 *213 Squadron* leaves Dover Marine with the up "Golden Arrow" on 21st August 1960. This engine, rebuilt only four months earlier, became the pride of Stewarts Lane and worked VIP specials until electrification forced the engine's transfer to Nine Elms where it lasted until March 1967.

R. Joanes

The up "Golden Arrow" in Southern Railway days with brand new light Pacific No. 21C157 (in malachite green) later to be named *Biggin Hill*. The engine was built at Brighton in March 1947, renumbered 34057 in 1949 and scrapped by BR in May 1967. Duty No. 4 is shown on the disc.

A. W. Cawston

Duty No. 3
8P MN class

	Stewarts Lane Loco	9.32am	‖
9.42am	Victoria	10. 0am	P
11.32am	Dover Marine	xx	‖
xx	Loco Yard	12.45pm	‖
xx	Dover Marine	1. 5pm	P
1.20pm	Folkestone Junction	1.35pm	P
	(1.20pm ex Folkestone Hbr)		
3. 7pm	Victoria (propel)	3.30pm	E
xx	Carriage Sidings	xx	‖
xx	Stewarts Lane loco		

Stewarts Lane men have the up and down Calais boat train which runs at 10.0am down during British wintertime. A nice little number for Stewarts Lane men but they have to prepare their own engine first.

Duty No. 4
7P/6F class Standard

	Stewarts Lane Loco	12. 5pm	‖
xx	Stewarts Lane Carriage Sidings (O/R)	12.20pm	E
12.32pm	Victoria	1. 0pm	P
2.26pm	Folkestone Junction	3.27pm	E
	(3.10pm ex F.Hbr)		
3.42pm	Dover Marine	xx	‖
xx	Loco Yard	4.30pm	‖
xx	Dover Marine	4.58pm	P
6.30pm	Victoria (O/R)	6.52pm	E
7. 2pm	Stewarts Lane Carriage Sidings	xx	‖
xx	Stewarts Lane Loco		

Stewarts Lane men have this most prestigious train which is the celebrated up and down "Golden Arrow" all-Pullman train. The duty uses the region's two 'Britannia' class Pacifics kept specially for the job. The engine travels 'on rear' from Stewarts Lane so that it is the right way round for the 1.0pm departure.

Duty Nos 5-9
7P/6F class or MN & BB summer only

Duty No. 10
5MT class Standard

	Stewarts Lane Loco	7.25am	‖
xx	Stewarts Lane	7.40am	E
7.50am	Victoria (bank 8.35am)	xx	‖
xx	Carriage Sidings	9. 0am	E
9.10am	Victoria (bank 10.0am)	xx	‖
xx	Victoria	10.35am	P
1.10pm	Ramsgate	1.25pm	‖
xx	Loco Yard	4. 0pm	‖
xx	Ramsgate	4.15pm	P
7.23pm	Victoria (shunt/bank 8.35pm)	8.37pm	‖
xx	Stewarts Lane	9. 0pm	E
9.10pm	Victoria (bank 9.35pm)	9.38pm	‖
xx	Stewarts Lane Loco		

Stewarts Lane men start the duty which includes banking the 8.35am Ramsgate and the 10.0am boat train. Ramsgate men take over at 10.10am and work the engine home. Ramsgate men bring the engine up in the afternoon. Stewarts Lane men relieve at 7.45pm and propel the empties off of the 4.15pm Ramsgate into the sidings at Victoria and out again for the 8.35pm departure which is banked out. The engine then goes down to Stewarts Lane to collect the 9.0pm empties for the 9.35pm departure which the Stewarts Lane men bank out before finishing.

Duty No. 11
5MT class Standard

	Stewarts Lane Loco	10.25am	‖
xx	Stew. Lane Carr. Sidings (O/R)	10.40am	E
10.50am	Victoria	11.35am	P
2.14pm	Ramsgate	xx	‖
xx	Loco Yard	5. 5pm	‖
	Ramsgate	5.22pm	P
8. 7pm	Victoria (O/R)	8.20pm	E
8.30pm	Stew. Lane Carr. Sidings	xx	‖
xx	Stewarts Lane Loco	xx	‖

Stewarts Lane men bring the 10.40am empties up and are relieved at Victoria at 11.15am. Ramsgate men work the 11.35am home and the 5.22pm back as far as Faversham where they are relieved by Stewarts Lane men at 6.27pm who finish the job including the 'on rear' 8.20pm empties from Victoria to Stewarts Lane.

U1 class 2-6-0 No. 31900 heads a down special through Shepherds Well on 18th August 1956. Eight U1 class 2-6-0s were allocated to Stewarts Lane and were used for excursions and boat extras.

E. Wilmshurst

Duty No. 12
7P/5F WC class

	Stewarts Lane Loco	4.50am	‖
4.57am	Victoria	5.10am	P
8.34am	Ramsgate	8.55am	‖
9. 0am	Loco Yard	11. 0am	‖
11. 3am	Ramsgate	11.15am	P
2.11pm	Victoria (propel)	2.20pm	E
2.25pm	Carriage Sidings	2.50pm	E
2.55pm	Victoria (bank 3.35pm)	xx	‖
xx	Victoria	4. 0pm	E
4.10pm	Stew. Lane Carr. Sidings	4.35pm	‖
4.40pm	Loco Yard		

Stewarts Lane men start the duty and are relieved at Ramsgate at 8.42am by Ramsgate men who work round to Victoria at 2.20pm. Stewarts Lane men take over at 2.20pm and propel the stock into the sidings returning at 2.50pm and banking the 3.35pm to Ramsgate. The engine then backs onto the 4.0pm empties off of the 1.10pm ex Ramsgate and takes them back to Stewarts Lane.

Duty No. 13
5MT class Standard

	Stewarts Lane Loco	8.10am	‖
8.17am	Victoria	8.35am	P
10.56am	Ramsgate	11. 5am	‖
11. 8am	Loco Yard	12.55pm	‖
12.58pm	Ramsgate	1.10pm	P
3.49pm	Victoria (bank 4.0pm)	xx	‖
xx	Victoria	4.40pm	E
4.50pm	Stewarts Lane	xx	‖
xx	Stewarts Lane Loco	6.35pm	‖
xx	Stewarts Lane	6.50pm	V
6.58pm	Victoria (C)	xx	‖
xx	Carriage Sidings (steam heat)	8. 0pm	E
8. 5pm	Victoria (bank 9.0pm)	xx	‖
xx	Stewarts Lane Loco		

Stewarts Lane men have all the work, after arrival at Victoria at 3.49pm the engine banks the 4.0pm departure. After release the engine works the 4.40pm empties to Stewarts Lane. The engine then works a 6.50pm vans to Victoria and then heats the "Night Ferry" stock which is worked in at 8.0pm from the sidings. After banking the 9.0pm "Night Ferry" out (10.0pm in summer) the engine returns to Stewarts Lane Loco.

Duty No. 14
5MT class Standard

	Stewarts Lane Loco	7.30am	‖
7.37am	Victoria Carr. Sidings	8. 0am	E
8. 5am	Victoria (bank 9.0am)	xx	‖
xx	Victoria	9.35am	P
12. 6pm	Ramsgate	xx	‖
xx	Loco Sidings	3. 0pm	‖
xx	Ramsgate	3.22pm	P
6.12pm	Victoria (bank 7.35pm)		
	C. shunting at Victoria		
	Victoria	8.20pm	E
8.30pm	Stew. Lane Carr. Sidings	xx	‖
xx	Stewarts Lane Loco		

Stewarts Lane men work the engine into Victoria and bank the 9.0am boat train. Ramsgate men take over at 9.20am and work the 9.35am home. Ramsgate men bring the 3.22pm up to Victoria and are relieved by Stewarts Lane men who bank the 7.35pm and shunt a 7.47pm van from the carriage sidings to the Central Section. The engine then takes the 8.20pm empties down to Stewarts Lane off of the 5.40pm Dover Priory.

Duty No. 15
5MT class Standard

	Loco Yard	10.25am	‖
xx	Stew. Lane Carr. Sidings	10.40am	E
10.50am	Victoria (bank 11.35am)	xx	‖
xx	Victoria	12.35pm	P
3.22pm	Ramsgate	3.37pm	‖
3.40pm	Loco Yard	5.40pm	‖
xx	Ramsgate	6. 0pm	F
9.40pm	Faversham	10.35pm	F
12.58am	Herne Hill S.S.	1.10am	‖
1.31am	Stewarts Lane Loco		
	Work No. 16		

The Class 5 4-6-0 works the 10.40am empties up to Victoria, banks the 11.35am out with Ramsgate men relieving the Stewarts Lane men at Victoria at 10.50am and taking the engine home. Faversham men relieve at Margate at 8.37pm and work to Faversham where a second set relieves at 10.10pm and takes the engine to Stewarts Lane for No. 16 duty which they work until 5.25am.

Stewarts Lane had an allocation of BR Standard Class 5 4-6-0s which replaced the ageing 'King Arthurs'. The Class 5 4-6-0s, when made redundant by electrification, were sent to Nine Elms. No. 73083 is seen at Ramsgate on a Stewarts Lane duty on 28th December 1958. The locomotive is on duty No. 18 (Sunday) 9.35am Victoria to Ramsgate (14 weekdays).

R. Joanes

U1 class 2-6-0s were shedded at Stewarts Lane and covered special traffic including summer extras to Ramsgate. No. 31895 works an up Ramsgate train and is seen on Bobbing bank in the summer of 1959, prior to electrification.

Duty No. 16
5MT class Standard

	Off No. 15		
	Stewarts Lane Loco	3.10am	‖
xx	Victoria	3.30am	V
7. 4am	Ramsgate	xx	‖
xx	Loco Yard	9.10am	‖
xx	Ramsgate	9.22am	P
11.49am	Victoria (propel)	12. 0pm	E
12. 5pm	Carriage Sidings	12.13pm	‖
12.20pm	Stewarts Lane Loco	3.15pm	‖
3.22pm	Victoria	3.35pm	P
6. 8pm	Ramsgate	xx	‖
xx	Loco Yard	7.30pm	‖
xx	Ramsgate	7.45pm	P
10.26pm	Victoria (O/R)	10.50pm	E
11.05pm	Stewarts Lane	xx	‖
xx	Stewarts Lane Loco		

The Faversham set work the 3.10am‖ and are relieved at 5.25am at Faversham by Dover men who work to Ramsgate and home pass. Ramsgate men prepare the 9.10am‖ and are relieved at 9.22am by Stewarts Lane men who then have the rest of the work. The engine finishes 'on rear' from Victoria to Stewarts Lane carriage sidings (next door to the loco shed).

Duty Nos 17-44 NOT USED

Duty No. 45
3P D1 class 4-4-0
OFF No. 46

	Gillingham Loco	7. 0pm	‖
xx	Gillingham	8.59pm	V
11.52pm	Cannon St.	12.35am	V
12.43am	Holborn	1. 3am	‖
1.14am	Ewer St.	2.30am	‖
2.40am	Holborn	3. 0am	P
6.10am	Ramsgate	6.20am	‖
6.25am	Loco Yard	8.25am	‖
8.33am	Ramsgate	8.44am	P
10.22am	Chatham	10.35am	E
10.40am	Strood	xx	‖
xx	Gillingham Loco		
	Work No. 47		

Gillingham men start the duty and have most of the work except from 8.25am until 9.44am when the duty is worked by Faversham men. The 3.0am passenger from Holborn is a three-coach set with newspaper vans and is advertised to the public. The train runs via Greenwich and Strood.

The D1 class 4-4-0s were a successful rebuild of the old Wainwright D class. No. 1743 is seen here in Southern Railway days heading a down Ramsgate train through Bickley with a hotch potch of former SECR stock. The duty number 38 is displayed with the train number 139. The top disc on the smokebox door is upside down and the number 'Special 1' has not been removed from a previous working.

A. Harvey

Duty No. 46
3P D1 class 4-4-0

	Stewarts Lane Loco	1.20am	‖
xx	Stewarts Lane	1.40am	EBV
2. 0am	Kensington	2.45am	M
3.27am	Stewarts Lane (via Lud Hill)	4.25am	E
5. 0am	Cannon St. (via Greenwich)	5.48am	P
9.11am	Dover Priory	xx	‖
xx	Dover Marine		
	C. shunting 9.20am to 11.0am		
	Dover Marine	xx	‖
xx	Loco Yard	12. 5pm	‖
xx	Dover Priory	12.35pm	P
2. 6pm	Gillingham	xx	‖
xx	Loco Yard		
	Work No 45.		

Stewarts Lane men have the work until relieved at Gillingham at 7.23am by Gillingham men who finish the job off. Interesting working is the milk train to Kensington, empty stock working, and main line work with the 5.48am Cannon St. to Dover Priory which has a three-corridor set and two vans for newspapers.

Duty No. 47
3P D1 class 4-4-0
OFF No. 45

	Gillingham Loco	1.25am	‖
xx	Gillingham	1.42am	F
4. 8am	Herne Hill S.S.	5.12am	‖
5.30am	Ewer St. (F/S 6.30am to 8.20am)	8.20am	‖
8.28am	Cannon St. (6.6 ex Ram)	8.33am	E
8.47am	Ludgate Hill	8.58am	‖
9.10am	Cannon St. (7.19 ex Ram)	9.31am	E
9.40am	Ludgate Hill	9.50am	‖
10.0am	Cannon St. (7.9 ex Marg)	10.36am	E
11.25am	Stewarts Lane	xx	‖
xx	Loco Yard	12.30pm	‖
xx	Stewarts Lane	12.45pm	M
1. 5pm	Kensington (via C. Junction)	1.30pm	M
2.12pm	Stewarts Lane	xx	‖
xx	Loco Yard	3.40pm	‖
3.50pm	Victoria (via Lud Hill)	4. 6pm	E
5.21pm	Cannon St.	5.46pm	‖
6.38pm	Stewarts Lane (via Lud Hill)	7. 0pm	V
8.15pm	Rotherhithe Rd. (via Lud Hill)	9.20pm	V
10.22pm	Stewarts Lane	10.45pm	‖
xx	Herne Hill	11.20pm	V
11.33pm	Holborn	1. 5am	V
1.35am	Victoria	1.50am	‖
1.58am	Stewarts Lane Loco		

A variety of work for an elderly D1 or E1 class 4-4-0. Gillingham men work round to Herne Hill where they are relieved at 5.10am by Stewarts Lane men who have the rest of the duty. Interesting work includes a 1.42am freight up from Gillingham (1.5am ex Sittingbourne) and empty stock working out of Cannon St. as well as some shunting at Southwark Depot (next door to Ewer Street). The afternoon sees the D1 working Kensington milk, empty stock working and van trains to Rotherhithe Road.

D1 class No. A735 struggles out of Victoria with a SECR 'birdcage' set bound for Ramsgate in pre-war days. The train number board has been placed over the smokebox disc.

A. Harvey

Duty Nos 48-51 NOT USED

Duty No. 52
1PT H class

	Loco Yard	6. 0am	‖
xx	Stew. Lane Carr. Sidings		
	C. shunting 6.10am–3.30pm		
	Stew. Lane (via Lud Hill)	4.15pm	E
5.36pm	Cannon St.	6. 5pm	‖
xx	Stewarts Lane Loco		

Stewarts Lane men shunt the carriage sidings and work empty stock to Cannon St. via Ludgate Hill. A place that is difficult to describe nowadays but was approximately where the present City Thameslink station has been built. Two sets of Stewarts Lane men are utilised.

Duty No. 53
1PT H class

	Loco Yard	6.50am	‖
xx	Stewarts Lane	7. 8am	Gas Tanks
7.23am	Clapham Junction (Pig Hill)	xx	‖
xx	Clapham Junction	8.16am	P
8.24am	Kensington	8.33am	P
8.41am	Clapham Junction	8.46am	P
8.54am	Kensington	9. 0am	P
9 .8am	Clapham Junction	11.25am	HB
11.35am	Kensington	12. 0pm	HB
12.11pm	Clapham Junction	1.45pm	HB
1.55pm	Kensington	2.28pm	P
2.38pm	Clapham Junction	4.15pm	P
4.23pm	Kensington	4.36pm	P
4.46pm	Clapham Junction	4.50pm	P
4.58pm	Kensington	5. 6pm	P
5.14pm	Clapham Junction	xx	‖
xx	Clapham Junction (Pig Hill)	6. 5pm	Gas Tanks
6.20pm	Stewarts Lane	xx	
xx	Loco Yard		

More interesting work for Stewarts Lane men. The gas tanks are taken round to Clapham Junction. The Kensington passenger service is worked in the morning and afternoon, known by railwaymen as the "Kensington Belle", the afternoon trains run half an hour later on Mondays, Tuesdays and Wednesdays for post office workers. Gas tanks are replenished (gas for the restaurant cars) and horse boxes are run from Kensington to Clapham Junction on inter-regional transfers.

14

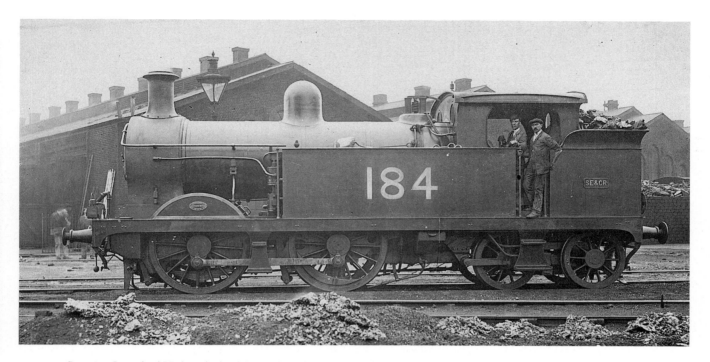

Stewarts Lane had H class duties (52 to 55) to shunt and work empty stock in the London area. H class 0-4-4T No. 184, later number 31184, is seen outside Longhedge shed (renamed Stewarts Lane in 1933) in SECR days. The locomotive, seen in the SECR wartime livery, was built at Ashford in 1915 and withdrawn by BR in 1958.

H. Gordon Tidy

Duty No. 54 NOT USED

Duty No. 55
1PT H class

	Stewarts Lane Loco	11.50pm	‖
12. 0mdt	Victoria		
	C. shunting 12.15am-11. 0pm		
	Victoria	xx	‖
xx	Stewarts Lane Loco		

Stewarts Lane men (three sets) have the work and take the engine 'on shed' midday for requirements.

Duty Nos 56 to 59 NOT USED

Duty No. 60
4P/5F N class

	Stewarts Lane Loco	9. 5am	‖
9.20am	Victoria (C)	9.50am	E
10. 7am	Eardley		
	C. shunting 10.10am to 3.10pm		
	Eardley	4.39pm	E
4.55pm	Victoria (C)	xx	‖
xx	Carriage Sidings	5.52pm	E
5.54pm	Victoria (C)	xx	‖
xx	Victoria (E)	7.26pm	E
7.36pm	Stewarts Lane Carr. Sidings	xx	‖
xx	Stewarts Lane Loco		
	Work No. 61		

Stewarts Lane men have all this work (two sets) which is on the Central District. After working the 9.50am empties off of the 8.24am ex Forest Row the engine shunts Eardley sidings for most of the day before returning to Victoria with a 4.39pm empties for the 5.9pm to Tunbridge Wells West. The engine pulls out the empty stock for the 6.10pm Brighton at 5.52pm and finishes with a 7.26pm empties to Stewarts Lane (off the 5.2pm ex Ramsgate).

Duty No. 61
4P/5F N class
OFF No. 60

	Stewarts Lane Loco	12.40am	‖
12.57am	Herne Hill S.S.	1.35am	F
4.45am	Faversham	6.44am	F
7.38am	Snowdown	7.50am	‖
8.10am	Dover Priory		
	C. shunting 8.40am to 11.50am		
	Dover Priory	11.50am	‖

(Continued)

12. 0 noon	Loco Yard	12.40pm	‖
1. 8pm	Snowdown	1.55pm	F
4. 5pm	Chatham Sidings	4.38pm	‖
4.46pm	Gillingham Loco	6.55pm	‖
7. 3pm	Chatham Sidings	7.35pm	F
9.10pm	Beckenham Junction	9.12pm	F
9.52pm	Waddon Marsh	11.15pm	F
11.52pm	New Cross Gate	12. 5am	‖
12.25am	Norwood Loco	1. 0am	‖
1. 5am	Norwood Down Yard	1.15am	F
1.25am	Norwood Up Yard	1.45am	F
2.22am	Battersea Yard	xx	‖
xx	Stewarts Lane Loco		
	Work No. 60		

Gillingham men work the 12.40am‖ which also conveys the crew for duty No. 70 and are relieved at 3.32am by Faversham men at Gillingham who work round to Dover. Dover men take the engine over at 12.40pm, and work to Gillingham Loco where Gillingham men work until 7.3pm. They are relieved by Stewarts Lane men at 7.3pm who take the engine over and work until relieved by Norwood men at 11.30pm at Norwood Junction who finish the job. The Stewarts Lane crew have the knowledge of the rare Birkbeck to Norwood Junction spur which brings coal trains into Waddon Marsh power station which burns Kentish coal.

Duty No. 62
4P/5F N class

	Stewarts Lane Loco	4.30am	‖
4.50am	Herne Hill S.S.	5.23am	F
7.15am	Chatham Sidings	7.57am	F
2. 5pm	Dover Town	2.15pm	‖
2.20pm	Dover Marine		
	C. shunting 2.45pm to 5.30pm		
	Dover Marine	5.30pm	‖
xx	Loco yard	7.30pm	‖
xx	Dover Town	8. 0pm	F
2.35am	Hither Green Sidings	xx	‖
xx	Hither Green Loco		
	Work No. 63		

Gillingham men take over at Herne Hill at 5.10am from Stewarts Lane men who have started the duty. Faversham men take over at Chatham at 7.15am and are responsible for the engine until Dover Loco. Dover men start the 7.30pm‖ and are relieved at Faversham at 11.15pm by Faversham men who are in turn relieved by Gillingham men at 12.20am who finish the job.

Opposite top: Stewarts Lane C and N class locomotives travelled all over the system (duties 60–74) and covered long distance freight and shunting work. Nos 31409 and 31293 are on shed during the afternoon of 26th May 1956. The C class 0-6-0 is a Bricklayers Arms engine.

Stewarts Lane engines were dispersed far and wide after the 1961 electrification of the South Eastern Division. N class No. 31812 built at Ashford in August 1920 was withdrawn in June 1964. This Stewarts Lane engine was transferred to Exmouth Junction in 1963, and is seen at Deepdene on 18th May 1962 with a Redhill to Reading train.

Duty No. 63
4P/5F N class
OFF No. 62

	Hither Green Loco	4.33am	‖
xx	Hither Green Sidings	4.58am	F
8.47am	Ashford Sidings	xx	‖
xx	Loco Yard	9.50am	‖
xx	Ashford Sidings	10. 5am	F
11.40am	St. Leonards W.M.	xx	‖
xx	Loco Yard	2.40pm	‖
xx	Galley Hill Sidings	3. 9pm	F
5.50pm	Ashford Sidings	xx	‖
xx	Loco Yard	7.20pm	‖
xx	Hump Sidings	7.45pm	F
xx	Ashford West Yard	8.40pm	F
11.36pm	Hither Green Sidings		
	Work No. 64		

Ashford men have all the work except the 8.40pm freight to Hither Green which is worked by Hither Green men.

Duty No. 64
4P/5F N class
OFF No. 63

	Hither Green Loco	2.47am	‖
xx	Hither Green Sidings	3. 7am	F
3.40am	Blackfriars	xx	‖
xx	Cannon St.		
	C. shunting 4.40am to 5.20am		
	Cannon St.	6.57am	P
8.32am	Gillingham	8.32am	P
10.17am	Ramsgate	10.25am	‖
xx	Loco Yard	4.30pm	‖
xx	Ramsgate	4.45pm	V
9.34pm	Sittingbourne	9.34pm	V
11.25pm	Stewarts Lane	xx	‖
xx	Loco Yard		

Gillingham men work the 3.7am freight and are relieved at 8.32am at Gillingham by Ramsgate men who work and dispose the engine. Faversham men work the 4.45pm vans to Sittingbourne where they are relieved by Gillingham men at 9.34pm who work the engine back to Stewarts Lane, change to No. 61 duty and work that to Gillingham, being relieved at 3.32am. The 4.30pm‖ is prepared by Ramsgate Shed Shunter.

<h2>Duty No. 65</h2>
4P/5F N class

	Stewarts Lane Loco	10.15am	‖
xx	Herne Hill S.S.	10.54am	F
3.40pm	Ashford West Yard	4.10pm	‖
4.19pm	Loco Yard	8.50pm	‖
xx	Ashford	9.19pm	P
10.18pm	Tonbridge	xx	‖
xx	West Yard	10.55pm	F
11. 0pm	East Yard	xx	‖
xx	Loco Yard	2.25am	‖
2.47am	Sevenoaks	3.25am	F
5.15am	Herne Hill S.S.	5.55am	‖
6.14am	Stewarts Lane Loco		

Ashford men take over from the Stewarts Lane crew at 10.35am in Herne Hill Sorting Sidings and work the engine home. Tonbridge men work the 8.50pm‖ off shed and work home. Stewarts Lane men work the 2.25am‖ off Tonbridge shed and take the engine back to Stewarts Lane at 5.55am.

<h3 align="center">Duty Nos 66-69 NOT USED</h3>

<h2 align="center">Duty No. 70</h2>
2F C class

	Stewarts Lane Loco	12.30am	‖
12.45am	Herne Hill S.S.	2.32am	F
11.26am	Gillingham	xx	‖
xx	Gillingham Loco	2. 0pm	‖
xx	Gillingham	2.22pm	E
3. 0pm	Strood		
	C. shunting 3.0pm to 5.25pm		
	Strood	5.25pm	‖
5.32pm	Chatham	6.20pm	P
7.1pm	Sheerness	7.10pm	‖
xx	Queenborough		
	F. shunting 7.30pm to 8.55pm		
	Queenborough	9.42pm	F

(Continued)

Stewarts Lane C class No. 31579, built in October 1903 and scrapped in October 1961, takes a rest on shed after working night freights (duties 70–74).

10.22pm	Gillingham	xx	‖
xx	Loco Yard	11.40pm	‖
xx	Gillingham	11.50pm	F
2.39am	Herne Hill S.S.	2.55am	‖
3.14am	Stewarts Lane Loco		

Work No. 73

A real mixture of work for the versatile C class which is worked by Stewarts Lane men as far as Fawkham where they are relieved by Gillingham men at 7.15am who take the engine home. Gillingham men start the 2.0pm‖ and have the work (two sets) until relieved by home going Stewarts Lane men at 12.15am at Chatham sidings.

Duty No. 71 NOT USED

Duty No. 72
2F C class

	Loco Yard	4.20pm	‖
xx	Stewarts Lane	4.35pm	E
5.14pm	Ludgate Hill	xx	‖
xx	Blackfriars	7.50pm	F
8.30pm	Hither Green	9.16pm	F
10.20pm	Herne Hill S.S.		
	shunting and trip working Camberwell, and Brockley Lane		
	Herne Hill S.S	xx	‖
xx	Ewer Street	xx	‖
xx	Cannon St. (Off 6.19am Ram)	9. 1am	E
9.21am	Ludgate Hill	9.45am	‖
9.55am	Cannon St.	10. 5am	E
	(off 8.20am ex Herne Bay)		
10.25am	Ludgate Hill	10.31am	E
10.55am	Stewarts Lane	xx	‖
xx	Stewarts Lane Loco		

Stewarts Lane men work the empties and shunt at Blackfriars. Hither Green men take over at 8.30pm, work the 9.16pm freight (on rear from Camberwell to Herne Hill) and are relieved at 12.45am by Stewarts Lane men who do a night freight to Camberwell and Brockley Lane. Stewarts Lane men finish off the duty in the morning which includes the engine taking a rest at Ewer Street where requirements are performed.

Duty No. 73
2F C class
OFF No. 70

	Stewarts Lane Loco	5.35am	‖
xx	Stewarts Lane	5.50am	EBV
6. 5am	Kensington (via Clap. Junction)	6.40am	M
7.25am	Stewarts Lane	8. 5am	‖
8.36am	Cannon St. (A/R)	9.31am	E
9.35am	Ludgate Hill	9.50am	E
10.15am	Stewarts Lane	11.40am	‖
12. 6pm	Herne Hill S.S.	12.28pm	F
3.33pm	Bromley South	4. 0pm	‖
4.40pm	Wandsworth Road	7.50pm	F
8.12pm	Camberwell (O/R)	8.15pm	F
8.22pm	Herne Hill S.S.	9.35pm	F
9.55pm	Stewarts Lane	xx	‖
xx	Stewarts Lane Loco		

Stewarts Lane men have this suburban work which includes the milk train for Kensington, empties from Cannon St. (assistance required) and a slow freight from Herne Hill to Bromley probably stopping off to shunt at Penge East and Beckenham. After shunting at Wandsworth Road the engine works a 7.50pm freight via Camberwell back to Herne Hill.

Duty No. 74
2F C class

	Stewarts Lane Loco	10. 2pm	‖
10.17pm	Herne Hill S.S.	10.32pm	F
11.14pm	Bromley South	1. 0am	F
2.24am	Herne Hill S.S. (including shunt)	6.12am	F
6.40am	Wandsworth Road	8.45am	F
8.55am	Battersea Yard	11. 0am	F
11.10am	Stewarts Lane	xx	‖
xx	Stewarts Lane Loco		

Stewarts Lane men have this night work which involves working freight in and out of Herne Hill sidings to local goods depots. Two sets used, a night and early turn.

19

Stewarts Lane had an allocation of ex-LBSCR E2 class 0-6-0Ts for shunting and local trip working (duties 75–76). No. 32100 is seen here in May 1956 shunting empty stock from the carriage sidings. The engine was withdrawn by BR in October 1961.

Right: Bricklayers Arms had four 'West Country' class duties for seven engines (duties 80–83) and these involved Cannon St. to Ramsgate commuter trains on weekdays. An up Ramsgate train is seen near Chestfield & Swalecliffe on a Sunday behind a rebuilt member of the class.

Duty No 75
3F E2 class

	Stewarts Lane Loco	9.45pm	‖
10. 5pm	Herne Hill S.S.		
	F.S. and trip working 10.5pm to 1.45am		
	Herne Hill S.S.	3.35pm	F
5.30pm	Stewarts Lane	xx	
xx	Loco Yard		

Stewarts Lane men work trip working in and out of Herne Hill sidings Camberwell and Blackfriars goods depots are visited.

Duty No. 76
3F E2 class

	Stewarts Lane Loco	5.35am	‖
xx	Camberwell	6.18am	F
6.23am	Herne Hill S.S.		
	F. shunting and trip working		
	Herne Hill S.S.	12.30am	‖
12.45am	Stewarts Lane Loco		

Stewarts Lane men work Camberwell goods and a trip to Blackfriars including pulling off the "Grand Vitesse" at Southwark Goods at 11.15pm (see duty No. 115).

Duty Nos 77–79 NOT USED

BRICKLAYERS ARMS

Duty No. 80
7P/5F WC class

	B'Arms Loco	4. 0pm	‖
4.20pm	Ewer St.	6.10pm	‖
6.15pm	Cannon St. (via Dover)	6.21pm	P
9. 9pm	Ramsgate	9.20pm	E
9.35pm	Margate	xx	‖
xx	Ramsgate Loco	5. 5am	‖
xx	Ramsgate (via Dover)	5.27am	P
8.35am	Charing Cross	10.38am	E
11. 2am	Grove Park	xx	‖
xx	B'Arms Loco		

Bricklayers Arms men work round to Ashford where they are relieved at 7.40pm by Ramsgate men who work the engine home. Ramsgate men sign on at 4.50am to start the 5.5am‖ and are relieved at Charing Cross at 8.50am by B'Arms men who finish the duty. The engine hides in Charing Cross sidings (by the Festival Hall) for two hours prior to working the 10.38am empties off the 8.25am ex Hastings. Pathways for light engines at that time of the day being non existent.

Duty No. 81
7P/5F WC class

	B'Arms Loco	2.30pm	‖
xx	Rotherhithe Road (P/O)	3. 0pm	E
xx	Surrey Canal Junction (O/R)	xx	E
3.25pm	Blackfriars (for 4.56pm Rams)	3.38pm	E
4.41pm	Cannon St. (via Fav)	5.44pm	P
8.1pm	Ramsgate	8.17pm	‖
xx	Ramsgate Loco	5.50am	‖
5.53am	Ramsgate (via Fav)	6. 6am	P
8.23am	Cannon St.	xx	‖
xx	Ewer St.	xx	‖
xx	Cannon St. (off 7.33am Rams)	10. 5am	E
10.27am	Rotherhithe Rd	xx	‖
xx	B'Arms Loco		

B'Arms men start the duty at 2.30pm‖ work the engine to pick up the stock which is pulled out at 3.0pm from Rotherhithe Rd. Engine then runs 'on rear' to Blackfriars then empty stock to Cannon St. After the 5.44pm from Cannon St. the B'layers Arms men are relieved by Ramsgate P & D men at 8.2pm who dispose the engine in Ramsgate Loco. Ramsgate men sign on at 4.50am and work the 5.50am‖ being relieved at Cannon St. at 8.25am by B'layers Arms men who finish off the rest of the duty.

Duty No. 82
7P/5F WC class

	B'arms Loco	6.25pm	‖
6.50pm	Charing Cross (via Dover)	7.8pm	P
9.57pm	Margate (with No. 488)	10.25pm	‖
10.40pm	Ramsgate Loco	6.24am	‖
xx	Ramsgate	6.45am	P
9.30am	Cannon St. (O/R)	9.52am	E
10.15am	Rotherhithe Road	10.30am	‖
10.44am	Blackheath (8.54am ex Willes)	11. 2am	F
11.25am	B'Arms	xx	‖
xx	B'Arms Loco		

B'Arms men start the duty off with the 6.25pm‖ up to Charing Cross but Ramsgate men relieve at 6.50pm to work the 7.8pm down to Margate running light at 10.25pm‖ coupled to duty No. 488 to Ramsgate Loco. Ramsgate men bring the engine up in the morning to Cannon St. where B'Arms men take over at 9.30am and work the engine 'on rear' to Rotherhithe Road before setting out for Blackheath for an 11.2am freight to B'Arms.

Duty No. 83
7P/5F WC class

	B'Arms Loco	2.30pm	‖
2.40pm	Rotherhithe Road	3. 0pm	E
3.25pm	Blackfriars O/R	3.38pm	E
4.41pm	Cannon St.	4.56pm	P
7.37pm	Ramsgate	7.52pm	‖
7.55pm	Ramsgate Loco	7.20am	‖
xx	Ramsgate	7.33am	P
9.36am	Cannon St.	10.35am	E
10.50am	Rotherhithe Road	xx	‖
xx	B'Arms Goods	11.50am	F
12.17am	Blackheath	xx	‖
xx	B'Arms Loco		

B'Arms men work the engine up to Cannon St. where Ramsgate men take over at 4.50pm and work the engine home. Ramsgate men bring the train up in the morning and are relieved at Rotherhithe Road at 10.50am by B'Arms men who finish the duty. The engine travels 'on rear' for the 3.38pm E Blackfriars to Cannon St. before setting out on the 4.56pm to Ramsgate.

Duty Nos 84-89 NOT USED

Duty No. 90
5P V class

	B'Arms Loco	3. 0am	‖
3.15am	London Bridge	3.40am	P
6. 6am	Hastings	6.10am	‖
6.17am	St. Leonards Loco	7.28am	‖
7.40am	Ore	8.12am	E
8.15am	Hastings	8.25am	P
10.30am	Charing Cross	xx	‖
xx	B'Arms Loco	3. 0pm	‖
xx	Rotherhithe Road P/O	3.30pm	E
xx	Surrey Canal Junction O/R	xx	E
3.53pm	Cannon St.	3.58pm	‖
4. 8pm	Charing Cross	4.20pm	P
6.10pm	Hastings	6.25pm	‖
6.32pm	St. Leonards Loco	7. 2pm	‖
7.11pm	Hastings	7.48pm	P
10.11pm	Charing Cross	11. 8pm	E
11.30pm	Rotherhithe Road	xx	‖
xx	B'Arms Loco		

Bricklayers Arms men work the engine round to St. Leonards. St. Leonards men take the engine as far as Robertsbridge where they are relieved at 9.0am by B'Arms men who take the engine home. In the afternoon B'Arms men have all the work including pulling out the empties from Rotherhithe Road to the main line at Surrey Canal Junction and working 'on rear' to Cannon St. prior to running light at 3.58pm to Charing Cross for the 4.20pm.

Duty No. 91
5P V class

	B'Arms Loco	2.55am	‖
xx	B'Arms Goods	3.20am	F
3.47am	Ewer St	xx	‖
xx	London Bridge (via Redhill)	4.50am	P
9. 7am	Margate	9.31am	‖
9.50am	Ramsgate Loco (with 492)	2. 0pm	‖
2.17pm	Margate (via Dover)	2.45pm	P
4.48pm	Ashford (via Redhill)	4.55pm	P
6.57pm	Cannon St.	xx	‖
xx	Charing Cross	7.51pm	E
8. 0pm	Cannon St.	xx	‖
xx	Ewer St.	10.30pm	‖
10.40pm	Charing Cross	10.50pm	P
12.55am	Dover Priory	xx	‖
xx	Loco Yard		
	stable for No. 96		

B'Arms men work the engine at 2.55am off shed and take loco coal to Ewer St. Loco sidings at 3.20am prior to working the 4.50am London Bridge to Margate via Redhill. Ashford men relieve at 7.33am and work to Canterbury West where Ramsgate men take over and finish the job. Ashford men (two sets) start the afternoon working with the 2.0pm‖ (D/H) and are relieved at Ashford by Dover men on the return at 12.16am. Dover men dispose the engine.

Duty No. 92
5P V class

	B'Arms Loco	3.50am	‖
xx	Rotherhithe Rd	4.20am	E
4.40am	Cannon St. (S.R.E.)	5. 0am	E
5. 9am	London Bridge	5.45am	P
8.25am	Hastings	8.34am	P
9.18am	Ashford	9.30am	P
10.22am	Tonbridge	10.30am	‖
xx	Loco Yard	3. 0pm	‖
xx	Tonbridge	3.22pm	P
4.16pm	Cannon St.	xx	‖
xx	Belvedere Sidings	xx	‖
xx	Charing Cross	6.28pm	P
8.47pm	Hastings	9.35pm	P
10.28pm	Ashford	xx	‖
xx	Loco Yard		
	stable for No. 94		

B'Arms men work the empties up to Cannon St. from Rotherhithe Rd, shunt round the empties at Cannon St. and work the 5.45am passenger as far as Crowhurst. Tonbridge men take over at Crowhurst at 8.7am and finish the duty off. Tonbridge men work the rest of the duty until 10.30pm when they are relieved by Ashford men who dispose the engine.

'Schools' class No. 30923 *Bradfield* arrives at Folkestone Central with empty stock for a Saturday evening train to Charing Cross on 21st May 1956. Bricklayers Arms had seven 'Schools'' duties for 14 engines.

G. Daniels

Duty No 93
5P V class

	B'Arms Loco	5.15am	‖
xx	R'hithe Road (for 7.0am Rams)	5.45am	E
6. 6am	Cannon St.	7. 0am	‖
7.14am	Charing Cross	8.20am	P
10.12am	Hastings	xx	‖
xx	St. Leonards Loco	1.25pm	‖
xx	Hastings	2.10pm	P
3.58pm	Charing Cross	xx	‖
xx	Ewer Street	xx	‖
xx	Charing Cross	7.20pm	P
9. 9pm	Hastings	9.15pm	E
9.18pm	Ore	xx	‖
xx	St. Leonards Loco		
	stable for No. 95		

B'Arms men take the loco off shed at 5.15am to work the 5.45am empties up to Cannon St. for the 7.0am Ramsgate and then follow the train out but run to Charing Cross for the 8.20am to Hastings probably spending time in the sidings at Charing Cross on the way. St. Leonards men take over at Robertsbridge at 9.57am and finish at St. Leonards. A late turn set of St. Leonards men take the engine off shed at 1.25pm‖, work the 2.10pm to Charing Cross, run light to Ewer St. Loco sidings to be out of the way of the evening down trains and complete the turn back to St. Leonards having taken the empties to Ore. Note that steam engines stable for the night - like horses.

Duty No. 94
5P V class

	stabled off No. 92		
	Ashford Loco Yard	2.10am	‖
xx	Ashford	2.33am	P
3.43am	Margate	xx	‖
xx	Loco Sidings	xx	‖
xx	Margate	7.58am	P
9. 4am	Ashford	xx	‖
xx	Loco Yard	3.50pm	‖
xx	Ashford	4.20pm	P
6.12pm	Charing Cross	xx	‖
xx	Cannon St.	7.26pm	E
7.46pm	Rotherhithe Road	xx	‖
xx	B'Arms Loco		

Ashford men have the work starting with the 2.33am from Ashford which is a connection off of the 11.50pm London Bridge. Ashford men take the 4.20pm to Charing Cross where they are relieved by B'Arms men who put the engine away after working the 7.26pm empties from Cannon St. to Rotherhithe Rd off of the 2.45pm from Margate. The engine and men have plenty of time to get to Cannon St. for the 7.26pm empties and could wait on the curve outside Cannon St.

Duty No. 95
5P V class

	stabled off No. 93		
	St. Leonards Loco	6.55am	‖
7. 5am	Ore	7.50am	E
7.53am	Hastings	8. 8am	P
9.50am	Cannon St.	xx	‖
xx	Ewer St.	xx	‖
xx	Charing Cross	12.20pm	P
2.22pm	Hastings	3.18pm	‖
3.25pm	St. Leonards Loco	4.13pm	‖
4.22pm	Hastings	5. 8pm	P
7.34pm	Charing Cross O/R	7.51pm	E
8. 0pm	Cannon St.	8.32pm	E
8.48pm	Rotherhithe Road	xx	‖
xx	B'Arms Loco		

Bricklayers Arms men have all the work and take the engine to Ewer St. for requirements prior to working the 12.20pm ex Charing Cross. After putting the empties away at Hastings the engine goes on St. Leonards loco prior to working the 5.8pm back to Charing Cross. The engine works 'on rear' on the 7.51pm empties from Charing Cross and the right way round on the 8.32pm to Rotherhithe Rd Carriage Sidings (now built upon).

Duty No. 96
5P V class

	stabled off No. 91		
	Dover Loco	5.30am	‖
5.48am	Shorncliffe	6.47am	V
6.55am	Folkestone Junction	7.35am	P
8.14am	Ashford	xx	‖
xx	Loco Yard (Turn)	8.50am	‖
xx	Ashford (7.59am Margate)	9.12am	P
9.53am	Hastings	10.10am	P
12. 4pm	Charing Cross	xx	‖
xx	Ewer St.	xx	‖
xx	Charing Cross	3.20pm	P
5.37pm	Hastings	5.50pm	‖
5.57pm	St. Leonards Loco	6.49pm	‖
6.55pm	Hastings	7.10pm	P
9. 3pm	Charing Cross O/R	9.20pm	E
9.45pm	Rotherhithe Road	xx	‖
xx	B'Arms Loco		

Ashford men work the engine round to Hastings where they are relieved by St. Leonards men at 10.5am. This interesting working shows the engine working a through train (the 7.59am Margate) from Ashford to Charing Cross via Hastings with the engine having to turn on Ashford Loco after working up from Dover. B'Arms men relieve the St. Leonards men at Robertsbridge at 10.38am and finish off the duty (two sets). The engine spends some time at Ewer St. sidings and finishes off by running 'on rear' from Charing Cross at 9.20pm to Rotherhithe Road with its own empties with late turn B'Arms men.

Duty No. 100
3P E1 class (4–4–0)

	Loco Yard	5. 0am	‖
xx	Rotherhithe Road	5.30am	E
6. 6am	Holborn S.R.E.	6.56am	E
7.12am	London Bridge	7.24am	P
8.52am	Ashford	8.58am	P
10.51am	Margate	xx	‖
xx	Loco Sidings	xx	‖
xx	Margate	11.44am	P
12.59pm	Ashford	1.15pm	‖
xx	Loco Yard	2.25pm	‖
xx	Ashford	2.48pm	P
3.30pm	Dover Priory (turn via Archcliffe)	5. 0pm	P
5.52pm	Ashford	7.42pm	V
	(C. shunting down side 6.0pm to 7.20pm)		
11.23pm	Cannon St.		
	(C. Shunting 11.25pm to 1.15am)		
	Cannon St.	1.34am	E
1.54am	Rotherhithe Rd	2. 0am	‖
2.10am	B'Arms Loco		

This is the celebrated duty 100, known to all railway enthusiasts as it gave some main line express running to a SECR 4-4-0. B'Arms men work the engine round to Ashford having worked the empties up for the 7.24am via Holborn where the engine has had to shunt round its own empties. Ramsgate men take over at 8.55am at Ashford and work round to Margate. Ashford men work the engine from 11.0am at Margate and are relieved at Dover at 4.35pm after turning the engine on the Archcliffe curve. Dover men work the engine from 4.35pm until 7.40pm when they are relieved by Ashford men who work to Paddock Wood where Hither Green men take over and work until 10.57pm where they are relieved by B'Arms men who finish the duty.

Duty No. 100 at Bricklayers Arms was a favourite with the enthusiasts as it gave main line work for the D1 and E1 4-4-0s, of which the shed had eight allocated for two duties. The 7.24am London Bridge to Ramsgate via Dover was a fast train with a light load. No. 31749 is seen at Sandwich on 20th December 1960.

Duty No. 101
3P E1 class (4-4-0)

	B'Arms Loco	9.50am	‖
xx	Rotherhithe Road (O/R)	10.20am	V
10.59am	Cannon St.	11.40am	V
11.46am	London Bridge (via Swanley)	12.44pm	V
3.52pm	Ramsgate	xx	‖
xx	Loco Yard	7. 0pm	‖
xx	Ramsgate (via Dover)	7.25pm	P
11.49pm	Holborn Viad.	12.30am	‖
12.55am	B'Arms Loco		

Faversham men relieve the B'Arms men at London Bridge at 12.30pm the engine having travelled up 'on rear' from Rotherhithe Rd on the 10.20am vans. Faversham men then take the train round to Ramsgate and dispose the engine. Ashford men work the 7.0pm‖ and are relieved at Ashford at 9.25pm by B'Arms men who work the engine back to B'Arms. E1 or D1 classes can work this duty.

Duty No. 102
3P L1 class 4-4-0

	B'Arms Loco	1.30pm	‖
xx	R'hithe Rd (forms the 3.20pm)	2. 0pm	E
3. 6pm	Charing Cross	3.28pm	‖
3.56pm	Cannon St. (via Faversham)	4.31pm	P
7.29pm	Ramsgate	xx	‖
xx	Loco Yard	8.55pm	‖
8.58pm	Ramsgate	9.10pm	P
12.29am	Charing Cross	12.50am	‖
1.13am	B'Arms Loco		

Here is main line work for the L1 class 4-4-0. The duty starts with the L1 taking the 2.0pm empties up from Rotherhithe Rd for the 3.20pm ex Charing Cross. The engine then works the 4.31pm Cannon St. via Faversham to Ramsgate. Faversham men have relieved the B'Arms men at 4.20pm and are relieved by Dover men at 6.11pm at Faversham. The Dover men take the engine to Ramsgate. B'Arms men take the 8.55pm‖ off shed and work the engine back to B'Arms.

Duty Nos 103-107 NOT USED

A close up of an L1 class 4-4-0, No. 31788, built in April 1926 by the North British Locomotive Company and withdrawn by BR in January 1960. The 15 4-4-0s were made redundant by the electrification of the South Eastern Division and the class was extinct by 1962. Bricklayers Arms had two engines for duty No. 102.

A. Harvey

The Class 2 2-6-2 tanks based at Bricklayers Arms (duties 108–109) worked empty stock and van trains in the London area. No. 41299 is seen passing Metropolitan Junction with a van train on 5th June 1960. Ewer Street loco servicing point was to the left of the engine.

R. Joanes

Duty No. 108
2P/2F Ivatt 2-6-2T

	B'Arms Loco	10.55am	‖
xx	Rotherhithe Road	11.23am	V
11.55am	Holborn Viaduct	xx	‖
xx	Charing Cross		
	shunting and empty stock working		
	Charing Cross		
	Cannon St. and Blackfriars		
	Blackfriars	8.30pm	F
9. 0pm	B'Arms (bank)	9.28pm	F
9.52pm	Forest Hill	9.56pm	‖
10.18pm	Rotherhithe Road	10.40pm	V
11. 3pm	Holborn Viad.		
	C. & F. Shunting 12.0mdt and trip		
	to Southwark Depot	4.50am	‖
	Holborn Viaduct	xx	‖
xx	Ewer St.		
	Work No. 109		

Bricklayers Arms men work the duty which is mainly empty stock working and carriage shunting. The engine does bank the 9.28pm freight as far as Forest Hill before returning to Rotherhithe Road for more shunting and van work. Three sets of men are used.

Duty No. 109
2P/2F Ivatt 2-6-2T
OFF No. 108

	Ewer St.	xx	‖
xx	Cannon St. (A/R)	9. 1am	E
9.21am	Ludgate Hill	9.33am	E
10. 0am	Stewarts Lane	xx	‖
xx	Stewarts Lane Loco	3.15pm	‖
xx	Stew. Lane Carr. Sidings (via Lud. Hill)	3.20pm	E
4.52pm	Cannon St.	5.23pm	‖
xx	Clapham Junction	7.15pm	V
7.59pm	Holborn Viad.	8.33pm	V
8.49pm	London Bridge		
	shunting 9. 0pm to 4.25am		
	London Bridge	4.30am	V
4.46am	Rotherhithe Road	4.55am	‖
5. 5am	B'Arms Loco		
	Work No. 108		

This duty is shared between Bricklayers Arms men and Stewarts Lane men and includes assisting the 9.1am empties from Cannon St. to Stewarts Lane. The engine does a shunting stint at Wandsworth Rd from 11.0am until 12.15pm before coming off shed at 3.15pm‖ for more empty stock and van working.

Duty Nos 110-111 NOT USED

Duty No. 112
1P H class
shunting B'Arms and Rotherhithe Road
from 4.30pm to 2.25pm

Bricklayers Arms men have the use of an H class for almost 24 hours, shunting empty stock at Rotherhithe Road. Three sets of men are used.

Duty Nos 113-114 NOT USED

Duty No. 115
4P/5F N class

	B'Arms Loco	3. 0am	‖
xx	Southwark Depot	3.48am	GV
8.10am	Dover Marine	xx	‖
xx	Loco Yard	11.45am	‖
xx	Dover Town	12.15pm	F
2.30pm	Sandwich	2.45pm	F
3.45pm	Dover Town	xx	‖
xx	Loco Yard	7.55pm	‖
xx	Dover Marine	8.15pm	GV
11.10pm	Southwark Depot	xx	‖
xx	B'Arms Loco		

This is an express freight working from Southwark Depot (next door to Ewer St.) of Continental "Grand Vitesse" freight to Dover. Gillingham men have the work going down with B'Arms men working the return in the evening. Dover men use the loco during the daytime to work a local freight to Sandwich and back.

Duty Nos 116-118 NOT USED

Duty No. 119
4P/5F N class

	Loco Yard	1. 0am	‖
xx	Bricklayers Arms Goods	1.40am	F
4.45am	Maidstone West	5.15am	F
5.45am	Paddock Wood	6.25am	F
7.55am	Maidstone West	8.15am	F
8.29am	Snodland	8.55am	F
11.25am	Maidstone West	2.34pm	F
5.14pm	Hoo Junction	8. 3pm	F
10.35pm	Paddock Wood	11.17pm	F
1. 2am	Hither Green Sidings	xx	‖
xx	Loco Yard		
	stable for No. 122		

An all night freight train worked by B'Arms, Hither Green, Tonbridge and Gillingham men. The engine spends most of the day working local freights and trip working in the Medway Valley and taking freights into Hoo Junction Yard. The engine is at Maidstone West for two hours to perform requirements on the loco siding which means attending to the fire.

H class duty No. 112 involved shunting at Rotherhithe Road carriage sidings (now an industrial estate) with Bricklayers Arms men. No. 1500 is seen in pre-war finery in Maunsell green with yellow numbering. The engine was built in November 1905 and withdrawn by BR in June 1961.

A. Harvey

N class No. 31870 is seen near Dunton Green on 15th May 1956 with a down freight. Bricklayers Arms had plenty of main line freight work and the engine is probably working a Hither Green to Ashford freight. Duties Nos 115–126 refer.

Duty No. 120
4P/5F N class
OFF No. 124

	B'Arms Loco	10. 2pm	‖
10.40pm	Angerstein Wharf	11.10pm	F
1.36am	Hoo Junction (via Strood)	2.15am	F
6.45am	Redhill (Ton Yard)	xx	‖
xx	Loco Yard		
	Work No. 124		

Another nocturnal freight working with B'Arms, Hither Green and Tonbridge men with Redhill men putting the engine away at Redhill.

Duty No. 121
4P/5F N class

	Loco Yard	12.30am	‖
xx	B'Arms	1. 0am	F
3.59am	Faversham	4.10am	‖
4.15am	Loco Yard	5.55am	‖
6. 0am	Faversham	6.14am	P
7.20am	Dover Priory (turn)	7.22am	‖
7.35am	Dover Marine	8. 0am	E
8. 4am	Dover Priory	8.16am	P
9.10am	Faversham	11.40am	F
11.57am	Whitstable	12.40pm	F
1.10pm	Faversham	2.30pm	‖
2.55pm	Canterbury East	4.20pm	F
9.42pm	North End Sidings	xx	‖
xx	B'Arms Loco		

Freight and passenger work on the main line to Dover via Faversham is shared by Faversham and Gillingham men. The loco turns via the Archcliffe curve at Dover to enable it to be facing in the up direction for the 8.16am passenger.

Duty No. 122
4P/5F N class
stabled off No. 119

	Loco Yard	3.30am	‖
xx	Hither Green (A. Section)	3.50am	F
4.30am	Bromley North	5. 0am	‖
5.16am	Hither Green Loco	2. 3pm	‖
2.13pm	Hither Green Sidings	2.28pm	F
5.13pm	Ashford Sidings	xx	‖
xx	Loco Yard	9.40pm	‖
xx	Ashford Hump Sidings	10. 0pm	F
11. 0pm	Paddock Wood	11.35pm	F
1.46am	B'Arms	xx	‖
xx	Loco Yard		

Hither Green men work an early freight to Bromley North with a spot of shunting. Ashford men work the 2.28pm freight via Maidstone East shunt at Ashford and Bricklayers Arms men work the engine back at 10.0pm stopping off to shunt at Paddock Wood and pick up a 10.40pm freight from Maidstone West.

Duty No. 123
4P/5F N class

	Loco Yard	10.25am	‖
xx	B'Arms (B. Section)	10.55am	F
11.20am	Hither Green Sidings	xx	‖
xx	Loco Yard	12.53pm	F
xx	Hither Green Sidings	1.18pm	F
2.38pm	Tonbridge West Yard	2.49pm	F
4.15pm	Hoo Junction	5.16pm	‖
5.25pm	Strood	6.57pm	F
7.20pm	Hoo Junction	xx	‖
xx	Dartford P/O 10.0pm F.	10.52pm	‖
11. 6pm	Crayford	11.54pm	F
1.35am	Blackheath	4.5am	F
4.31am	Hither Green Sidings	4.40am	F
5. 5am	B'Arms	xx	‖
xx	Loco Yard		

Bricklayers Arms men start the turn off at 10.25am and are relieved at Hither Green by Hither Green men who work to Tonbridge West Yard. Tonbridge men work the 2.49pm to Hoo Junction where they are relieved by Gillingham men who work round to Crayford at 11.6pm. B'Arms men relieve at Crayford and complete the duty. An interesting feature is the light run to Dartford to pull off a 10.0pm freight to release another engine.

Duty No. 124
4P/5F N class
Off No. 120

	Redhill Loco	8.50am	‖
xx	Redhill Up Yard	9. 5am	F
12.19pm	Reading Spur Junction	12.41pm	F
12.51pm	Scours Lane	xx	‖
xx	Reading Loco	3.50pm	‖
xx	Reading South	4.20pm	P
6.16pm	Redhill	xx	‖
xx	Up Yard	7. 5pm	F
8. 3pm	Norwood Yard	9.10pm	F

(Continued)

9.40pm	New Cross Gate	10. 0pm	‖
10.12pm	B'Arms Loco	11.25pm	‖
xx	B'Arms	11.45pm	F
11.59pm	New Cross Gate (bank)	12.36am	F
12.46am	Forest Hill	12.48am	‖
1. 7am	B'Arms	xx	‖
xx	B'Arms Loco		
	Work No. 120		

Redhill men work the morning freight and return passenger. Redhill men work round to the evening where the engine is left at B'Arms. B'Arms men finish off the duty from 11.25pm including banking the 12.36am to Forest Hill.

Duty No. 125
4P/5F N class

	Loco Yard	1.45am	‖
xx	B'Arms	2.10am	F
3.22am	Hoo Junction (turn)	4.22am	F
5.30am	Hither Green Sidings	xx	‖
xx	Loco Yard	10.25am	‖
xx	Hither Green Sidings	10.50am	F
3. 4pm	Faversham	5. 5pm	‖
xx	Loco Yard		
	Work No. 126		

Hither Green men start the duty and turn the engine on the Hoo Junction triangle before working the 4.22am freight back home. Hither Green men work the 10.50am freight to Chatham to be relieved at 1.10pm by Gillingham men who finish the job.

Duty No. 126
4P/5F N class

	OFF No. 125		
	Faversham Loco	6.13pm	‖
6.24pm	Teynham	7.17pm	F
9.40pm	Gillingham	10.40pm	F
2.15am	B'Arms	xx	‖
xx	Loco Yard		

Gillingham men have all the work which includes a spot of shunting at Teynham.

Duty Nos 127-131 NOT USED

Duty No. 132
2F C2X class

	OFF No. 134		
	Loco Yard	11.12pm	‖
11.24pm	B'Arms (B. Section)	11.40pm	F
1.20am	Lower Sydenham	2. 0am	F
2.45am	B'Arms (B. Section)	3.15am	F
4.30am	Dartford	xx	‖
xx	North End Sidings	5.30am	F
5.35am	Slade Green		
	F. shunting including a trip to Erith		
	Slade Green	8.50am	F
8.56am	North End Sidings	9.27am	‖
10.10am	B'Arms Loco	3.10pm	‖
xx	Rotherhithe Road	3.40pm	E
3.56pm	Blackheath (for 6.24pm Dover)	4.25pm	E
4.57pm	Ludgate Hill (for 6.14pm Rams)	5.29pm	E
5.54pm	Cannon St.	6.34pm	‖
6.50pm	Rotherhithe Road	7.35pm	E
7.54pm	London Bridge L.L.	8.15pm	‖
xx	Charing Cross (off 7.10pm Hast.)	9.20pm	E
9.45pm	Rotherhithe Road	xx	‖
xx	B'Arms Loco		
	Work No. 135		

Bricklayers Arms men have all the work with freights in the morning and empty stock in the afternoon. The C2X had to be steam heat fitted for the afternoon empty stock working. The most interesting working is that of the empty stock for the 6.24pm Cannon St. to Dover Priory which leaves Rotherhithe Road at 3.40pm and runs via Blackheath and Ludgate Hill before arriving at Cannon St. to form the 6.24pm. The pathways were so tight at that time of the day that empty stock had to be kept on the move to prevent upsetting the scheduled passenger services which were, of course, mainly electric multiple units. The empties go forward at 5.58pm from Ludgate Hill—see Duty No. 200.

Duty No. 133
2F C class
OFF No. 142

	B'Arms Loco	1.25am	‖
1.30am	B'Arms (N Section)	1.55am	F
4.10am	North End Sidings	4.40am	F
6. 8am	Plumstead	9.45am	F
	(F. shunting 6.10am to 8.20am)		
9.53am	Crabtree Sidings	10.41am	F
10.51am	Plumstead	11.15am	F
11.25am	B.B.H. Siding	12.35am	F
12.50pm	Plumstead	2.45pm	F
2.55pm	Crabtree Sidings	4. 5pm	F
4.19pm	Plumstead	12.0 mdt	‖
	(F. shunting 4.30pm to 11.55pm)		
12.45am	B'Arms Loco		
	Work No. 136		

Hither Green men have the work except the finish of the duty which is taken over by B'Arms men from 5.33pm at Plumstead where a lengthy shunting stint is involved.

Duty No. 134
2F C2X class
OFF No. 135

	B'Arms Loco	8. 5pm	‖
8.33pm	Elmers End	8.50pm	F
9.45pm	Hayes	10.45pm	F
11.52pm	Elmers End	12.0mdt	F
12.8am	Addiscombe	12.45am	F
2.27am	B'Arms (B. Section)	3. 0am	F
4.25am	Addiscombe (via Lewisham)	4.40am	‖
5. 7am	Hither Green	5.50am	F
6.15am	B'Arms	xx	‖
xx	B'Arms Loco	7.25am	‖
7.42am	Southwark Depot	xx	‖
	(F. shunting 8.0am to 12.0 noon)		
xx	Ewer St.	12.15pm	F
12.41pm	B'Arms	xx	‖
xx	B'Arms Loco	2. 0pm	‖
xx	Blackheath	5. 6pm	E
	(C. shunting 3.15pm to 3.45pm)		
5.48pm	Ludgate Hill	6. 5pm	‖
6.20pm	Ewer St.	6.56pm	‖
7.25pm	Angerstein Wharf	7.43pm	F
8.25pm	B'Arms (L. Section)	xx	‖
xx	Loco Yard		
	Work No. 132		

Nocturnal freights around the suburbs, shunting the "Grand Vitesse" stock at Southwark and empty stock working up from Blackheath are all part of the duty worked by B'Arms men. The engine has to shunt out the empty stock at Blackheath and heat the 5.6pm empties. Three sets of B'Arms men are used.

Duty No. 135
2F C2X class
OFF No. 132

	Loco Yard	3.37am	‖
3.47am	B'Arms (B. Section)	4. 7am	F
5.18am	Hayes		
	F. shunting including W. Wycombe trip		
	Hayes	9.33am	‖
9.40am	Elmers End	10.58am	F
11. 6am	Addiscombe		
	F. shunting 11.15am to 12.15pm		
	Addiscombe	xx	‖
xx	Rotherhithe Road	4.30pm	Gas-holders
4.35pm	B'Arms Goods	xx	‖
xx	Loco Yard		
	Work No. 134		

Bricklayers Arms men work freights and trip working on the Mid Kent line including a trip working from Rotherhithe Road to B'Arms with the gas tanks (used for cooking in the restaurant cars). Two sets of men used.

The C class roamed all over the system and worked nocturnal freights to suburban goods depots (duties 133/6/42). No. 1592, now on the Bluebell, is seen shunting at New Cross Gate in 1934.

H. N. James

C2X classes had plenty of suburban freight work at Bricklayers Arms (duties 132/4/5). The engines were a Marsh rebuild of the 1893 Billinton 0-6-0s with larger boiler and extended smokebox. These ex-LBSCR engines came to Bricklayers Arms after New Cross Gate shed closed in 1948. No. 32434 is seen at Eastbourne.

Walter Gilbert

Duty No. 136
2F C class

Off No. 133

	B'Arms	2. 0am	‖
xx	New Cross Gate (10.2pm ex Newhaven)	2.35am	F
2.52am	Blackfriars	3.10am	‖
xx	Hither Green Loco	4.40am	‖
xx	Hither Green Sidings	5. 5am	F
5.40am	Blackfriars	6.15am	‖
6.20am	Ewer Street	8.27am	‖
8.20am	Cannon St. A/R	8.33am	E
8.47am	Ludgate Hill	8.56am	E
9.28am	Victoria (propel)	9.42am	E
9.45am	Carriage Sidings	10. 5am	‖
10.27am	Holborn	11. 0am	V
11. 8am	Cannon St.	11.50am	‖
12. 0 noon	Blackfriars	12.35pm	F'Q'
1.12pm	B'Arms	1.20pm	‖
xx	New Cross Gate		
	F. shunting up Side 1.45pm to 3.30pm		
	New Cross Gate	3.30pm	‖
3.45pm	B'Arms Loco		

Work No. 142

Bricklayers Arms men have all the work which includes night freight working and the 8.33am empties from Cannon St. to Victoria Carriage sidings off of the 6.6am from Ramsgate. The engine is assisted from Cannon St. to Ludgate Hill. The engine also has a 'Q' freight from Blackfriars to B'Arms. Two sets of men are used.

Duty Nos 137 to 141 & 143 to 169 NOT USED

Duty No. 142
2F C class
OFF No. 136

	B'Arms Loco	7.39pm	‖
7.49am	New Cross Gate	8.17pm	F
8.56pm	Waddon Marsh	9.11pm	‖
9.24pm	Norwood Down Yard	10.30pm	F
10.41pm	Selsdon	11. 7pm	F
11.40pm	Lower Sydenham	12.18am	F
12.53am	Selsdon	1.34am	F
2. 8am	New Cross Gate	2.30am	‖
xx	Charing Cross	3.20am	F
4.15am	Lower Sydenham	4.25am	‖
4.30am	Catford Bridge	4.50am	F
5. 5am	Beckenham Junction	5.50am	EBV
6. 0am	Bromley South	6.20am	F
6.30am	Beckenham Junction	6.49am	‖
7.19am	Hither Green Loco	10.10am	‖
xx	Hither Green Sidings	10.30am	F
11.10am	Camberwell O/R	11.14am	F
11.21am	Herne Hill S.S. O/R	12.55pm	F
1. 3pm	Camberwell	1. 9pm	F
1.43pm	Hither Green Sidings	2. 5pm	‖
xx	Hither Green Loco	4. 0pm	‖
4.20pm	Bromley North	6.49pm	F
8. 7pm	Hither Green Sidings	xx	‖
xx	Plumstead	9. 8pm	F
9.55pm	B'Arms	xx	‖
xx	B'Arms Loco		

Another around the houses night working visiting some of the long lost goods depots of the Southern suburbs. B'Arms men have the engine round to 7.19am and Hither Green men have the engine from 10.10am onwards. The rare working must be the 3.20am freight from Charing Cross which must be rubbish or loco ash from the sidings. Rare track includes the Beckenham spur and the closed line from Woodside to Selsdon. The engine also works on rear from Camberwell to Herne Hill and back.

HITHER GREEN

Duty No. 170
4P/5F N class

	Loco Yard	3.30am	‖
xx	Hither Green Sidings	3.50am	F
4.58am	Hoo Junction	5.20am	‖
5.35am	Strood	8.46am	F
	(F. shunting 7.0am to 8.0am)		
	(Continued)		

(Duty No. 170 continued)

9.40am	Hoo Junction	10. 2am	F	
12.50pm	Maidstone West	12.50pm	F	
2.23pm	Tonbridge W. Yard	xx	‖	
xx	Loco Yard	4. 0pm	‖	
xx	Tonbridge	4.27pm	P	
4.41pm	Sevenoaks	5.15pm	‖	
5.30pm	Orpington			
	F. shunting 5.30pm to 7.30pm			
	Orpington	7.30pm	‖	
7.50pm	Hither Green Loco Sidings	10.55pm	‖	
xx	Hither Green Sidings	11.20pm	F	
3.35am	Ashford	3.35am	F	
5.35am	Dover Town	5.37am	‖	
5.42am	Loco Yard			
	stable for No. 172			

Hither Green men work the 3.30am‖ round to Strood at 7.30am where Gillingham men take over and do a spot of shunting before working the 8.46am freight round to Maidstone West where they are relieved at 12.50pm. Tonbridge men take over at 12.50pm and work round to Tonbridge Loco Yard. Hither Green men work the 4.0pm‖ off Tonbridge Loco and work the engine back to Hither Green Loco. Ashford men work the 10.55pm‖ and are relieved at Ashford at 3.35am. Dover men come on at Ashford and work the engine back to Dover.

Duty No. 171
4P/5F N class
OFF No. 181

	Loco Yard	5.28am	‖	
xx	Hither Green Sidings	5.53am	F	
7.35am	Paddock Wood	8.38am	F	
10.18am	Hoo Junction	12.50pm	F	
	(F. shunting 11.0am to 12.0noon)			
2.35pm	Grain	5.20pm	F	
7.38pm	Hoo Junction	8.12pm	‖	
8.54pm	Gillingham Loco			
	stable for No. 180			

Hither Green men work round to 11.30am at Hoo Junction when they are relieved by Gillingham men who have the rest of the work.

Duty No. 172
4P/5F N class
OFF No. 170

	Dover Loco	7.10am	‖	
xx	Bulwark Street	7.35am	F	
7.45am	Dover Priory	8.30am	V	
8.35am	Dover Marine	9.38am	‖	
10. 7am	Shepherdswell	10.40am	F	

(Continued)

Hither Green N class 2-6-0s (duties 170–181) had plenty of main line freight work, shared with the Q1 and N1 classes. N class engines were a favourite for night ballast work and No. 31826 is seen here on a track relaying job between St Mary Cray and Brickley on 14th December 1958.

R. Joanes

12.54pm	Hoo Junction	1.40pm	‖
2. 0pm	Gillingham Loco	8.12pm	‖
8.50pm	Northfleet	9.38pm	F
9.53pm	Hoo Junction	10.45pm	F
11. 5pm	Chatham Sidings	11.25pm	‖
11.38pm	Hoo Junction	12.30am	F
2. 0am	Tonbridge W. Yard	xx	‖
xx	Tonbridge Loco		
	Work No. 173		

Dover men work to Faversham where they are relieved at 11.45am. Faversham men work from 11.45am and work round to Gillingham Loco at 2.0pm. Gillingham men work the engine from 8.12pm‖ until 10.30pm at Hoo Junction. Tonbridge men come on at Hoo Junction at 10.30pm and finish off the job.

Duty No. 173
4P/5F N class
OFF No. 172

	Tonbridge Loco	7.45am	‖
7.57am	Paddock Wood	9. 0am	F
12.24pm	Hoo Junction	12.45pm	F
1. 5pm	Chatham Sidings	xx	‖
xx	Gillingham Loco	8.15pm	‖
xx	Chatham Sidings	8.55pm	F
9.13pm	Hoo Junction	10.25pm	F
11.30pm	Hither Green Sidings (O/R)	12.50am	F
1. 3am	St. Johns	1. 7am	F
1.15am	Blackheath	2. 0am	F
2.12am	Eltham W.H.	2.45am	‖
3. 0am	Blackheath	3.32am	F
5.52am	Plumstead	6. 0am	‖
6.48am	Hither Green Loco		

Tonbridge men work round to Paddock Wood where they are relieved at 8.0am by Gillingham men who take the engine home. Late turn Gillingham men work the 8.15pm‖ until 9.25pm at Hoo Junction when they are relieved by Hither Green men who complete the duty. The engine travels 'on rear' from Hither Green to St. Johns.

Duty No. 174 NOT USED

Duty No. 175
4P/5F N class

	Loco Yard	10.55am	‖
xx	Hither Green Sidings	11.20am	F
12.53pm	Paddock Wood	1.18pm	‖
1.31pm	Tonbridge Loco	3.50pm	‖
4.23pm	Otford	5.10pm	F
7.30pm	West Malling	9.15pm	F
12.26am	St. Mary Cray	3.45am	F
4.10am	Hither Green Sidings	xx	‖
xx	Loco Yard		

Hither Green men start the 10.55am‖ and leave the engine at Tonbridge Loco. Tonbridge men on at 3.35pm start the 3.50pm‖ and are relieved at Kemsing at 10.5pm by Hither Green men who finish the job.

Duty No. 176
4P/5F N class
stabled off No. 177

	B'Arms Loco	6.58pm	‖
xx	B'Arms (B Section)	7.28pm	F
7.54pm	Hither Green Sidings	xx	‖
xx	Loco Yard	9.35pm	‖
xx	Hither Green Sidings	10. 0pm	F
5.25am	Dover Town (via Faversham)	xx	‖
xx	Loco Yard	7.25am	‖
7.30am	Dover Marine	xx	‖
xx	Dover Town	10. 0am	F
1.50pm	Hoo Junction	3. 5pm	F
4.12pm	Hither Green Sidings	xx	‖
xx	Loco Yard		
	Work No. 177		

Bricklayers Arms men work to Hither Green. Hither Green men get the 9.35pm‖ ready for Stewarts Lane men who relieve at 9.45pm and work to Chatham Sidings where they are relieved by Gillingham men at 12.15am. Faversham men take over from the Gillingham men at 1.20am at Gillingham and are relieved by Dover men at 2.30am at Faversham who work and dispose. Dover men work round to Hoo Junction at 2.10pm. Hither Green men take over at Hoo Junction at 2.10pm and finish the job.

Duty No. 177

4P/5F N class
OFF No. 176

	Loco Yard	7.50pm	‖
xx	Hither Green Sidings	8.15pm	F
9.34pm	Tonbridge W. Yard	11.26pm	F
4.56am	Angerstein Wharf	5.30am	‖
6. 0am	Hither Green Loco	9.50am	‖
xx	Hither Green Sidings	10.12am	F
10.40am	B'Arms	12.25pm	F
12.55pm	Blackfriars	xx	F
xx	Ewer Street	xx	‖
xx	B'Arms Loco		

stable for No. 176

Tonbridge men (two sets) work round to Charlton where they are relieved at 4.40am by Hither Green men who work round to B'Arms where they are relieved at 12.0 noon by B'Arms men who take over and dispose.

Duty No. 178

5F Q1 class

	Hither Green Loco (tender first)	4. 0pm	‖
4.22pm	Crayford	4.53pm	‖
5.15pm	Eltham (Well Hall)	8. 8pm	F
	(F. shunting 5.45pm to 7.30pm)		
8.18pm	Blackheath	9.38pm	‖
	(F. shunting 8.20pm to 9.30pm)		
9.49pm	Woolwich Arsenal	10.18pm	‖
	(C. shunting 9.55pm to 10.5pm)		
10.22pm	Plumstead	10.58pm	F
12.50am	Feltham	1. 0am	‖
1.10am	Loco Yard	2. 0am	‖
2.10am	Feltham	2.35am	F
4.23am	Hither Green Sidings	4.35am	‖
4.45am	Loco Yard		

Hither Green men have all the work including the freight to Feltham for which Hither Green men have the route knowledge.

Duty No. 179 NOT USED

Duty no 180

4P/5F N class
stabled off No. 171

	Gillingham Loco	10. 8pm	‖
10.28pm	Hoo Junction		
	F. shunting 10.30pm to 12.40am		
	Hoo Junction (via Maidstone West)	1.15am	F
4.40am	Redhill	4.58am	‖
xx	Loco Yard	6.25am	‖
xx	Redhill	6.57am	F
7.44am	Tonbridge W.Yard (via Maidstone West)	9. 0am	F
2.27am	Plumstead	xx	‖
xx	Hither Green Loco		

Work No. 181

Gillingham men convey men and work the light engine at 10.8pm‖ to Hoo Junction and are relieved at 12.40am by Tonbridge men who work round until 8.52am at Tonbridge West Yard. Hither Green men take over from Tonbridge men at 8.52am and work the engine home.

Duty No. 181

4P/5F N class
OFF No. 180

	Hither Green Loco	7.18pm	‖
xx	Hither Green C. Section	7.43pm	F
9.16pm	Paddock Wood	10.55pm	F
11.25pm	Maidstone West	11.40pm	F
2. 5am	Hither Green Sidings	2.10am	F
2.15am	Up Side	2.25am	‖
2.30am	Loco Yard		

Work No. 171

Hither Green men work round to Paddock Wood at 10.30pm. Tonbridge men relieve at 10.30pm and work round to Hoo at 12.40am. Gillingham men relieve at 12.40am and dispose in Hither Green Loco.

The first Q1, later known as No. 33001, was Bulleid's 0-6-0 creation for heavy goods work. The ugliest engines ever built they started to appear from Brighton Works in 1942 and a total of 40 were eventually built. The engines were powerful and were classified 5F by BR. This is the official SR photograph of the new No. C1 at Brighton. The engine now resides on the Bluebell Railway where it is a great favourite in the winter as the cab is fairly enclosed. Hither Green had four members of the class.

Hither Green had a 'King Arthur' allocated to work duty No. 182. No. 30806 *Sir Galleron* is seen on shed in 1955, along with one of the shed's numerous diesel shunters.

R. Gillham

Duty No. 182
5P N15 class

	Hither Green Loco	3.15pm	‖
3.39pm	Ewer Street	5.34pm	‖
5.34pm	Cannon Street	5.47pm	P
7.47pm	Dover Priory	8.15pm	‖
8.23pm	Loco Yard	9.15pm	‖
xx	Dover Town	9.35pm	F
10.55pm	Ashford Sidings	11.20pm	‖
11.23pm	Loco Yard	12.45am	‖
xx	Ashford Sidings	1.15am	F
4. 0am	Hither Green Sidings	xx	‖
xx	Hither Green Loco		

Hither Green men work the only 'King Arthur' duty and their only passenger train, the 5.47pm from Cannon St. to Dover Priory. Ashford men take over at 7.10pm and work back to Ashford Loco where they are relieved by Hither Green men at 11.55pm who return the engine to Hither Green Loco after working the 1.15am freight.

Duty No. 183
5F Q1 class

	Loco Yard	4. 5am	‖
4.10am	Hither Green (C. Section)	4.30am	F
5.49am	Tonbridge W. Yard	6.30am	F
11.20am	Battle	12.10pm	‖
12.36pm	St. Leonards Loco	2.45pm	‖
2.53pm	Hastings	5.25pm	F
	(F. shunting 3.0pm to 5.0pm)		
9.53pm	Tonbridge W. Yard	10.40pm	F
10.45pm	Tonbridge Long Sidings	11. 5pm	F
12.45pm	Hither Green Sidings	xx	‖
xxam	Hither Green Loco		

Tonbridge men work the 4.5am‖ round to Battle where they are relieved at 12.5pm by St. Leonards men who work and dispose. A late turn set work the 2.45pm‖ off shed to Hastings where they are relieved at 4.40pm by Tonbridge men who finish the duty at Hither Green Loco.

Hither Green had the entire allocation of N1 2-6-0s in 1957, and the six engines had two duties allocated, (184–185), which included freight working on the Central Section. Following electrification of the South Eastern Division the engines were sent to the Central Division. The prototype N1 can be seen arriving at Chilworth on 18th May 1962, the engine having been built at Ashford in 1923 was withdrawn by BR in November 1962.

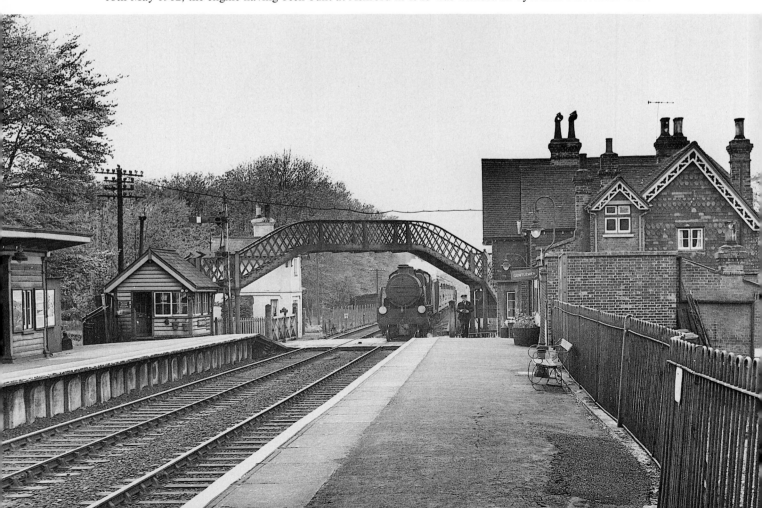

Duty No. 184

4P/5F N1 class

	Loco Yard	10. 3am	‖
10.10am	Hither Green Sidings	10.28am	F
2.15pm	Ashford Sidings	2.30pm	‖
2.33pm	Loco Yard (with No. 366)	4.10pm	‖
xx	Ashford		
	C. shunting 4.25pm to 5.0pm		
	Ashford	xx	‖
xx	Ashford Sidings	5.40pm	F
7.33pm	St. Leonards	xx	‖
xx	St. Leonards Loco		
	stable for No. 185		

Ashford men have the work until relieved by St. Leonards men at 4.30pm who work and dispose.

Duty No. 185

4P/5F NI class

stabled off No. 184

	St. Leonards Loco	3. 5am	‖
3.17am	Hastings	3.40am	F
6.20am	Tonbridge W. Yard	7.50am	F
7.55am	East Yard	xx	‖
xx	Loco Yard	9.30am	‖
xx	Tonbridge W. Yard	10. 0am	F
11.15am	Redhill Up Yard	xx	‖
xx	Redhill Loco	12. 2pm	‖
12.13pm	Merstham	1.23pm	F
	(F. shunting 12.15pm to 1.20pm)		
2. 6pm	Redhill Up Yard	xx	‖
xx	Redhill Down Yard	3.18pm	F
4. 5pm	Tonbridge W. Yard	4.25pm	‖
4.30pm	Tonbridge Loco	6. 8pm	‖
	(coupled to 301 to Sevenoaks)		
7.25pm	Hither Green Loco	8.25pm	‖
8.50pm	Blackheath	9.25pm	F
9.30pm	Kidbrooke	10. 7pm	F
10.15pm	Blackheath	10.56pm	F
11.19pm	B'Arms (A/R)	12.28am	F
1. 0am	Hither Green	xx	‖
xx	Loco Yard		

St. Leonards men start the 3.5am‖ and are relieved at Battle at 4.26am by Tonbridge men who have the engine until 7.50pm at Hither Green Loco (three sets). An interesing feature of this duty is the double headed light running from Tonbridge to Sevenoaks, scope for special traffic arrangements here. Hither Green men relieve at 7.50pm and finish the job including being assisted from B'Arms to Hither Green.

Duty No. 186

2F C class

	Loco Yard	3.35am	‖
xx	Hither Green Sidings	4. 0am	F
	(via Maidstone East)		
1.40pm	Ashford West	1.55pm	‖
2.0pm	Loco Yard	4.30pm	‖
xx	Ashford West	5.20pm	F
1.58am	Hither Green Sidings	xx	‖
xx	Loco Yard		

A slow pick up freight from Hither Green to Ashford via Maidstone East occupies most of the engine's time. Ashford men relieve the Hither Green crew at West Malling at 8.45am and have the engine until 9.30pm (two sets). Hither Green men relieve at 9.30pm at Maidstone East work and dispose.

Duty No. 187

2F C class

stabled off No. 194

	Stewarts Lane Loco	7. 5pm	‖
xx	Battersea Yard	7.37pm	F
8.38pm	Hither Green Sidings	10.15pm	F
12.58pm	Knockholt	2.25am	F
	(F. shunting 1.15am to 2.15am)		
5.0am	Hither Green Sidings	xx	‖
xx	Loco Yard		
	Work No. 188		

Hither Green men take over from a Stewarts Lane crew at 9.45pm and finish the duty.

Duty No. 188
2F C class
OFF No. 187

	Hither Green Loco	7.47am	‖
7.58am	Hither Green Sidings		
	CCE & MP shunting 8.0am to 12.0 noon		
	Hither Green Sidings	2.47pm	F
5. 3pm	Farningham Road	6. 2pm	‖
6.25pm	Gravesend West	8.15pm	F
11.38pm	B'Arms	12.30am	F
1. 0am	Hither Green Sidings	xx	‖
xx	Loco Yard		
	Work No. 194		

Hither Green men have all the work which includes a trip to Sole Street and shunting at Farningham Road as well as Gravesend West. Two sets of men are used.

Duty Nos 189-190 & 192-193 NOT USED

Duty No. 191
2F C class
OFF No. 200

	Hither Green Loco	11.15pm	‖
xx	Hither Green (B. Section)	11.35pm	F
1.45pm	Plumstead	3. 0am	F
3.46am	Brockley Lane	3.54am	F
4.30am	Hither Green Sidings	4.20am	‖
xx	Loco Yard		
	Work No. 195		

Hither Green men out on a night sortie visiting Brockley Lane, the ex Great Northern depot on the Nunhead to Lewisham line.

Duty No. 194
2F C class
OFF No 188

	Loco Yard	5. 0am	‖
xx	Hither Green Sidings	5.26am	F
7. 2am	Gravesend West		
	F. shunting and trip to Farningham Rd		
	Gravesend West	12.50pm	‖
1.38pm	Hither Green Loco	8.50pm	‖
xx	Hither Green Sidings	9.10pm	F
10.14pm	Hoo Junction (turn)	11.30pm	F
12.58am	Camberwell (O/R)	1.10am	F
1.17am	Herne Hill S.S.	2.25am	‖
2.45am	Stewarts Lane Loco		
	Work No. 187		

Gillingham men take over the engine at 5.0am and are relieved at Gravesend West at 7.50am by Hither Green men who work the engine back home. Stewarts Lane men work the engine from 8.50pm onwards. The Gravesend West branch closed to all traffic on 25th March 1968 from Southfleet.

Duty No. 195
2F C class
OFF No. 191

	Loco Yard	9.56am	‖
10.10am	Hither Green Sidings	10.16am	F
11.26am	Plumstead	12.38pm	F
2.30pm	Willesden	xx	‖
xx	Loco Yard	xx	‖
xx	Sudbury Sidings	7. 5pm	F
8.46pm	Blackheath	9. 9pm	‖
9.30pm	Hither Green Loco		

Hither Green men work this inter-regional transfer freight over to Willesden, an early set and a late set are utilised.

Duty Nos 196 & 198 NOT USED

Duty No. 197
2F C class
OFF No 195

	Loco Yard	12.30am	‖
xx	Hither Green Sidings	12.50am	F
1. 3am	St. Johns	1.10am	‖
1.15am	Hither Green	2.45am	F
3. 3am	Brockley Lane	3.13am	F
3.38am	Plumstead	4.25am	F
4.33am	Charlton	5.35am	F
6.45am	Plumstead	8.23am	F
8.37am	Woolwich Dockyard	10.10am	F
10.21am	Plumstead	11. 7am	F
11.28am	Angerstein Wharf	1.28pm	F
3.32pm	Hither Green Sidings	xx	‖
xx	Loco Yard	7. 3pm	‖
xx	Hither Green Sidings	7.20pm	F
8.13pm	Erith	xx	‖
xx	North End Sidings	10.28pm	F
	(F. shunting 8.50pm to 10.15pm)		
11.30pm	Camberwell (O/R)	11.38pm	F
11.45pm	Herne Hill S.S.	12.12am	‖
12.43am	Hither Green Loco		
	Work No. 200		

All night around the North Kent with Hither Green men (three sets) including a morning visit to 'Hole in Wall' sidings at Plumstead at 10.21am. B'Arms men take over from Hither Green men at 8.20am and work until 1.47pm.

Duty No. 199
2F C class

	Hither Green Loco	8.50am	‖
9.32am	Bickley		
	F. shunting 9.40am to 10.30am		
	Bickley	10.40am	‖
11.2am	Herne Hill S.S. (via Bfrs)	11.15am	F
12.4pm	Hither Green Sidings	xx	‖
xx	Loco Yard	2.18pm	‖
xx	Hither Green Sidings (B. Sect)	2.38pm	F

(Continued)

Chelsfield in Southern Railway days with C class No. A287 on a down passenger train which could be empty stock. The C class 0-6-0s worked freight and trip workings on weekdays but could be utilised for all sorts of specials at weekends, including excursions to the coast. BR No. 31287, built in May 1908, was withdrawn in October 1960 and was a Hither Green engine. The train could be a "Pankhurst" special.

H. Gordon Tidy

(*Duty No. 199 continued*)

3. 9pm	Crayford		4.36pm	F
9. 5pm	Hither Green Sidings			
	F. shunting 9.10pm to 5.0am			
	Hither Green Sidings		5. 0am	‖
xx	Hither Green Loco			

Hither Green men work the 8.50am‖ via St. Mary Cray then light to Herne Hill for a 11.15am freight to Hither Green via Blackfriars. Late turn men work the Crayford freight and night shunting in Hither Green Yard. Three sets of Hither Green men are used.

Duty No. 200
2F C class
OFF No. 197

	Hither Green Loco		9. 0am	‖
xx	Hither Green Sidings		9.20am	F
9.32am	Lee		xx	‖
xx	Mottingham		12.50pm	M
1.20pm	Clapham Junction		1.45pm	‖
1.55pm	Stewarts Lane Loco		4.30pm	‖
4.35pm	Stewarts Lane		4.45pm	E
5.32pm	Ludgate Hill		5.58pm	E
	(3.40pm ex R.Rd for 6.24pm DP)			
6.11pm	Cannon St. (P/O 2.45pm Marg.)		7.10pm	‖
xx	Southwark Depot			
	F. shunting and C. shunting L. Bdge,			
	Bfrs. and Southwark Depot		xx	‖
xx	Holborn		11.16pm	V
11.40pm	Victoria		12. 1am	‖
12. 8am	Stewarts Lane Loco		2. 0am	‖
2. 8am	Clapham Junction		2.35am	M
3.14am	Mottingham		4.35am	F
5. 8am	Crayford		5.18am	‖
6. 1am	Dartford			
	F. shunting 6.5am to 10.40am			
	Dartford		10.43am	‖
11.15am	Hither Green Loco			
	Work No. 191			

Hither Green men work freight to Lee and milk from Mottingham to Clapham Junction. Stewarts Lane men start with the 4.30pm‖ and work empties and shunting at Southwark Depot, London Bridge and Blackfriars. Hither Green men take over at 2.0am and work the Mottingham milk, finishing at 11.15am.

Duty No. 201
2F C class

	Hither Green Loco		3.45am	‖
4. 5am	London Bridge L.L.		4.20am	V
6.37am	Maidstone West		7.35am	P
7.59am	Paddock Wood		8.20am	P
8.29am	Tonbridge		xx	‖
xx	Tonbridge Loco		10.20am	‖
xx	Tonbridge W. Yard		10.48am	F
12.15pm	Maidstone West		1. 5pm	‖
1.30pm	Strood (coupled to 257)		1.42pm	‖
1.54pm	Gillingham Loco		4.42pm	‖
	(coupled to 257 to Gravesend Ctl)			
5.56pm	Dartford			
	F. shunting 6.0pm to 9.0pm			
	Dartford		9.20pm	‖
9.29pm	Bexleyheath		9.43pm	F
9.57pm	North End Sidings		xx	
xx	Erith			
	F. shunting 10.15pm to 10.45pm			
	Erith		11.38pm	F
1.11am	Hither Green Sidings		xx	‖
xx	Loco Yard			

Gillingham men work the 3.45am‖ off shed and take the engine up to London Bridge. Tonbridge men take over at 8.0am and work until 12.50pm at Maidstone West. Gillingham men work round from 12.50pm to 5.35pm including the light running with 257 duty. Hither Green men take over at Gravesend Central at 5.35pm and complete the job.

Duty No. 202 NOT USED

Duty No. 203
6F W. class

	Loco Yard	9.20am	‖
xx	Hither Green (A. Section)	9.50am	F
11.40am	Willesden	xx	‖
xx	Sudbury Sidings	1.50pm	F
3.37pm	Hither Green Sidings	xx	‖
xx	Loco Yard	11.55pm	‖
xx	Hither Green (A. Section)	12.15am	F
2.10am	Willesden	xx	‖
xx	Sudbury Sidings	4. 0am	F
5.52am	Hither Green Sidings	xx	‖
xx	Hither Green Loco		

Inter-regional transfer freights worked by Hither Green men. W class 2-6-4 tanks were not permitted to work passenger trains but were useful on heavy inter-regional freights.

Duty No. 204
6F W. class

	Loco Yard	10.32am	‖
xx	Hither Green (A. Sect)	10.52am	F
12. 4pm	Old Oak Common	1.35pm	F
3. 0pm	Hither Green Sidings	3.10pm	‖
3.20pm	Loco Yard	6.22pm	‖
6.53pm	Blackheath	7. 8pm	F
7.34pm	Bexleyheath	9.15pm	‖
9.25pm	Dartford	10. 0pm	F
10.24pm	Plumstead	11.25pm	F
1.30am	Willesden	xx	‖
xx	Sudbury Sidings	2.55am	F
4.36am	Hither Green Sidings	4.45am	‖
4.50am	Loco Yard		

Hither Green men working over to the Western Region as well as the London Midland on transfer freight. W class 2-6-4 tanks were not allowed to work passenger trains. Three sets of Hither Green men are used.

Duty No. 205 NOT USED

Duty No. 206
6F W. class

	Loco Yard	4.33am	‖
4.41am	Hither Green Up Yard	4.58am	F
6.35am	Willesden	xx	‖
xx	Sudbury Sidings	9.54am	F
10.48am	Blackheath	xx	‖
xx	Hither Green Loco	2. 5pm	‖
2.16pm	Hither Green Up Yard	2.30pm	F
4.35pm	Willesden	xx	‖
xx	Sudbury Sidings	5.55pm	F
8. 5pm	Hither Green Sidings	8.15pm	‖
xx	Hither Green Loco	10.15pm	‖
xx	Hither Green Sidings	10.35pm	F
11.58pm	Old Oak Sidings	1.30am	F
2.44am	Hither Green Sidings	xx	‖
xx	Hither Green Loco		

Hither Green men work Willesden and Old Oak transfer freights with the 5.55pm from Sudbury Sidings not returning to the Southern until after the evening rush hour is over. Three sets of Hither Green men are used.

Duty No. 207
6F W. class

	Loco Yard	5.25am	‖
xx	Hither Green Sidings	5.45am	F
7. 0am	Old Oak Common	10.10am	F
11.42am	Hither Green Sidings	xx	‖
xx	Loco Yard	2.33pm	‖
xx	Hither Green Sidings	2.53pm	F
4.10pm	Old Oak Common	6.44pm	F
8.12pm	Hither Green Sidings	xx	‖
xx	Loco Yard	10.58pm	‖
xx	Hither Green (A. Section)	11.18pm	F
12.30am	Old Oak Common	2.35am	F
3.51am	Hither Green Sidings	xx	‖
xx	Loco Yard		

Night transfer freight work to Old Oak worked by Hither Green men. Western Region engines could not work a reciprocal arrangement. Three sets of Hither Green men are used early, late, and night.

Hither Green had W class 2-6-4Ts to work duties 204 to 209 which involved inter-regional transfer freights from Hither Green to the London Midland and Western Regions. No. 31924 is seen 'on shed' on 11th September 1954.

Brian Morrison

Duty No. 208
6F W. class

	Loco Yard	4.57am	‖
5. 7am	Hither Green Up Yard	5.22am	F
7.10am	Willesden	xx	‖
xx	Sudbury Sidings	10.30am	F
12.20pm	Hither Green Sidings	xx	‖
xx	Hither Green Loco	7.37pm	‖
xx	Hither Green Sidings	7.57pm	F
9.45pm	Willesden	xx	‖
xx	Sudbury Sidings	11.55pm	F
1.40am	Hither Green Sidings	xx	‖
xx	Hither Green Loco		

Hither Green men work to Willesden and back via Nunhead and the West London line which was a very busy freight route. Two sets of Hither Green men used; an early, and late.

Duty No. 209
6F W. class

	Loco Yard	12.40am	‖
xx	Hither Green (C. Sect)	1. 5am	F
2.25am	Sevenoaks	3.45am	F
5.15am	Hither Green Sidings	6.15am	F
6.30am	Down Yard	xx	‖
xx	Loco Yard	11. 8am	‖
xx	Hither Green (A. Sect)	11.28am	F
1.14pm	Feltham	2.22pm	F
4.10pm	Hither Green	xx	‖
xx	Loco Yard		

Hither Green men do a night trip to Sevenoaks and return and a transfer trip to Feltham Yard on the South Western District. An early and night set are used.

44

Duty Nos 210 to 233

Diesel Electric shunters 350hp.
These versatile locomotives worked pilot duties
all over the district but were Hither Green
based for maintenance.

Duty No			
210	Plumstead	24hrs	shunt
211	Bricklayers Arms	24hrs	shunt
212	Hither Green	24hrs	shunt and trips
213	Bricklayers Arms	24hrs	shunt
214	Hither Green	24hrs	shunt and trips
215	Bricklayers Arms	24hrs	shunt and trips
216	Bricklayers Arms	24hrs	shunt
217	Bricklayers Arms	24hrs	shunt
218	Hither Green	24hrs	shunt
219	Hither Green	24hrs	shunt
220	Hither Green	24hrs	shunt
221	Hither Green	24hrs	shunt
222	Tonbridge	10am to 12.0mdt	shunt
223	Tonbridge	8am to 12.0mdt	shunt
224	NOT USED		
225	Gillingham	24hrs	shunt
226	NOT USED		
227	Hither Green	24hrs	shunt
228	Stewarts Lane	3.30am to 12.0mdt (204hp Drewry)	
229	NOT USED		
230	NOT USED		
231	Angerstein Wharf	6.30am to 12.0mdt	shunt and trips
232	Bricklayers Arms	7.0am to 12.0mdt	shunt
234	to 239 NOT USED		
240	Hither Green CCEs	8.0am to 4.0pm	shunt
241	to 244 NOT USED		

The appropriate drivers worked where the engine was based but a fireman had to ride the locos as second man when the engines ran light on running lines.

The P class 0-6-0T No. 31323 is seen shunting at Stewarts Lane on 26th May 1956, but the duty was soon taken over by a 204 hp diesel shunter on No. 228 duty. The engine is now on the Bluebell Railway who bought it from BR in June 1960.

GILLINGHAM

Duty No. 245
3P L1 class

	Gillingham Loco	3.30am	‖
3.42am	Strood	4.33am	P
5. 3am	Maidstone West	7.17am	P
8.38am	Redhill	xx	‖
xx	Loco Yard (turn)	10. 0am	‖
xx	Redhill	10.16am	P
11.48am	Reading South	11.55am	‖
12. 0 noon	Loco Yard (turn)	1.20pm	‖
1.25pm	Reading South	1.50pm	P
3.42pm	Redhill	4. 5pm	‖
xx	Loco Yard (turn)	7.25pm	‖
xx	Redhill (5.39pm ex-Reading)	7.44pm	P
8.23pm	Tonbridge	9.35pm	P
10.44pm	Maidstone West	12. 1am	F
2.18am	Strood (bank 2.28am F)	2.32am	‖
2.44am	Gillingham Loco		

An interesting working if ever there was one, with a Gillingham L1 class straying as far as Reading. Tonbridge men come on the engine at 3.50am and work round to Redhill. Redhill men take the 10.0am‖ off shed and work round to Tonbridge at 8.30pm (two sets) where they are relieved by a Gillingham crew who finish the turn including banking the 2.28am freight at Strood.

Gillingham had one L1 class duty (No. 245) but three L1s to cover it. The engines worked right through to Reading and back during which they had to turn three times. No. 31787 is seen here leaving Paddock Wood on 27th September 1958 on the Saturday version of the duty.

H class 0-4-4 tanks worked from Gillingham on duties 246 and 247. Here, H class No. 31322 is seen near Newington on a Sheerness to Gillingham stopping train, just prior to electrification on 13th June 1959.

Duty No. 246
1P H class P & P fitted

	Gillingham Loco	4.45am	‖
4.51am	Chatham		
	C. shunting 5.0am to 6.50am		
	Chatham	6.50am	‖
6.56am	Rochester	7.26am	E
7.28am	Chatham (via Sittingbourne)	7.40am	P
8.34am	Sheerness	xx	‖
xx	Dockyard	9.15am	E
9.20am	Sheerness	9.38am	P
9.58am	Sittingbourne	10.19am	P
10.39am	Sheerness (via Sittingbourne)	11.11am	P
11.50am	Gillingham	xx	‖
xx	Loco Yard	3.20pm	‖
3.45pm	Gravesend Central	4.10pm	P
4.46pm	Allhallows		
	works Allhallows branch until		
	Allhallows	8.49pm	P
9.26pm	Gravesend Central	9.42pm	‖
10. 7pm	Gillingham Loco		

Gillingham men work the Sheerness branch in the morning and the Allhallows branch in the afternoon including the Grain branch passenger.

Duty No. 247
1P H class P & P fitted

	Loco Yard	4.25am	‖
4.27am	Gillingham	4.41am	P
5. 8am	Gravesend Central		
	Work Allhallows branch until		
10.14pm	Gravesend Central	11. 7pm	P
11.36pm	Gillingham	xx	‖
xx	Loco Yard		

Gillingham men work the Allhallows branch from Gravesend Central. The branch closed to passengers on 4th December 1961. Grain is still used by oil trains. Three sets of men were used.

Duty Nos 248 & 249 NOT USED

Duty No. 250
4P/5F N class

	Loco Yard	2. 0am	‖
xx	Gillingham	2.22am	F
4. 0am	Northfleet	5.30am	F
7. 2am	Gillingham	xx	‖
xx	Loco Yard	10.20am	‖
xx	Maidstone West	11.30am	F
12.48pm	Hoo Junction	xx	‖
xx	Gillingham Loco	2.33pm	‖
	(coupled to 444 to Rochester)		
3.18pm	Hoo Junction	3.34pm	F
4.52pm	Maidstone West	6. 5pm	‖
6.12pm	Aylesford	8. 5pm	F
9.23pm	Hoo Junction	10.15pm	F
10.50pm	Rainham	xx	‖
xx	Gillingham Loco		

Gillingham men work North Kent freights and go off shed at 2.33pm‖ coupled light with No. 444, a Dover 4MT 2-6-4 tank. Three sets used.

Duty Nos 251 & 252 NOT USED

Duty No. 253
2F C class
OFF No. 254

	Gillingham Loco	9.50am	‖
xx	Gillingham	10.10am	F
11.42am	Hoo Junction		
	F. shunting 12.15pm to 8.50pm		
	Hoo Junction	9. 5pm	F
9.37pm	Chatham Sidings	10. 0pm	‖
10.10pm	Gillingham Loco		
	Work No. 255		

Gillingham men work freights to Hoo Junction and shunt in the marshalling yard. Two sets of men are used, one early and one late.

C class 0-6-0s worked from Gillingham on freights which included a stint on the Allhallows branch, on passenger and freight work. No. 31689 is seen at Allhallows on the last train on 3rd December 1961.

R. Joanes

Duty No. 254
2F C class
OFF No. 256

	Hither Green Loco	10.50pm	‖
11.22pm	Herne Hill S.S.	11.40pm	F
1.55am	Chatham Sidings	xx	‖
xx	Gillingham Loco	3. 0am	‖
3.10am	Chatham Sidings	3.45am	F
4.35am	Queenborough		
	F. shunting 4.45am to 7.40am		
	Queenborough	7.40am	‖
8.35am	Gillingham Loco		
	Work No. 253		

Hither Green men work through the night, being relieved by Gillingham men who work the 3.0am‖ and complete the duty at 8.35am in Gillingham Loco.

Duty No. 255
2F C class
OFF No. 253

	Gillingham Loco	2.25am	‖
xx	Hoo Junction	3.10am	F
4.55am	Hither Green Sidings	xx	‖
xx	Loco Yard	11. 0am	‖
xx	Hither Green (B. Sect)	11.20am	F
12.27pm	Plumstead	2. 9pm	F
	(F. shunting 12.30pm to 2.0pm)		
2.31pm	Angerstein Wharf		
	CCE shunting 2.40pm to 3.40pm		
	Angerstein Wharf	3.45pm	‖
4.12pm	Hither Green Loco	6.45pm	‖
xx	Hither Green (B. Sect)	7. 5pm	F
7.23pm	Mottingham		
	F. shunting 7.25pm to 9.55pm		
	Mottingham	9.58pm	‖
10. 8pm	Lee	10.30pm	F
2.50am	Hoo Junction	3.38am	‖
4. 3am	Gillingham Loco		
	Work No. 257		

Hither Green men relieve the Gillingham men at 5.10am and work round to Plumstead at 1.47pm. B'Arms men take over at Plumstead and work to Charlton where Hither Green men come back on at 2.17pm, and work until relieved at 10.8pm by B'Arms men. Gillingham men take over at Crayford at 11.6pm and work the engine home. The 3.38am‖ from Hoo Junction also conveys staff.

Duty No. 256
2F C class
OFF No. 258

	Gillingham Loco	1. 3am	‖
1.30am	Hoo Junction		
	F. shunting 1.40am to 4.30am		
	Hoo Junction	4.38am	F
6.55am	Allhallows	7. 5am	P
7.45am	Gravesend Central	8.56am	P
9.30am	Allhallows	9.48am	P
10.29am	Gravesend Central	10.47am	‖
11.25am	Hither Green Loco	1.15pm	‖
1.20pm	Hither Green (A. Section)	1.35pm	F
1.53pm	Brockley Lane	2. 3pm	F
2.15pm	Blackheath		
	F. & C. shunting 2.15pm to 3.45pm		
	Blackheath	3.58pm	‖
4.18pm	Erith	7.10pm	F
	(F. shunting 5.0pm to 6.15pm)		
8.30pm	Hither Green Sidings	xx	‖
xx	Loco Yard		
	Work No. 254		

Gillingham men have the opportunity of freight and passenger work on the Allhallows branch. Hither Green men work the branch from 8.45am and finish off with freights on the late turn.

Duty No. 257
2F C class
OFF No. 255

	Loco Yard	4.55am	‖
4.58am	Gillingham	5.25am	F
7.22am	Teynham	8. 0am	‖
8.10am	Faversham Loco (turn)	8.25am	‖
xx	Faversham	8.48am	P
9.29am	Chatham	xx	‖
xx	Hoo Junction	11. 2am	F
1.35pm	Strood (coupled to 201)	1.42pm	‖
1.54pm	Gillingham Loco (coupled to 201)	4.42pm	‖
5.20pm	Gravesend Central	5.39pm	P
6.16pm	Allhallows	7. 0pm	F
8.45pm	Hoo Junction	10.45pm	F
11.11pm	Littlebrook Sidings	11.42pm	F
3. 3am	Dartford	4. 0am	F
4.30am	Hoo Junction	4.40am	‖
5. 1am	Gillingham	xx	‖
xx	Loco Yard		

Gillingham men have all the work after 8.25am when they relieve Faversham men who have turned the engine to work the 8.48am passenger. Passenger and freight work follows on the late turn on the Allhallows branch. The engine runs light coupled to another C class (201 duty) at 1.42pm and 4.42pm.

Duty No. 258
2F C class
OFF No. 257

	Loco Yard	9.12am	‖
9.22am	Chatham Sidings	9.55am	F
10.49am	Queenborough	11.33am	F
12.9pm	Sittingbourne	1.55pm	P
2.20pm	Sheerness	3. 2pm	P
3.21pm	Sittingbourne		
	F. shunting 3.50pm to 6.20pm		
	Sittingbourne	6.39pm	‖
6.57pm	Gillingham Loco		
	Work No. 256		

Gillingham men work round to Queenborough at 10.50am where Faversham men take over for a stint on the Sheerness branch. Gillingham men relieve at Sittingbourne at 6.5pm work and dispose.

Duty No. 259
2F C class

	Gillingham Loco	6.30am	‖
xx	Chatham		
	C. shunting 6.50am to 7.20am		
	dockyard trip working and shunting to 5.30pm		
	Chatham	xx	‖
xx	Gillingham Loco		

Local shunting of empty stock and freight trips to Chatham Dockyard occupy this C class duty with Gillingham men (three sets).

FAVERSHAM

Duty No. 260
4P/3F U1 class

	Loco Yard	2.15am	‖
xx	Faversham	2.30am	F
5.43am	Hoo Junction	7. 6am	F
7.19am	Strood	7.32am	‖
7.44am	Hoo Junction	8.40am	F
9. 2am	Chatham Sidings	9.42am	‖
9.52am	Gillingham Loco	10.57am	‖
11.20am	Hoo Junction	11.40am	F
12.45pm	Hither Green Sidings	xx	‖
xx	Hither Green Loco	2.15pm	‖
xx	St. Johns	2.53pm	V
3. 6pm	Southwark Depot	xx	‖
xx	Ewer St.	xx	‖
xx	Cannon St.	5.18pm	P
8. 6pm	Dover Priory	8. 8pm	‖

(Continued)

8.15pm	Loco Yard	9.40pm	‖
xx	Dover Marine	9.50pm	E
9.55pm	Dover Priory		
	C. shunting 10.5pm to 10.35pm		
	Dover Priory	10.47pm	P
11.38pm	Faversham	xx	‖
xx	Loco Yard		

Faversham men start the duty but Gillingham men take over at 4.5am and work round until 7.30am at Strood when Hither Green men take over. Hither Green men work the loco back to Gillingham. Gillingham men take the 10.57am‖ off shed and change with Hither Green men at Hoo Junction at 11.30am. Hither Green men work round until relief at Cannon St. where Gillingham men take over at 4.50pm, work the 5.18pm passenger to Gillingham and are relieved at 6.18pm. Dover men finish off the rest of the duty.

Chatham Dockyard was shunted by a C class (duty No. 259). On this occasion a railtour has visited the branch behind an H class, No. 31177, and 350 hp diesel shunter No. D3721. The 350 hp shunters worked the Gillingham shunts on duty No. 225. The H class locomotives worked the Allhallows push and pull trains.

Faversham had two U1 class duties on weekdays, working freights in the morning and passenger trains in the afternoon. Here, a U1 2-6-0, possibly a Stewarts Lane engine, passes Sydenham Hill with an up Ramsgate train on 8th June 1957.

Duty No. 261 NOT USED

Duty No. 262
3P L class

	Loco Yard		9. 0am	‖
9. 5am	Faversham		9.21am	P
10.18am	Dover Priory		10.23am	V
10.28am	Dover Marine		10.35am	‖
10.46am	Dovery Priory		11.21am	P
12.16pm	Faversham		12.30pm	‖
xx	Loco Yard		1.20pm	‖
xx	Faversham		2.20pm	P
3.19pm	Dover Priory		3.20pm	E
3.25pm	Dover Marine		xx	‖
xx	Loco Yard		5.20pm	‖
5.27pm	Dover Priory		5.40pm	P
6.30pm	Faversham		7.39pm	P
8. 6pm	Gillingham		8.11pm	E
8.15pm	Chatham		8.25pm	‖
xx	Gillingham Loco		10.20pm	‖
10.26pm	Chatham		11.22pm	P
11.55pm	Faversham		xx	‖
xx	Loco Yard			

Local passenger work by an SECR 4-4-0 to Dover and back worked by Faversham men down on the 9.21am and 11.21am back. Faversham men (2nd set) are relieved at 2.2pm and hand over to Dover men who take the 2.20pm down. Faversham men bring the engine back at 5.40pm and are relieved at 6.30pm by a 3rd set who work and dispose the engine after the 11.22pm passenger.

Faversham had two duties for L class 4-4-0s. Duty No. 264 took the engine to Ashford via Ramsgate. Engine No. 31767 is seen arriving at Walmer with a six-coach train of two sets, the leading vehicles consisting of Maunsell coaches in red and cream, with a three-coach birdcage set on the rear.

J. Stredwick

Duty Nos 263 & 265 to 268 NOT USED

Duty No. 264
3P L class

	Loco Yard	4.10am	‖
xx	Faversham		
	C. shunting 4.15am to 8.5am		
	Faversham	8. 8am	P
8.52am	Margate	xx	‖
xx	Loco Sidings	9.30am	‖
xx	Margate	10.10am	P
11.38am	Ashford	12.42pm	P
1.33pm	Tonbridge	xx	‖
xx	Loco Yard	3.30pm	‖
xx	Tonbridge	4. 9pm	P
5. 0pm	Ashford	5. 9pm	P
6.16pm	Ramsgate	6.26pm	P
7.30pm	Faversham	xx	‖
xx	Loco Yard		

A grand tour by L class takes the engine to Tonbridge. Faversham men having started the duty are relieved by Gillingham men at 6.35am who take the engine to Margate where Ashford men step onto the footplate at 9.30am and have the rest of the work which includes turning on Tonbridge shed and running out at 3.30pm‖ for the 4.9pm passenger.

Duty No. 269
2MT Ivatt 2-6-2T

	Loco Yard	4.20am	‖
xx	Faversham	4.45am	E
5.25am	Margate	5.57am	P
7.28am	Rochester	7.42am	E
7.46am	Strood		
	F. shunting 8.0am to 10.45am		
	Strood	xx	‖
xx	Gillingham	12.15pm	E
12.20pm	Chatham (via Sitt.)	12.56pm	P
1.48pm	Sheerness	4.15pm	P
	(F. shunting Queenboro 2.0pm to 3.35pm)		
4.26pm	Sittingbourne	4.56pm	P
5.21pm	Sheerness	5.40pm	P
6. 0pm	Sittingbourne		
	F. shunting 6.20pm to 8.40pm		
	Sittingbourne	9.10pm	P
9.33pm	Sheerness	10.11pm	P
10.20pm	Sittingbourne	10.45pm	P
11. 4pm	Sheerness (A.N.R.)	11.13pm	P
11.31pm	Sittingbourne	1. 5am	F
1.28am	Gillingham	xx	‖
xx	Loco Yard		
	stable for No. 272		

Faversham men work the engine to 7.20am when they are relieved by Gillingham men who work the engine until 6.0pm at Sittingbourne (two sets). Faversham men work from 6.0pm until 7.0pm when Gillingham men come on briefly again until Faversham men take over the engine at 7.25pm and finish the job. The much travelled Ivatt 2-6-2T class double heads the 11.13pm Sheerness to Sittingbourne with a C class on 278 duty.

Duty No. 270
2MT Ivatt 2-6-2T

	Loco Yard	4. 0am	‖
xx	Faversham	4.40am	P
4.55am	Sittingbourne		
	Work Sheerness Passenger until		
	Sittingbourne	7.30pm	P
7.53pm	Chatham	8.38pm	P
9.17pm	Faversham	xx	‖
xx	Loco Yard		

Faversham men start off with the 4.0am‖ and are relieved by Gillingham men who come on to the engine at 10.30am. Gillingham men work the engine shuttling up and down the Sheerness branch until 7.0pm (two sets) when Faversham men take over and finish the duty.

Duty No. 271
2MT Ivatt 2-6-2T
OFF No. 272

	Faversham Loco	11.30pm	‖
xx	Sittingbourne	12.20am	F
1.35am	Faversham A/R with 279	2. 0am	F
2.20am	Sittingbourne A/R with 279	2.50am	F
3.40am	Queenborough	4. 0am	‖
4.16am	Sittingbourne	5. 5am	P
5.23am	Sheerness A.N.R. with 278	5.31am	P
5.54am	Sittingbourne	6.11am	P
6.33am	Sheerness	7.11am	P
7.39am	Sittingbourne	7.48am	P
8.9am	Sheerness	8.25am	E
8.30am	Dockyard	xx	‖
xx	Sheerness	9.10am	E
9.15am	Dockyard		
	F. shunting Dockyard and Queenborough		
	Queenborough	12.10pm	‖
12.40pm	Faversham Loco	1.55pm	‖
xx	Faversham	3.11pm	P
3.51pm	Chatham	4.37pm	P
5.2pm	Sittingbourne	5.29pm	P
5.52pm	Sheerness	6. 6pm	P
6.26pm	Sittingbourne	7.32pm	E
7.44pm	Faversham	xx	‖
xx	Loco Yard		

Faversham men work freights through the night including double heading the 2.0am freight and the 5.31am passenger. Gillingham men take over at 10.50am and work the engine until 6.26pm when Faversham men take over and complete.

Duty No. 272
2MT Ivatt 2-6-2T
OFF No. 269

	Gillingham Loco	3.40am	‖
3.50am	Strood	4.22am	V
4.40am	Gillingham	5. 0am	‖
5. 6am	Chatham	5.44am	P
6. 8am	Sittingbourne	6.16am	P
6.30am	Faversham	6.36am	P
6.51am	Canterbury East	7.10am	P
7.29am	Faversham		
	C. & CCE shunting 7.30am to 10.15am		
	Faversham	xx	‖
xx	Loco Yard	3.25pm	‖
xx	Sittingbourne	4. 0pm	P
	work Sheerness shuttles until		
	Sheerness	9.22pm	P
10.20pm	Faversham	xx	‖
xx	Loco Yard		
	Work No. 271		

Gillingham men work round to 7.29am when Faversham take over and work until 7.25pm (three sets) at Sittingbourne. Gillingham men work the engine from 7.25pm until 9.42pm when Faversham men resume working the engine until finish.

Duty Nos 273 to 275 NOT USED

Duty No. 276
4P/3F U1 class

	Loco Yard	4. 0am	‖
xx	Faversham	4.23am	F
6.37am	Ramsgate		
	F. shunting 7.0am to 10.30am		
	Ramsgate	10.30am	‖
xx	Loco Yard	4.23pm	‖
4.55pm	Margate	5.35pm	P
5.59pm	Minster	6. 9pm	P
6.58pm	Dover Priory	xx	‖
	(turn via Archcliffe)		
xx	Dover Priory	7.49pm	P
8.45pm	Faversham	9. 5pm	‖
xx	Loco Yard		

Faversham men start the duty and are relieved by Ramsgate men at 7.45am who work round to 5.50pm (two sets). Faversham men take the engine home after relieving at 5.50pm at Ramsgate.

Ivatt Class 2 2-6-2 tank No. 41312 is seen arriving at Newington with a Sheerness to Gillingham train, on 13th June 1959, the penultimate day of steam finishing on the line. Duties 269–272 refer.

Faversham had N class 2-6-0s which worked passenger and freight trains. The Ns could be used on summer weekends when passenger traffic was heavy. One of these locomotives pounds uphill with a Ramsgate to Victoria relief train on the last day of steam working, 14th June 1959. The train is ascending the steep bank to Sole Street out of the Medway valley.

Duty No. 277
4P/5F N class

	Loco Yard	4.45am	‖
4.50am	Faversham	5. 5am	P
6. 0am	Dover Priory	6. 5am	‖
	(turn via Archcliffe)		
6.41am	Dover Priory	7.42am	P
8.39am	Faversham	xx	‖
xx	Loco Yard	11.24am	‖
11.40am	Sittingbourne	1. 0pm	F
	(F. shunting 11.45am to 12.55pm)		
4.18pm	Dover Town	xx	‖
xx	Loco Yard	6.30pm	‖
xx	Dover Marine	6.50pm	P
7.14pm	Shorncliffe	8.55pm	F
1.20am	Faversham	xx	‖
xx	Loco Yard		

Faversham men work the 4.45am‖ off loco and work until relieved at 1.45pm (two sets). Dover men work the 1.0pm freight as from Faversham at 1.45pm and work round to Shorncliffe at 7.50pm where Faversham men take over and complete the duty. The loco turns via the Archcliffe triangle after the 6.0am arrival.

Duty No. 278
2F C class (Fully Coaled)
OFF No. 283

	Loco Yard	2.45am	‖
xx	Faversham	3. 6am	F
4.17am	Queenborough	xx	‖
xx	Sheerness (D/H with 271)	5.31am	P
5.54am	Sittingbourne		
	(F. shunting 6.5am to 10.30am)		
	Sittingbourne	11.53am	P
12.13pm	Sheerness	1.20pm	P
1.41pm	Sittingbourne	2.36pm	P
2.58pm	Sheerness	3.30pm	‖
3.35pm	Queenborough	4.30pm	‖
	(F. shunting 3.35pm to 4.30pm)		
xx	Sheerness	xx	‖
xx	Dockyard	5.22pm	F
5.32pm	Queenborough	7.15pm	‖
xx	Sheerness	7.28pm	P
8. 3pm	Faversham	9.40pm	P
10.24pm	Sheerness (via Sitt)	10.35pm	E
10.40pm	Dockyard	xx	‖
xx	Sheerness (D/H with 269)	11.13pm	P
11.32pm	Sittingbourne	11.49pm	P
12.11am	Sheerness	12.30am	‖
12.36am	Queenborough	12.56am	F
3.10am	Faversham	xx	‖
xx	Loco Yard		
	Work No. 283		

Faversham men have all the work on this C class which works a mixture of freight and passenger on the Sheerness branch.

Duty No. 279
2F C class

	Loco Yard	1.35am	‖
xx	Faversham Yard D/H with 271	2. 0am	F
3.40am	Queenborough	5.45am	F
5.53am	Sheerness Dockyard		
	C. & F. shunting 5.55am to 7.10am		
	Sheerness Dockyard	7.15am	E
7.20am	Sheerness	7.55am	P
8.15am	Sittingbourne	8.27am	P
8.42am	Faversham	xx	‖
xx	Loco Yard	11.50am	‖
xx	Faversham	12.13pm	F
2.57pm	Margate Goods (turn in Loco Sidings)	3.45pm	F
6.48pm	Faversham	xx	‖
xx	Loco Yard		

Faversham men have this interesting turn of duty which starts with the double headed 2.0am freight to Queenborough before working passenger trains on the Sheerness branch. A late turn set works the goods to Margate and back which goes to Birchington only on Mondays, Wednesdays and Fridays. (Three sets used).

SECR Brunswick green with polished dome, as seen on the new C class No. 684 plodding away on a down freight at Sydenham Hill. The engine was built by Neilson, Reid in June 1900 and withdrawn in October 1961. No. 684 was a Faversham engine when new and is probably working a heavy goods from Herne Hill Sorting Sidings.

Duty Nos 280 to 282 NOT USED

Duty No. 283
2F C class
OFF No. 278
Faversham shunting 1.30pm to 1.0am
including loco coal empties
Work No. 278

Faversham men have the work which includes three sets of men.

Duty No. 284
2F C class
Faversham Creek F. shunting 6.0pm to 9.30pm
Faversham F. shunting 9.30pm to 1.30pm
including loco coal and CCE sidings

Faversham men work the shunting which uses three sets of men.

Duty Nos 285 to 289 NOT USED

TONBRIDGE

Duty No. 290
3P L class

	Redhill Loco	7.55am	‖
xx	Redhill	8. 9am	P
8.41am	Tonbridge	8.49am	P
9.35am	Ashford	9.42am	P
11.20am	Ramsgate	12.34pm	P
12.48pm	Margate (via Dover)	1.50pm	P
3.40pm	Ashford		
	C. shunting 4.0pm to 5.30pm		
	Ashford (5.0pm ex D.P.)	6. 2pm	P
7.26pm	Tonbridge	7.44pm	P
8.21pm	Redhill	xx	‖
xx	Loco Yard		

Tonbridge men start with the 7.55am‖ off Redhill Loco and are relieved at Tonbridge by St. Leonards men who work to Ashford. Ramsgate men take over at Ashford at 9.35am and work round to Ramsgate where Ashford men take over at 12.30pm and complete the duty (two sets). The engine works from Redhill and goes over light from Tonbridge at 5.15am on Mondays – an unusual arrangement.

Tonbridge had two U1 duties, including the 5am triple header to Sevenoaks. No. 31896 is seen leaving Redhill on duty No. 293 (which, in 1958 worked the 5.8pm to Tonbridge). The engine was built at Eastleigh in 1931 and withdrawn in 1962. Photographed on 26th September 1958.

Duty N. 291
3P L class

	Loco Yard	4.10am	‖
xx	Tonbridge		
	C. shunting 4.20am to 5.25am		
	Tonbridge	5.55am	E
6. 4am	Paddock Wood	6.30am	P
6.39am	Tonbridge	6.58am	P
7.37am	Redhill	xx	‖
xx	Loco Yard (turn)	8.45am	‖
xx	Redhill	9. 6am	P
9.41am	Tonbridge	10.12am	P
11.42am	Brighton		
	C. shunting 12.0noon to 1.0pm		
	Brighton	xx	‖
xx	Loco Yard (turn)	2.30pm	‖
xx	Brighton	2.55pm	P
4.27pm	Tonbridge		
	C. shunting 5.30pm to 6.0pm		
	Tonbridge	6.15pm	P
6.52pm	Redhill	xx	‖
xx	Loco Yard (turn)	8.45pm	‖
xx	Redhill	9. 5pm	P
9.42pm	Tonbridge		
	C. shunting 10.0pm to 11.30pm		
	Tonbridge	xx	‖
xx	Loco Yard		

Tonbridge men are relieved at Redhill from 7.37am by Redhill men who turn the engine for Tonbridge men to work the 9.6am who are in turn relieved at Tonbridge at 9.41am by Tunbridge Wells West men. Brighton men relieve the Tunbridge Wells West men at 10.30am and work the engine until relieved by another set of Tunbridge Wells West men at 4.10pm on the return of the engine from Brighton. Tonbridge men finish the job by relieving at 4.10pm and completing the duty.

Duty No. 292
3P L class
stabled off No. 293

	St. Leonards Loco	5.20am	‖
5.27am	Hastings	6.17am	P
7.36am	Tonbridge	xx	‖
xx	Loco Yard	9. 0am	‖
xx	Tonbridge	9.32am	P
10.10am	Redhill	xx	‖
xx	Loco Yard (turn)	11.58am	‖
xx	Redhill	12. 7pm	P
12.44pm	Tonbridge	xx	‖
xx	Loco Yard	3.35pm	‖
xx	Tonbridge		
	C. shunting 3.45pm to 6.15pm		
	Tonbridge	6.44pm	P
7.30pm	Ashford	7.52pm	P
8.40pm	Hastings	9.10pm	P
10.32pm	Tonbridge	xx	‖
xx	Loco Yard		

St. Leonards men work round to Tonbridge at 7.36am. Tonbridge men work to Redhill and back from 7.36am. Late turn Tonbridge men have the afternoon 6.44pm circular tour back to Tonbridge.

Duty No. 293
3P L class

	Loco Yard	7.10am	‖
xx	Tonbridge	7.43am	P
9.10am	Brighton	xx	‖
xx	Top Table (turn)	10.42am	‖
xx	Brighton	10.47am	P
11.29am	Redhill (coupled to 485)	11.52am	‖
xx	Loco Yard (turn)	1.50pm	‖
xx	Redhill (7.35am Birkenhead)	2.45pm	P
3.26pm	Brighton	xx	‖
xx	Top Table (turn)	4.42pm	‖
xx	Brighton	4.55pm	P
6.22pm	Tonbridge	xx	‖
xx	Loco Yard (turn)	8.15pm	‖
xx	Tonbridge	8.40pm	P
9.55pm	Hastings	xx	‖
xx	St. Leonards Loco		
	stable for No. 292		

A rare working with a Tonbridge L class working to Brighton and heading the Hastings to Birkenhead from Brighton to Redhill and back. Three Bridges men relieve the Tonbridge men at Brighton where the engine is turned. Brighton men relieve at 3.35pm and turn the engine again for the 4.55pm to Tonbridge. Tonbridge men relieve at Tunbridge Wells West on the way back at 6.5pm. St. Leonards men take the engine home. The engine turns four times.

Tonbridge L class No. 31763 is seen leaving Redhill on the 1.5pm to Tonbridge. The duty (No. 294) was for a D1 class but an L has been substituted as the power classification is the same. Photograph taken on 16th January 1959.

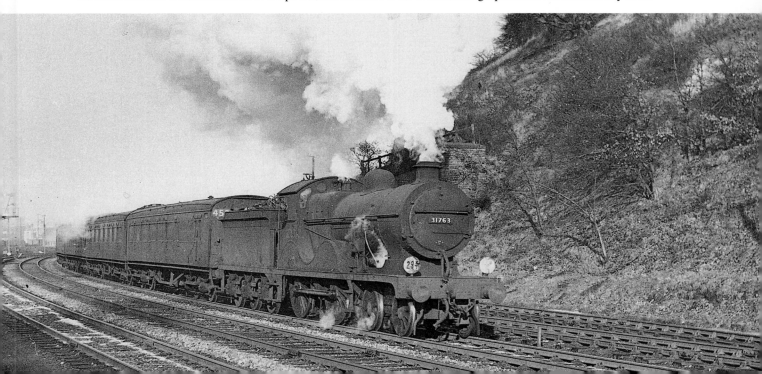

Duty No. 294
3P D1 class

	Loco Yard	5.45am	‖
xx	Tonbridge	6.10am	P
7.40am	Brighton	xx	‖
xx	Top Table (turn)	xx	‖
xx	Brighton		
	C. shunting 8.25am to 8.50am		
	Brighton	9. 0am	P
10.32am	Tonbridge	10.38am	P
11.16am	Redhill	11.30am	‖
xx	Loco Yard (turn)	12.50pm	‖
xx	Redhill	1. 5pm	P
1.47pm	Tonbridge	2.12pm	P
3.42pm	Brighton		
	C. shunting 3.50pm to 5.40pm		
	Brighton	5.40pm	‖
xx	Loco Yard (turn)	9.50pm	‖
xx	Carriage Sidings propel	xx	E
xx	Brighton	10.30pm	P
11.54pm	Tonbridge	xx	‖
xx	Loco Yard		

B'Arms men work to Tunbridge Wells West. Tunbridge Wells West men relieve at 6.30am at Tunbridge Wells West and work to 10.11am. Tonbridge men work from 10.11am at Tunbridge Wells West until 2.5pm at Tonbridge where Brighton men relieve and work home. Tonbridge men prepare and work the 9.50pm‖ and finish the duty at Tonbridge after having propelled the stock into the platform at Brighton for the 10.30pm departure.

Duty No. 295
3P D1 class

	Loco Yard	7.40am	‖
xx	Tonbridge	8.12am	P
9.40am	Brighton	xx	‖
xx	Top Yard	10. 5am	Coal
10.15am	Loco Yard (turn)	xx	‖
xx	Brighton		
	C. shunting 10.50am to 12.15pm		
	Brighton	12.55pm	P
2.27pm	Tonbridge	xx	‖
xx	Loco Yard (turn)	5. 5pm	‖
xx	Tonbridge	5.30pm	E
5.40pm	Tunbridge Wells Ctl Goods	6.10pm	E
6.13pm	Tunbridge Wells Ctl	6.14pm	P
7.41pm	Brighton		
	C. shunting 8.0pm to 9.0pm		
	Brighton	9. 0pm	‖
9. 4pm	Top Table (turn)	9.42pm	‖
xx	Brighton	9.55pm	P
11.25pm	Tonbridge	xx	‖
xx	Loco Yard		

Tonbridge men work round to Eridge at 8.43am to be relieved by Brighton men who work the engine until 2.27pm at Tonbridge. Tonbridge men take over at 2.27pm and finish the job.

Duty No. 296
4P/3F U1 class

	Loco Yard	4.30am	‖
xx	Tonbridge (triple headed)	5. 0am	P
5.15am	Sevenoaks (via Ton.)	6. 9am	P
8.18am	Brighton	9. 1am	‖
9.40am	Top Table (turn)	9.25am	‖
xx	Brighton	9.55am	P
11.59am	Victoria (propel)	xx	E
xx	Carriage Sidings	12.25pm	‖
12.35pm	Stewarts Lane Loco	6.20pm	‖
6.37pm	Victoria	6.48pm	P
8. 3pm	East Grinstead	8.55pm	‖
9.44pm	Tunbridge Wells West	9.46pm	‖
10. 9pm	Tonbridge Loco		

Tonbridge men start up the 4.30am‖ and work a triple headed 5.0am passenger to Sevenoaks with 310 and 325 duties. Triple headed passenger trains are very rare on BR. The Tonbridge men are relieved at 6.45am by Tunbridge Wells West men who work round to Stewarts Lane at 12.35pm. Stewarts Lane men start the 6.20pm‖ and are relieved at East Grinstead at 8.3pm by Tunbridge Wells West men who take the engine to Tunbridge Wells West to be relieved by Tonbridge men at 9.44pm who complete the duty.

Duty No. 299
4P/3F U1 class

	Loco Yard	6.40am	‖
xx	Tonbridge	7. 6am	P
7.24am	Sevenoaks	8.21am	P
8.56am	Tunbridge Wells West	9.47am	P
	(C. shunting 9.0am to 9.30am)		
11.28am	Victoria (propel)	11.40am	E
xx	Carriage Sidings	11.48am	E
11.50am	Victoria	12.10am	‖
xx	Carriage Sidings		
	C. shunting 12.15pm to 2.0pm		
	Carriage Sidings	2. 2pm	‖
2.12pm	Stewarts Lane Loco	3.30pm	‖
3.48pm	Victoria	4.50pm	P
7.11pm	Brighton		
	C. shunting 7.40pm to 8.5pm		
	Brighton	8. 5pm	‖
8.10pm	Top Table (turn)	8.42pm	‖
xx	Brighton	8.55pm	P
10.27pm	Tonbridge	xx	‖
xx	Loco Yard		

Tonbridge men are relieved at Tunbridge Wells West at 9.45am by Brighton men who work round to Stewarts Lane. Stewarts Lane men start the 3.30pm‖ and work to Brighton at 7.11pm where Tonbridge men take over and complete.

Duty Nos 297-298 NOT USED

Duty No. 300 NOT USED

Tunbridge Wells West (now a restaurant) with H class No. 31519 in the bay with the 4.45pm to Sevenoaks, consisting of SECR stock. A Class 4 2-6-4 tank can be glimpsed on the far left. The photograph was taken on Sunday 21st February 1960 and duty No. 305 (Sundays only) applied. The crew are preparing to depart and the guard is concerned about a right time start.

Duty No. 301
1P H class P & P fitted

	Location	Time	
	Loco Yard	7.45am	‖
xx	Tonbridge	8.10am	P
8.47am	Maidstone West	9.39am	P
10. 3am	Paddock Wood	10.32am	‖
10.46am	Tonbridge	11.38am	P
12.37pm	Oxted	1. 4pm	P
1.56pm	Tonbridge	xx	‖
xx	Tonbridge Loco (coupled to No. 185)	6. 8pm	‖
6.30pm	Sevenoaks	7.31pm	P
7.45pm	Tonbridge		
	C. shunting 8.0pm to 9.30pm		
	Tonbridge	9.45pm	P
10.22pm	Redhill	11.10pm	P
11.47pm	Tonbridge	xx	
xx	Loco Yard		

Tonbridge men have all the work one early turn set on at 7.0am and a late turn set on at 5.23pm.

Duty Nos 302-305 & 307 NOT USED

Duty No. 306
1P H class P & P fitted

	Location	Time	
	Loco Yard	5. 5am	‖
xx	Tonbridge	5.35am	P
6.0am	Wadhurst	6.24am	P
7.16am	Sevenoaks	7.24am	‖
7.40am	Tonbridge		
	C. shunting 8.10am to 9.30am		
	Tonbridge	10.38am	P
11.37am	Oxted	12.45pm	P
12.56pm	Tonbridge	2.10pm	P
2.48pm	Maidstone West	3. 8pm	P
3.43pm	Tonbridge	5. 0pm	P
5.40pm	Maidstone West		
	F. shunting 6.5pm to 7.30pm		
	Maidstone West	7.47pm	P
8.53pm	Sevenoaks	10.10pm	P
10.43pm	Wadhurst	11. 0pm	P
11.17pm	Tonbridge	xx	‖
xx	Loco Yard		

Tonbridge men work push and pull to Wadhurst, Oxted, Maidstone West and Sevenoaks. Tonbridge Loco had ten H class locomotives allocated for the local passenger trains.

Duty No. 308
1P H class P & P fitted

	Location	Time	
	Loco Yard	6.15am	‖
xx	Paddock Wood	6.53am	P
7.19am	Maidstone West	8.30am	P
9.11am	Tonbridge	9.28am	P
10. 5am	Maidstone West	10.45am	P
11.22am	Tonbridge	11.31am	‖
11.36am	Loco Yard	12.48pm	‖
12.58pm	Paddock Wood	1.20pm	P
1.46pm	Maidstone West		
	F. shunting 2.15pm to 4.0pm		
	Maidstone West	4.16pm	P
4.43pm	Paddock Wood	5.42pm	P
6. 7pm	Maidstone West	6.39pm	P
7.17pm	Tonbridge	8.48pm	P
9.24pm	Maidstone West	9.53pm	P
10.55pm	Sevenoaks	11.40pm	P
11.54pm	Tonbridge	xx	‖
xx	Loco Yard		

Tonbridge men work push and pull to Maidstone West and indulge in a spot of freight shunting. Three sets cover the turn, early on at 5.30am, middle on at 11.45am and late on at 7.15pm.

Duty No. 309
1P H class P & P fitted

	Location	Time	
	Loco Yard	5.35am	||
5.40am	Tonbridge	6. 3am	P
6.19am	Sevenoaks	6.47am	P
7. 1am	Tonbridge		
	C. shunting 7.30am to 9.35am		
	Tonbridge	10.30am	P
11. 7am	Maidstone West	11.46am	P
12.24pm	Tonbridge		
	C. shunting 1.50pm to 3.45pm		
	Tonbridge	3.50pm	P
4.51pm	Maidstone West	5.20pm	P
5.57pm	Tonbridge	6.20pm	P
6.29pm	Paddock Wood	7.30pm	P
7.56pm	Maidstone West	8.44pm	P
9.21pm	Tonbridge		
	C. shunting 9.30pm to 1.15am		
	Tonbridge	xx	||
xx	Loco Yard		

Tonbridge men have the work as far as 9.21pm when they are relieved by Redhill men who finish the duty with the carriage shunting.

Duty No. 310
1P H class P & P fitted

	Location	Time	
	Loco Yard	4.50am	||
xx	Tonbridge A.N.R. with 299 & 325	5. 0am	P
5.15am	Sevenoaks	5.17am	||
5.21am	Dunton Green	5.45am	F
6. 0am	Westerham	6.14am	P
	work Westerham branch shuttles to		
10. 4am	Dunton Green	10.10am	E
10.14am	Sevenoaks	10.20am	P
10.35am	Tonbridge	10.58am	||
xx	Loco Yard	11.50am	||
xx	Tonbridge	12.16pm	P
12.51pm	Maidstone West	1.12pm	P
1.46pm	Tonbridge	xx	||
xx	Loco Yard	3.40pm	||
xx	Tonbridge	4. 0pm	E
4.19pm	Dunton Green	4.20pm	P
	work Westerham shuttles until		
8. 1pm	Westerham	8.50pm	F
9.30pm	Dunton Green	9.55pm	||
xx	Tonbridge Loco		

Tonbridge men work the rare 5.0am passenger to Sevenoaks before running light to Dunton Green for the 5.45am freight to Westerham. After working the branch passenger, the loco and men work back to Tonbridge by taking the empties with them at 10.10am to Sevenoaks. The late turn Tonbridge men take the empties back to Dunton Green for the branch. Having completed the branch passenger working, the engine finishes off with an evening freight to Dunton Green at 8.50pm. Three sets of Tonbridge men are used.

Duty Nos 311 & 313 NOT USED

Duty No. 312
1P H class P & P fitted

	Location	Time	
	Tonbridge Loco	6.35am	||
xx	Tonbridge		
	(C. shunting 6.45am to 6.55am)		
	Tonbridge	6.58am	||
7.10am	Paddock Wood	7.28am	P
8.3am	Hawkhurst	8.20am	P
	Work Hawkhurst branch until		
	Hawkhurst	1. 5pm	P
1.35pm	Paddock Wood	1.47pm	||
2.0pm	Tonbridge Loco	3.30pm	||
3.44pm	Paddock Wood	4.25pm	P
	Work Hawkhurst branch until		
7.58pm	Hawkhurst	8. 6pm	P
8.36pm	Tonbridge	xx	||
xx	Loco Yard		

Tonbridge men work the Hawkhurst branch and take the engine with them to couple up to the P & P set at Paddock Wood in the morning. A late turn crew take the 3.30pm\|\| engine off shed and complete the duty by taking the whole train back to Tonbridge. The P & P set returns to Paddock Wood at 9.35pm and is berthed for the 7.28am next day.

Duty No. 314
5F Q1 class

	Location	Time	
	Loco Yard	4.35am	‖
xx	Tonbridge West Yard	5. 2am	F
8.11am	Bexhill West	xx	‖
xx	Loco Yard (turn)	9. 0am	‖
9.11am	Battle	11. 5am	F
12.50pm	Tonbridge West Yard	xx	‖
xx	Loco Yard	4.55pm	‖
xx	Tonbridge (A.N.R.)	5.16pm	P
6.30pm	Hastings	xx	‖
xx	St. Leonards Loco	7.40pm	‖
xx	Battle	8.35pm	F
10.19pm	Tonbridge West Yard	xx	‖
xx	Loco Yard	11.30pm	‖
xx	Tonbridge	11.51pm	P
12.16am	Wadhurst	12.25am	E
12.43am	Tonbridge	xx	‖
xx	Loco Yard		

Tonbridge men start the duty and are relieved at Crowhurst at 7.58am. St. Leonards men take over at 7.58am, work to Bexhill West, turn the engine and hand over to Tonbridge men off No. 317 at 8.55am. Tonbridge men take over at 8.55am and finish the duty including a late turn crew who work the 5.16pm passenger double headed.

Duty No. 315
5F Q1 class
OFF No. 323

	Location	Time	
	Loco Yard	3.45am	‖
xx	Tonbridge West Yard	4. 8am	F
7. 5am	Hastings	9.18am	F
	(C. shunting 8.15am to 9.0am)		
9.28am	Ore	11.35am	F
	(F. shunting 9.30am to 11.0am)		
11.40am	Hastings	xx	‖
xx	St. Leonards Loco	2.12pm	‖
2.43pm	Battle	4. 0pm	F
	(F. shunting 3.0pm to 3.45pm)		
7.16pm	Tonbridge West Yard	xx	‖
xx	Loco Yard		
	Work No. 323		

Tonbridge men start up the duty, leave the engine at St. Leonards and home pass. St. Leonards men start the 2.12pm‖ and finish the duty.

Duty No. 316 NOT USED

Duty No. 317
5F Q1 class

	Location	Time	
	Tonbridge Loco	6.15am	‖
6.58am	Etchingham	8.11am	P
8.48am	Bexhill West	10.45am	F
1.53pm	Tonbridge West Yard	xx	‖
xx	Loco yard	3. 0pm	‖
xx	Tonbridge West Yard	3.20pm	F
6.42pm	Redhill Up Yard	xx	‖
xx	Loco Yard (turn)	8. 0pm	‖
xx	Redhill	8.14pm	F
	(12.15pm ex Moreton Cutting)		
9. 9pm	Tonbridge West Yard	xx	
xx	Tonbridge East Yard	9.48pm	F
xx	West Yard	xx	‖
xx	Loco Yard		

Tonbridge men work to Bexhill West where they are relieved at 8.55am by St. Leonards men who work until 12.5pm at Battle. Tonbridge men have the rest of the work which includes the 12.15pm Moreton Cutting (near Didcot) which is 8.14pm off Redhill station.

Duty No. 319 NOT USED

Tonbridge had six H class duties covering local branch lines (Nos 301–312), and worked to Maidstone West, Westerham, Hawkhurst, Oxted, and Redhill. H class 0-4-4Ts with push and pull trains worked the Hawkhurst branch with Tonbridge men. No. 31500 is seen at Horsmonden on the Saturday version of No. 312 duty (302) on 6th May 1961, shortly before closure.

Tonbridge had seven Q1 duties; 314–317, 320–323 and 325 to work heavy freights. No. 33028 belts up Wadhurst bank on 7th July 1956 with the 11.5am Battle to Tonbridge West Yard on duty No. 314.

G. Daniels

Duty No. 318
2F C class
OFF No. 327

	Tonbridge Loco	5. 5am	‖
5.18am	Paddock Wood	5.50am	F
10. 4am	Ashford	xx	‖
xx	Loco Yard	12.15pm	‖
xx	Ashford		
	C. & W. shunting 12.30pm to 1.0pm		
	CCE shunting 1.30pm to 2.30pm		
	Ashford	xx	‖
xx	Loco Yard	4. 0pm	‖
xx	Ashford Sidings	4.23pm	F
9.40pm	Paddock Wood		
	F. shunting 9.45pm to 3.30am		
	Paddock Wood	5. 0am	F
5.20am	Tonbridge East Yard	xx	‖
xx	Loco Yard		

Ashford men have the work until Paddock Wood in the evening where they are relieved at 10.0pm by Tonbridge men who complete the duty.

Duty No. 320
5F Q1 class

	Loco Yard	2.20am	‖
xx	Tonbridge West Yard	2.45am	F
3.45am	Redhill Up Yard	4.10am	‖
xx	Loco Yard	7.25am	‖
xx	Redhill Down Yard	8.15am	F
11.15am	Tonbridge West Yard	xx	‖
xx	Loco Yard	6.50pm	‖
xx	Tonbridge West Yard	7.16pm	F
9.31pm	Snodland	10.27pm	F
1.33am	Tonbridge West Yard	xx	‖
xx	Loco Yard		

Tonbridge men have all the work except the start up of the 7.25am‖ ex Loco Yard which is covered by Redhill men. Two sets are used.

Duty No. 321
5F Q1 class

	Tonbridge Loco	2.20pm	‖
3.15pm	Hither Green Loco	10. 5pm	‖
xx	Hither Green (A. Sect)	10.25pm	F
10.53pm	B'Arms (N. Sect)	11.58pm	F
1.43am	Tonbridge West Yard	2.35am	F
5.10am	Hastings	5.20am	‖
5.27am	St. Leonards Loco	7.58am	‖
8. 7am	Hastings	8.40am	F
11. 7am	Tonbridge West Yard	xx	‖
xx	Loco Yard		

Hither Green men work the 2.20pm‖ and the 10.5pm‖ being relieved by Stewarts Lane men at 11.55pm at B'Arms. The Stewarts Lane men work the 11.58pm freight round to Tonbridge at 1.43am where Tonbridge men take over and work to Battle where they are relieved by St. Leonards men at 4.26am. St. Leonards men have the engine until Hastings at 8.10am where Tonbridge men relieve and take the engine home. The 2.20pm‖ Tonbridge to Hither Green is an engine balance but the light engine is very useful for any special traffic on offer like engineeers empties.

Duty No. 322 NOT USED

Duty No. 323
5F Q1 class
OFF No. 315

	Loco Yard	11.40pm	‖
xx	Tonbridge West Yard	12.10am	F
4.30am	Hoo Junction		
	F. shunting 4.30am to 10.30am		
	Hoo Junction	10.42am	F
11. 7am	Crayford	12.17am	F
1.20pm	Hoo Junction	2.10pm	F
3.22pm	Brookgate Sidings	3.26pm	‖
3.43pm	Maidstone West	4.40pm	F
4.58pm	Snodland	6.30pm	F
7.53pm	Maidstone West	10.40pm	F
11. 6pm	Paddock Wood	11.29pm	‖
11.47pm	Tonbridge Loco		
	Work No. 315		

Tonbridge men work round to Hoo Junction where Gillingham men take over at 8.50am. The Gillingham men are relieved at Brookgate Sidings (New Hythe) at 3.22pm by Tonbridge men who complete the job. After working the 10.40pm Maidstone West to Paddock Wood, the crew off duty No. 119 are conveyed home to Tonbridge.

Duty No. 324
2F C class

	Loco Yard	1.10am	‖
xx	Tonbridge West Yard	1.45am	F
2. 5am	Tonbridge Ctl Goods	4.15am	F
5.35am	Tonbridge West Yard	xx	‖
xx	Tonbridge	6.56am	V
7.32am	Tunbridge Wells West		
	C. shunting 7.35am to 9.15am		
	Tunbridge Wells West	9.32am	‖
9.47am	Tonbridge West Yard	10.22am	F
11.40am	Tunbridge Wells West	xx	‖
xx	Loco Yard	1.30pm	‖

(Continued)

xx	Tunbridge Wells West	1.52pm	F
6.31pm	Polegate	6.59pm	‖
7. 9pm	Eastbourne Loco		
	stable for No. 327		

Tonbridge men have all the work on this local freight working but Central Section drivers and firemen take over from 11.40am for the 'Cuckoo Line' freight.

Duty No. 325
5F Q1 class

	Tonbridge Loco with 310	4.50am	‖
xx	Tonbridge A.N.R. 299 & 310	5. 0am	P
5.15am	Sevenoaks	5.46am	F
6.10am	Swanley		
	F. shunting 7.00am to 8.0am		
	Swanley	8.23am	F
12.29pm	Tonbridge West Yard	1.25pm	F
4.20pm	Etchingham	4.45pm	F
5.56pm	Tonbridge West Yard	xx	‖
xx	Tonbridge		
	C. shunting 6.30pm to 7.45pm		
	Tonbridge	xx	‖
xx	Loco Yard	9.30pm	‖
xx	Tonbridge	10.12pm	P
11.2pm	Ashford	xx	‖
xx	Loco Yard	12. 5am	‖
xx	Ashford Sidings	12.30am	F
1.30am	Paddock Wood	xx	‖
xx	Tonbridge Loco		

Tonbridge men have all the work except from 10.21pm at Paddock Wood where Ashford men take the 10.12pm passenger home to be relieved at 11.10pm at Ashford shed by Tonbridge men who complete the job. The engine is one of the trio on the triple headed 5.0am Tonbridge to Sevenoaks.

Duty No. 326
2F C class

	Tonbridge Loco	4.50am	‖
5. 5am	Paddock Wood	5.25am	F
7. 6am	Hawkhurst	7.34am	P
8. 4am	Paddock Wood	xx	‖
xx	Tonbridge Loco	10.40am	‖
xx	Tonbridge West Yard	10.55am	F
	trip workings West to East Yard		
	Tonbridge West Yard	2.20pm	F
2.54pm	Tunbridge Wells Ctl Goods		
	F. shunting 3.0pm to 4.50pm		
	Tunbridge Wells Ctl Goods	4.55pm	‖
xx	Tunbridge Wells West	5.56pm	P
6.11pm	Tonbridge	xx	‖
xx	Tonbridge West Yard	7. 8pm	F
9.14pm	Bat & Ball	10.35pm	F
2.50am	Tonbridge West Yard	xx	‖
xx	Loco Yard		

Tonbridge men have this mixed bag of passenger and freight work which includes an early turn on the Hawkhurst branch closed in 1961. Three sets are used; early, middle, and late.

Duty No. 327
2F C class
stabled off No. 324

	Eastbourne Loco	5.25am	‖
5.38am	Polegate	7.13am	F
11.20am	Tunbridge Wells West	12.18pm	F
12.28pm	Tunbridge Wells Ctl Goods	12.33pm	‖
12.45pm	Tonbridge Loco	3. 5pm	‖
xx	Tonbridge West Yard	3.30pm	F
3.35pm	East Yard	5. 2pm	F
	(F. shunting 3.45pm to 5.0pm)		
5. 7pm	West Yard		
	C. shunting 6.0pm to 9.40pm		
	Tonbridge West Yard	10. 5pm	F
10.40pm	Sevenoaks	12. 1am	P
12.16am	Tonbridge	xx	‖
xx	Loco Yard		

Central District men work the goods up the "Cuckoo Line" and are relieved by Tonbridge men from 11.50am. Tonbridge men have the rest of the work and finish off with the 12.1am passenger ex Sevenoaks.

The Hawkhurst branch also saw C class working but on this occasion No. 31588 is seen at Cranbrook, working the branch on the last day, 10th June 1961. The normal push and pull H class working was suspended on this day, duty No. 338 being the Saturday working amended for the occasion.

E. Wilmshurst

Duty Nos 328 to 329 NOT USED

ASHFORD

Duty No. 345
3P D1 class
stabled off No. 348

	St. Leonards Loco	5. 3am	‖
5.10am	Hastings		
	F. shunting 5.30am to 8.50am and steam heat stock		
	Hastings	11.35am	P
12.31pm	Ashford	xx	‖
xx	Loco Yard	3.25pm	‖
xx	Ashford	3.48pm	P
5.10pm	Ramsgate	7.53pm	P
8. 7pm	Margate	9.58pm	P
11.18pm	Ashford	xx	‖
xx	Loco Yard		

St. Leonards men start up the duty which includes heating passenger stock at Hastings. Ashford men take over at 10.5am and have the rest of the work back to Ashford in the evening.

Duty No. 346
3P L1 class

	Loco Yard	5.45am	‖
xx	Ashford (via Cant. West)	6.10am	P
6.39am	Margate (turn)	9.18am	P
10.22am	Ashford	10.40am	P
11.29am	Tonbridge	11.38am	P
12.17pm	Redhill (C. shunting to 1.10pm)	xx	‖
xx	Loco Yard (turn)	3.46pm	‖
xx	Redhill	4.15pm	P
4.54pm	Tonbridge D/H with 314	5.16pm	P
6.30pm	Hastings D/H with 347	6.52pm	P
7.46pm	Ashford (coupled to 347)	8. 0pm	‖
xx	Loco Yard		

Tonbridge men take over from Ashford men at 10.25am and work to Redhill. Redhill men come on at 12.30pm where they turn the loco and work the 4.15pm to Tonbridge after shunting. The Redhill men are relieved by Tonbridge men at 4.54pm who complete the duty including the double headed 5.16pm Tonbridge to Hastings, and 6.52pm Hastings to Ashford.

An Ashford L1 class 4-4-0, No. 31758, approaches Redhill on the 11.38am Tonbridge to Redhill on 9th January 1959. The engine is working a D1 duty (No. 346) but as the power classification was the same for the two classes both were suitable for the work.

Duty No. 347
3P L1 class

	Loco Yard	9.20am	‖
xx	Ashford Engineers Sidings		
	CCE shunting 9.30am to 12.0noon		
	Ashford Engineers Sidings	xx	‖
xx	Ashford	1.12pm	P
1.58pm	Hastings	xx	‖
xx	St. Leonards Loco	3.30pm	‖
xx	St. Leonards W.M.	4.26pm	F
4.31pm	Galley Hill	5.35pm	‖
xx	Hastings A.N.R. with 346	6.52pm	P
7.46pm	Ashford (with 346)	8. 0pm	‖
xx	Loco Yard		

Ashford men start the duty and are relieved at 11.25am by St. Leonards men who have the engine until 6.45pm when Ashford men take over and complete the duty. The 6.52pm passenger from Hastings is double headed with No. 346, an Ashford L1 class.

Duty No. 348
3P D class

	Loco Yard	6. 5am	‖
xx	Ashford C. shunting 6.15am to 7.40am	8. 0am	P
8.57am	Hastings	9.25am	P
9.58am	Eastbourne	xx	‖
xx	Loco Yard	3.50pm	‖
xx	Eastbourne	4.20pm	P
4.53pm	Hastings	5.18pm	‖
5.25pm	St. Leonards Loco		
	stable for No. 345		

Ashford men have the duty to Hastings where they are relieved by St. Leonards men at 8.57am who have the rest of the duty. The 9.25am from Hastings is the first leg of the through train to Birkenhead which reverses at Eastbourne, Brighton, Redhill and Chester. The train ran throughout the year. The D class 4-4-0s were all withdrawn in 1956 and the reference to the class is, a printer's error left in from the previous year.

Duty Nos 349 to 353 NOT USED

No. 1488 is seen at Ashford in Southern Railway days in tip top condition; built in 1902 and withdrawn in 1956 it was one of the last D class 4-4-0s to work. Duty No. 348 shows an Ashford D class to work over to Eastbourne and back on the first stage of the Hastings to Birkenhead train. As the last Ds were withdrawn in 1956 the reference to the class on No. 348 duty is obviously an item left in the workings and should read D1.

A. Harvey

Duty No. 354
4MT 2-6-4T LMR class
stabled off No. 355

	Loco Yard	4. 5am	‖
xx	Dover Priory	4.42am	P
6. 1am	Gillingham	6.30am	E
7. 0am	Faversham	7.37am	P
8.46am	Dover Priory	11.45am	P
12.33pm	Ashford	1. 4pm	P
1.43pm	Maidstone East	3.35pm	P
4.19pm	Ashford	4.35pm	P
5.54pm	Margate	6.15pm	‖
6.33pm	Ramsgate	7.18pm	P
8.27pm	Ashford		
	C. and F. shunting 8.45pm to 12.55am		
	Ashford	12.55am	‖
xx	Loco Yard		

Dover men start the duty and work until Ashford men take over at 11.45am and work the engine until 8.27pm (two sets). Ramsgate men take over at 8.27pm and are relieved at 10.15pm by Ashford men who finish the duty.

Margate, with Fairburn Class 4 2-6-4 tank No. 42099 on Duty No. 354, one of four duties at Ashford for these engines. It is seen on 20th December 1958.

E. Wilmshurst

Duty No. 355
4MT 2-6-4T LMR class
stabled off no 356

	Dover Loco	4.30am	‖
xx	Dover Priory	4.50am	P
5.35am	Ashford	xx	‖
xx	Ashford Sidings	6.21am	F
7.20am	Sandling	8.12am	F
10.50am	Ashford Sidings	xx	‖
xx	Ashford		
	F. and C. shunting 11.30am to 2.45pm		
	Ashford	3.13pm	P
3.44pm	Maidstone East	4.35pm	P
5.16pm	Ashford (via Dover)	5.45pm	P
7.27pm	Faversham	xx	‖
xx	Loco Yard	9. 1pm	P
10. 0pm	Dover Priory	xx	‖
xx	Loco Yard		
	stable for No. 354		

Ashford men have all the work until at 6.15pm at Folkestone Junction (two sets) when Dover men take over and finish the job. LMR 2-6-4 tanks were built at Brighton and numbered in the LMR series but were Southern built and used being the predecessors of the Standard class 4MT tank.

Duty No. 356
4MT 2-6-4T LMR class

	Loco Yard	3.40am	‖
xx	Ashford Sidings	3.55am	F
5.45am	New Romney	6.10am	P
6.39am	Appledore	7. 0am	E
7.13am	Ashford	8. 8am	P
8.48am	Maidstone East	9.35am	P
10.13am	Ashford	10.35am	P
11.30am	Ramsgate	xx	‖
xx	Loco Yard	1.20pm	‖
xx	Ramsgate	1.40pm	P
2.11pm	Canterbury West	3. 0pm	P
3.47pm	Margate	4.25pm	P
5.45pm	Ashford	6. 8pm	P
6.44pm	Maidstone East	7.10pm	P
8.19pm	Folkestone Junction	9.15pm	E
9.32pm	Dover Marine	xx	‖
xx	Loco Yard		
	stable for No. 355		

Ashford men work the engine until 10.15am when Ramsgate men take over (two sets). Dover men relieve at Ashford at 7.50pm on the return and complete the duty.

Duty Nos 357-359 NOT USED

Duty No. 360
4MT 2-6-4 tank LMR class

	Loco Yard (coupled to 365)	7.30am	‖
xx	Ashford	7.51am	P
8.40am	Dover Priory	8.46am	P
9.41am	Faversham	xx	‖
xx	Loco Yard	11.30am	‖
xx	Faversham	12. 6pm	P
1. 7pm	Dover Priory		
	C. shunting 1.10pm to 2.25pm		
	Dover Priory	3.28pm	P
4.25pm	Faversham	5.12pm	P
6.17pm	Dover Priory	6.38pm	P
6.43pm	Dover Marine	xx	‖
7. 9pm	Dover Priory	7.16pm	P
8.41pm	Maidstone East	10.30pm	P
11.11pm	Ashford	xx	‖
xx	Loco Yard		

Ashford men work round to Dover Priory where they are relieved at 8.40am by Dover men. Ramsgate men take over at 9.41am and are on the engine until 12 noon when Dover men take over and work to Dover Priory at 1.7pm. Faversham men relieve at Dover Priory at 1.7pm and work round until relieved by Dover men at Shepherdswell at 5.58pm who complete the duty.

Duty No. 361
2MT 2-6-2T Ivatt or BR Standard
OFF No. 362

	Ramsgate Loco	2.20am	‖
2.50am	Canterbury West		
	F. and C. shunting 3.0am to 10.30am		
	Canterbury West	10.30am	‖
11. 2am	Ashford Loco	11.40am	‖
xx	Ashford	12. 2pm	P
12.40pm	Maidstone West	1.45pm	P
2.28pm	Ashford	3.58pm	P
4.36pm	Maidstone East	5.15pm	P
5.55pm	Ashford	6.12pm	P
6.39pm	Rye	6.53pm	P
7.16pm	Ashford	7.21pm	P
8. 0pm	Maidstone East	8.32pm	P
9.12pm	Ashford	xx	‖
xx	Loco Yard		
	Work No. 362		

Ramsgate men are relieved at Canterbury West at 8.7am by Ashford men who have the rest of the work. BR Standard Class 2MTs were also allocated to Ashford as well as the LMR type.

Duty No. 362
2MT 2-6-2T Ivatt
OFF No 361

	Loco Yard	6. 5am	‖
xx	Ashford	6.28am	P
7. 6am	Maidstone East	7.36am	P
8.19am	Ashford	8.26am	P
9.51am	Margate		
	C. shunting 10.0am to 12.0 noon		
	Margate	1.18pm	P
1.33pm	Ramsgate	2.22pm	P
2.36pm	Margate		
	C. shunting 3.0pm to 9.15pm		
	Margate	9.20pm	P
10. 5pm	Canterbury West	11. 2pm	P
11.53pm	Margate	xx	‖
xx	Ramsgate Loco		
	stable for No. 361		

Ashford men are relieved at Margate at 11.0am by Ramsgate men who finish the duty. (Several sets involved.)

Duty No. 363 NOT USED

Duty No. 364
1P H class

	Loco Yard	7.50am	‖
xx	Folkestone Junction	8.35am	E
8.48am	Dover Marine		
	C. shunting 8.50am to 11.35am		
	Dover Marine D/H with 449	12.45pm	E
1. 1pm	Folkestone Cent.		
	steam heat and shunting including Shorncliffe		
	Folkestone Cent.	5.50pm	‖
xx	Folkestone Junction	6.50pm	V
7.30pm	Ashford	xx	‖
xx	Loco Yard		

Ashford men work local empty stock and shunting but are relieved by Dover men at 10.45am. Ashford men come back at 5.55pm at Folkestone Junction and finish the duty. Double heading of the 12.45pm empties from Dover Marine to Folkestone Central is also a feature of this duty.

Duty No. 365
1P H class P & P fitted

	Loco Yard (with 360)	7.30am	‖
xx	Ashford		
	C. shunting 7.40am to 9.40am		
	Ashford	9.48am	P
10. 2am	Appledore	10.11am	P
	Work New Romney branch until		
10.49pm	New Romney	11. 0pm	‖
11.46pm	Ashford Loco		

Ashford men work the New Romney push and pull train. Three sets of men are utilised.

Duty No. 366
1P H class P & P fitted

	Loco Yard (with 487)	5.10am	‖
xx	Ashford	5.50am	P
6.46am	New Romney	7.17am	P
7.50am	Appledore	8.21am	P
8.52am	New Romney	9.25am	P
10.16am	Ashford		
	C. shunting 10.30am to 11.30am		
	F. shunting 12.30pm to 2.30pm		
	Ordnance Sidings	2.10pm	F
2.20pm	West Yard	xx	
xx	Loco Yard (with 184)	4.10pm	‖
xx	Ashford	4.35pm	P
5.20pm	New Romney	5.50pm	P
6.41pm	Ashford	xx	‖
xx	Loco Yard		

Ashford men (two sets) work the New Romney branch passenger and local shunts. The New Romney branch closed on 6th March 1967.

Duty Nos 367 to 369 NOT USED

Duty No. 370
4P/5F N class

	Loco Yard	4.55am	‖
4.55am	Ashford Sidings	5.15am	F
11.17am	Deal (turn)	12. 5pm	F
1.13pm	Minster		
	F. shunting 1.25pm to 4.0pm		
	Minster	4. 5pm	F
4.20pm	Ramsgate	6.55pm	F
7. 8pm	Minster	7.20pm	‖
7.30pm	Ramsgate	8.10pm	F
8.50pm	Deal (turn)	9.28pm	F
12.43am	Ashford (Hump Sidings)		
	F. shunting 12.55am to 2.15am		
	Ashford	xx	‖
xx	Loco Yard		

Ashford men start the duty and are relieved at Minster at 10.0am. Ramsgate men work the engine until 3.13pm. Ashford men relieve at 3.13pm at Minster and work round to Ramsgate at 4.20pm. Ramsgate men work the 6.55pm and complete the duty. Note that the engine turns on the Deal turntable.

Duty No. 371
4P/5F N class

	Loco Yard	9.40am	‖
xx	Ashford Up Sidings	9.58am	F
1. 1pm	Hither Green Sidings	1.55pm	F
2.22pm	B'Arms	xx	‖
xx	B'Arms Loco	11.55pm	‖
xx	B'Arms Goods	12.20am	F
3.18am	Ashford	3.45am	F
5.20am	Ramsgate	xx	
xx	Loco Yard		
	stable for No. 372		

Ashford men are relieved at Hither Green at 1.1pm by B'Arms men who take the engine back to B'Arms. Ashford men take over at 11.50pm, work and are relieved at 3.45am by Ramsgate men who finish the duty.

Standard Class 2 2-6-2 tank No. 84020 at work on the New Romney branch is seen crossing an H class (duties 364 Sats, 365/366 Mon to Fri.) at Lydd Town. The branch closed on 6th March 1967. Standard Class 2 2-6-2Ts in the 84000 series worked on the Ivatt duties; the Region had ten of the locomotives in this series.
J. H. Aston

Ashford had eight N class duties (Nos 370–377) for freight and local passenger work. No. 31406 is shown passing Hollingbourne on a down fast freight on 31st August 1960.

G. Daniels

Duty No. 372
4P/5F N class
OFF No 371

	Ramsgate Loco	6.50am	‖
7. 0am	Minster		
	F. shunting 7.0am to 8.30am		
	Minster	8.47am	‖
8.57am	Ramsgate	9.19am	F
xx	Ramsgate	9.19am	F
12.18pm	Ashford Sidings	1.40pm	F
2.40pm	Paddock Wood	4. 5pm	F
4.17pm	Wateringbury	5.17pm	F
6.15pm	Paddock Wood	6.30pm	‖
6.44pm	Tonbridge Loco	7.30pm	‖
xx	Tonbridge West Yard	7.57pm	F
9.12pm	Ashford Sidings	xx	‖
xx	Loco Yard		
	Work No. 373		

Ramsgate men start the duty with the 6.50am‖ and run the engine light to Minster for 1½ hours shunting, before returning for the 9.19am freight which is worked to Minster where the crew are relieved at 10.0am by Ashford men who finish the duty.

Duty No. 373
4P/5F N class
OFF No. 372

	Loco Yard	12.40am	‖
xx	Ashford Sidings	1.10am	F
3.25am	Dover Town	4. 0am	F
7.55am	Ashford Sidings		
	F. shunting 8.0am to 9.25am		
	Ashford Sidings	11. 0am	F
1. 7pm	St. Leonards W.M.	1.43pm	‖
2.15pm	Rye	2.30pm	F
4.30pm	Hastings		
	C. shunting 4.30pm to 6.10pm		
	Hastings	6.35pm	F
10. 2pm	Brighton Top Yard	xx	‖
xx	Loco Yard		
	stable for No. 377		

Ashford men work round to 9.25am (two sets) when they are relieved by St. Leonards men who work until 6.10pm (early and late set) at Hastings. Brighton men take over at 6.10pm and complete the duty.

Duty No. 374
4P/5F N class

	Loco Yard	7.50am	‖
xx	Ashford Sidings	8. 5am	F
2.30pm	Dover Town	xx	‖
xx	Loco Yard	12.10am	‖
xx	Dover Town	12.40am	F
2.56am	Ashford (Hump Sidings)	xx	
xx	Loco Yard		

Ashford men work round to Minster where they are relieved at 11.5am by Dover men who complete the duty. Early and night set of Dover men are utilised.

Duty No. 375
4P/5F N class

	Loco Yard	5.50am	‖
xx	Ashford	6.40am	P
7.29am	Tonbridge (turn)	10.14am	P
12.28pm	Ramsgate (turn)	1.45pm	‖
1.56pm	Minster	2.42pm	F
4. 0pm	Ashford (turn)	6.15pm	P
7.42pm	Dover Priory	7.46pm	E
7.50pm	Dover Marine	xx	‖
xx	Loco Yard		
	stable for No. 376		

Ashford men work round to Tonbridge at 7.29am, take the engine on to the Loco and are relieved by St. Leonards men who work round to Ashford at 4.0pm. Dover men take over the engine at 5.45pm and finish the duty. The engine turns three times during the course of the duty.

Duty No. 376
4P/5F N class
stabled off No. 375

	Dover Loco	1.15am	‖
xx	Snowdown	2.15am	F
3. 1am	Faversham	xx	‖
xx	Loco Yard	7. 0am	‖
7. 5am	Faversham	7.15am	F
12. 5pm	Dover Town	1.10pm	F
2.16pm	Ashford	2.26pm	‖
xx	Loco Yard	4.25pm	‖
xx	Ashford Sidings	4.45pm	F
5.17pm	Canterbury West		
	F. shunting 5.20pm to 8.50pm		
	Canterbury West	10. 0pm	F
10.58pm	Ashford Sidings	xx	‖
xx	Loco Yard		

Dover men work the engine round to 12.15pm at Dover Town where Ashford men take over and complete the duty.

Duty No. 377
4P/5F N class
OFF No. 374

	Brighton Loco	2. 5am	‖
xx	Top Yard	2.40am	F
6. 0am	St. Leonards	6.15am	F
9.13am	Ashford Sidings		
	F. shunting 9.40am to 11.20am		
	Ashford Sidings	12.50pm	F
3.13pm	Minster	xx	‖
xx	Deal		
	F. shunting 3.45pm to 5.0pm		
	Deal	5.25pm	‖
5.33pm	Sandwich		
	F. shunting 5.35pm to 6.50pm		
	Sandwich	6.55pm	F
7. 5pm	Minster	7.40pm	F
9. 2pm	Ashford (Hump Sidings)	xx	‖
xx	Loco Yard		

St. Leonards men work round to Ashford at 9.25am (two sets) where they are relieved by Ashford men who work the engine until relieved by Ramsgate men at 3.13pm. Ramsgate men work from 3.13pm until 6.20pm at Sandwich where Ashford men take over and complete the duty.

Ashford had plenty of freight work and the C class 0-6-0s were kept busy day and night. C class No. 31218 takes the through line at Ashford station on 31st August 1960.

G. Daniels

Duty No. 378
2F C class (fully coaled)

	Loco Yard	8.20am	‖
xx	Ashford Sidings	8.45am	F
9.28am	Rye	9.30am	F'Q'
9.40am	Rye Harbour	10.20am	F'Q'
10.30am	Rye	11.30am	‖
11.44am	Appledore	12.10pm	F
12.55pm	Lydd Town	3.45pm	F
5.20pm	Ashford West Sidings	xx	‖
xx	Loco Yard		

Ashford men take the morning freight to Rye which has a 'Q' working to Rye Harbour before working a freight from Appledore. The Rye Harbour branch closed on 29th February 1960.

Duty No. 379
2F C class

	Loco Yard	11.10am	‖
xx	Ashford Sidings	11.30am	F
1.13pm	Sturry	2.30pm	F
7.21pm	Ashford Sidings	xx	‖
xx	Loco Yard		

Ashford men work an extremely slow pick up freight from Sturry which shunts en route. One set of men sign on at 10.55am and work the engine which is prepared by Ashford No. 1 P & D men.

Duty No. 380 NOT USED

Duty No. 381
6F Z class

	Loco Yard	5.10am	‖
xx	Hump Yard		
	F. shunting and trip working 5.20am to 8.30pm		
	Ashford	8.30pm	‖
xx	Loco Yard		

Ashford men work the rare Maunsell Z class 0-8-0 shunting tank which covers trip workings and hump shunts. Two sets of Ashford men are used.

Duty No. 382
2F O1 class

	Loco Yard	6.30am	‖
xx	Kimberley Sidings		
	shunting 7.0am to 6.0pm		
	Ashford	6. 0pm	‖
xx	Loco Yard		

A duty for the O1 class 0-6-0, the Wainwright rebuild of the South Eastern O class of 1878. Two sets of Ashford men employed.

Ashford had a Z class 0-8-0 tank to shunt the hump yard on duty No. 381. Introduced in 1929 Maunsell's heavy duty shunting class consisted of eight engines only. No. 30956 was an Exmouth Junction engine.

Ashford shed with O1 class 0-6-0 No. 1377 in early BR days, with the engine still bearing the Southern number and lettering. Duty No. 382 shows all-day shunting at Kimberley Sidings.

Duty No. 383 shows an R1 class 0-6-0T to shunt Ashford Works. Most of the class were used at Folkestone Junction to work the harbour branch. No. 31337 is shown in ex-works condition in early BR days.

Duty No. 383
2F R1 class

	Loco Yard	7.25am	‖
xx	Erecting Shops		
	shunting 7.30am to 5.30pm hauling ex works engines		
	Erecting shops	5.30pm	‖
xx	Loco Yard		

This is one of the works shunting duties which could be worked by any engine available. Sometimes an engine working out its last days before scrapping. Ashford men (two sets) work with the SER R1 0-6-0T class.

Duty No. 384
1P H class

	Loco Yard	6.18am	‖
xx	Carriage Works		
	C. shunting 6.30am to 7.0pm		
	Carriage Works	7.30pm	‖
xx	Loco Yard		

An H class is rostered for the carriage work but any engine might be found on the duty. Ashford men (two sets)

Duty Nos 385 to 393
Diesel electric shunters 350 hp
based at Ashford for fuelling
and maintenance purposes

Duty No.	385	Ashford Hump Yard 6.15am to 12.0mdt shunt
”	386	Ashford sorting sidings 9.25am to 12.0mdt shunt
”	387	Dover Bulwark Street 6.0am to 8.0pm shunt
”	388	Dover Town and Bulwark Street 3.15am to 12.0mdt shunt
”	389	Paddock Wood (inc. Hawkhurst) 4.40am to 12.0mdt shunt
”	390	Tonbridge West Yard 24 hrs shunt
“	391	”　　　”　　　” 8.0am to 12.0 mdt shunt
”	392	”　　　East　　” 24 hrs shunt
”	393	Maidstone West　” 3.45am to 12.0mdt shunt
”	394 to 399 NOT USED	

ST LEONARDS

Duty No. 400
3P L class

	St. Leonards Loco	7. 0am	‖
xx	Hastings	7.48am	P
9. 2am	Tonbridge (turn)		
	C. shunting 9.30am to 1.35pm		
	Tonbridge	3.19pm	P
4.37pm	Hastings	5.10pm	P
5.57pm	Ashford (turn)	7.12pm	P
7.57pm	Hastings		
	C. shunting 8.0pm to 9.0pm		
	Hastings	9.10pm	P
10.32pm	Tonbridge (turn)	11.51pm	P
1. 3am	Hastings	xx	‖
xx	St. Leonards Loco		

St. Leonards men work and are relieved at Tonbridge at 9.5am by Tonbridge men. St. Leonards men work the 3.19pm passenger and work the engine until relieved by Ashford men at 7.5pm. St. Leonards men finish the job having taken over at 8.0pm at Hastings. The engine must turn three times during the duty.

Duty No. 401
1P H class P & P fitted

	St. Leonards Loco (with 410)	5.15am	‖
5.40am	Crowhurst	5.54am	V
6.4am	Bexhill West	7. 7am	P
	work Bexhill West branch until		
7.18pm	Bexhill West	7.25pm	‖
xx	St. Leonards Loco		

St. Leonards men (two sets) work the Bexhill West branch and take the engine with them from St. Leonards Loco. The branch closed to passengers on 15th June 1964. Two sets of men are used, an early and a late.

Ashford duties 383 and 384 are the works shunters and their duties were covered by two C class 0-6-0s, Nos 31271 and 31592 survived, after steam was abolished in 1961. The two engines are seen here on Ashford shed on 24th February 1963 when they were fitted out for snowplough work during the severe winter of that year. No. 31271 was eventually scrapped in 1967 but No. 31592 was preserved and went to the Bluebell Railway in 1967.

J. Smallwood

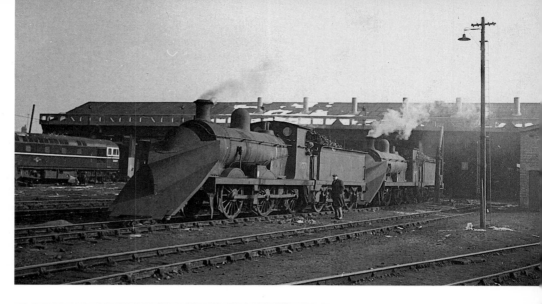

St Leonards had an L class duty for local passenger work between Ashford and Tonbridge via Hastings. No. 31764 was built by Beyer Peacock in 1914 and withdrawn by BR in 1961. The engine is seen at Crowhurst with a pristine ex-works birdcage set. Regrettably none of these fine engines reached preservation.

Lens of Sutton

'Schools' class No. 30909 *St. Paul's* is seen passing Frant on the 10.25am Charing Cross to Hastings on 7th July 1956. Duty No. 396 shows on the disc and is a Saturday working.

G. Daniels

Duty Nos 402 to 406 NOT USED

Duty No. 407
1P H class P & P fitted

	Loco Yard	6.50am	‖
xx	Hastings	7.25am	P
8.21am	Ashford		
	C. shunting 8.30am to 9.45am		
	Ashford	10.40am	P
11.26am	New Romney	1. 0pm	P
1.34pm	Appledore	1.47pm	P
2.30pm	Hastings	2.58pm	P
3.40pm	Appledore	3.50pm	P
4.38pm	Hastings		
	F. shunting 5.0pm to 7.20pm		
	Hastings A/R	9.15pm	E
9.20pm	Ore	xx	‖
xx	St. Leonards Loco		

St. Leonards men have all the work which includes the New Romney branch. The engine finishes working the 9.15pm empties from Hastings to Ore; assistance required. Two sets of St. Leonards men, an early and a late, work the duty.

Duty No. 408
1P H class P & P fitted

	St. Leonards Loco	6.53am	‖
7. 5am	Ore		
	C. shunting 7.5am to 7.40am		
	Ore	7.45am	‖
7.48am	Hastings	8. 3am	P
8.40am	Rye	9.50am	P
10.20am	Hastings		
	F. shunting 10.30am to 11.0am		
	Hastings	11. 5am	‖
11.12am	St. Leonards Loco (with 494)	12.41pm	‖
12.50pm	Hastings	1.24pm	P
2.20pm	Ashford	2.53pm	P
3.39pm	Hastings	5.23pm	P
5.53pm	Rye	6. 8pm	P
6.40pm	Hastings A/R (with 486)	6.55pm	E
6.58pm	Ore	xx	‖
xx	St. Leonards Loco	8.30pm	‖
9. 3pm	Eastbourne Loco	1.30am	‖
xx	Eastbourne	1.56am	V
2.39am	Hastings	xx	
xx	St. Leonards Loco		

St. Leonards men have all the work but Eastbourne men bring the engine off shed at 1.30am. The engine works the 6.55pm empties 'assisting required' from Hastings to Ore. Three sets of men work the duty.

Duty No. 409
5P V class

	St. Leonards	5.43am	‖
5.52am	Hastings		
	C. shunting 6.10am to 6.40am		
	Hastings	6.45am	‖
6.48am	Ore		
	C. shunting 7.50am to 8.10am		
	Ore	8.15am	‖
8.18am	Hastings		
	C. and F. shunting 9.30am to 12.25pm		
	Hastings	12.59pm	P
1.58pm	Ashford (turn)	4.55pm	P
5.40pm	Hastings		
	C. shunting 6.10pm to 7.0pm		
	Hastings	xx	‖
xx	St. Leonards		

Ashford men take over from the St. Leonards crew at 11.50am at Hastings and work until 6.45pm when St. Leonards men take over to finish the duty. Shunting with a 'Schools' – not the ideal engine for the job.

St Leonards had H class 0-4-4Ts to work the Bexhill West branch and A1X class 0-6-0Ts to work the Tenterden goods. In the hop-picking season empty stock had to be worked from Hastings to Robertsbridge and H class No. 31279 is seen double heading A1X class No. 32636 near Crowhurst on Sunday 20th September 1953.

S. C. Nash

The Tenterden goods with A1X No. 32678 on duty No. 413 in July 1957. The A1X class still work the line which has become part of the preserved Kent & East Sussex Railway.

St Leonards' H class No. 31519 at Sidley on duty No. 409 before the line was closed to passenger traffic, which occurred on 15th June 1964. St Leonards shed had five H class 0-4-4Ts for four duties.

Lens of Sutton

Duty No. 410
1P H class P & P fitted

	St. Leonards Loco (with 401)	5.15am	‖
5.40am	Crowhurst	5.41am	‖
5.50am	Bexhill West	6.20am	P
	work Bexhill West branch until		
9.57pm	Bexhill West	xx	
xx	St. Leonards Loco		

St. Leonards men work the Bexhill West branch coming off shed with No. 401 to start the duty. Three sets of men work this duty.

Duty Nos 411 & 412 NOT USED

Duty No. 413
OP A1X class

	St. Leonards Loco	6.30am	‖
7.10am	Robertsbridge	7.55am	F
9.30am	Tenterden Town		
	F. shunting 9.30am to 10.25am		
	Tenterden Town	10.35am	F
1. 9pm	Battle	1.20pm	‖
1.45pm	St. Leonards Loco		

St. Leonards men sign on at 6.15am and take the A1X to Robertsbridge for the Tenterden goods; a nice little number.

Duty No. 414 NOT USED

FOLKESTONE JUNCTION

Duty No. 415
2F R1 class 0-6-0T.

	Loco Yard	4.30am	‖
xx	Folkestone Junction	4.50am	E
5. 6am	Dover Marine	5.16am	E
	C. shunting 5.35am to 8.45am inc. steam heating		
	and work trips to Folkestone Hbr until		
9.10pm	Folkestone Junction	xx	‖
xx	Loco Yard		

Folkestone Junction men work the branch assisting in banking and double or even triple heading boat trains. Three sets of men cover the duty.

Folkestone Junction shed had an allocation of seven aged South Eastern Railway 0-6-0 tanks dating from 1888 to work the steeply graded harbour branch. A triple headed boat train is being worked up the 1 in 30 grade on 21st May 1956. The centre engine of the trio has cut down cab and boiler mountings for the closed Canterbury & Whitstable branch. Duties 415–418 refer.

G. Daniels

R1 class 0-6-0 tanks await the next boat train at Folkestone Junction in January 1959. The R1s were eventually replaced by ex-GWR pannier tanks. Note the unusual track with weighbridge, left.

Duty No. 416
2F R1 class 0-6-0T

	Loco Yard	4. 0am	‖
xx	Folkestone Junction		
	F. & C. shunting 4.5am to 11.30am		
	and work trips and boat trains until		
	Folkestone Junction	1.30am	‖
xx	Loco Yard		

Folkestone Junction men have an early start and spend the duty working boat trains and shunting. Three sets of men are utilised.

Duty No. 417
2F R1 class 0-6-0T

	Loco Yard	12.55pm	‖
	assist on Folkestone Harbour branch until		
	Folkestone Junction	7.15pm	‖
xx	Loco Yard		

Folkestone Junction men work the branch and shunt as required. Two sets used, one early, and one late turn.

Duty No. 418
2F R1 class 0-6-0T

	Loco Yard	6. 0am	‖
	work freight and passengers on the branch until		
9.10pm	Folkestone Junction	xx	‖
xx	Loco Yard		

An early and late turn set of Folkestone Junction men work freights and empty stock as well as assisting on boat trains with their elderly SER 0-6-0Ts, replaced by panniers in 1959.

Duty Nos 419 & 420 NOT USED

DOVER

Duty No. 421
4MT 4-6-0 BR Standard

	Loco Yard	9.10am	‖
xx	Dover Marine	9.28am	F 'Q'
	(Via Chatham)		
12.47pm	Southwark Depot	xx	‖
xx	Hither Green Loco	7.25pm	‖
xx	Southwark Depot	8.10pm	F 'Q'
	(Via Maidstone East)		
11. 7pm	Dover Marine	xx	‖
xx	Loco Yard		

Gillingham men work this "Grand Vitesse" express freight when required and Hither Green with Ashford men bring it back.

Dover had an allocation of five BR Standard Class 4 4-6-0s to work express, freight, and special passenger trains. No. 75066 is seen working a Dover to Victoria passenger train on the last day of steam working on Sunday 14th June 1959 and is near Rochester Bridge Junction. Duty Nos 421–429 refer.

Duty No. 422
4MT 4-6-0 BR Standard

	Loco Yard	2. 5am	‖
xx	Dover Marine	2.25am	F 'Q'
6.25am	B'Arms	12.45pm	F 'Q'
3.47pm	Dover Marine	xx	‖
xx	Loco Yard		

Dover and Bricklayers Arms men work this "Grand Vitesse" express freight as required.

Duty Nos 423 to 428 NOT USED

Duty No. 429
4MT 4-6-0 BR Standard

	Loco Yard	9.45am	‖
xx	Dover Marine	10. 5am	V
2.18pm	Rotherhithe Road	xx	‖
xx	B'Arms Loco	6.15pm	‖
xx	Rotherhithe Road	6.45pm	E
7.15pm	Charing Cross	xx	‖
xx	Southwark Depot		
	F. shunting 8.0pm to 10.30pm		
	Southwark Depot	10.30pm	‖
xx	B'Arms (F. Sect)	11.10pm	F
2.36am	Dover Marine	xx	‖
xx	Loco Yard		

Ashford men work round to Ashford at 11.13am where B'Arms men take over. B'Arms men work the duty until 1.45am when Ashford men take over and finish the duty. B'Arms have a late and a night set to work the trains.

Duty No. 430
8P MN class

	Loco Yard (with 437)	6.50am	‖
6.55am	Dover Marine D/H	7. 8am	P
9.10am	Victoria (propel)	9.42am	E
9.46am	Carriage Sidings	xx	‖
xx	Stewarts Lane Loco	11.40am	‖
xx	Stewarts Lane O/R	11.50am	E
12. 2pm	Victoria	12.30pm	P
2. 6pm	Folkestone Junction	2. 9pm	‖
2.20pm	Dover Loco	4.50pm	‖
xx	Dover Marine	5.10pm	P
6.51pm	Victoria (propel)	7.10pm	E
7.15pm	Carriage Sidings	xx	‖
xx	Stewarts Lane Loco (with 437)	8.35pm	‖
8.42pm	Victoria D/H	9. 0pm	P
10.40pm	Dover Marine	xx	‖
xx	Dover Loco		

Dover men have this prestige turn working the up and down "Night Ferry" with the 'Wagon Lits', the only through train from Britain to the Continent. The train proved to be very heavy so was double headed with a Dover L1 (No. 437 duty). The 12.30pm down and 5.10pm up boat trains were also Dover worked. An early and a late turn set of Dover men are used.

Dover had an allocation of two 'Merchant Navies' to work the "Night Ferry". No. 35029 is seen at Stewarts Lane in 1954 in BR blue, having worked the up train on duty No. 430. No. 35029 *Ellerman Lines* has survived in its rebuilt form as a sectioned exhibit at the National Railway Museum, York.

P. J. Winding

Bulleid 'West Country' No. 34103 *Calstock* is seen working the 2.35pm Victoria to Dover Priory on 27th June 1959 at Paddock Wood on duty No. 431.

E. Wilmshurst

Duty No. 431
7P/5F WC class

	Loco Yard	8.55am	‖
xx	Dover Marine	9.10am	E
9.14am	Dover Priory	9.20am	P
11.28am	Victoria (propel)	11.40am	E
11.44am	Carriage Sidings	xx	‖
xx	Stewarts Lane Loco	2.15pm	‖
2.22pm	Victoria	2.35pm	P
5. 6pm	Dover Priory	xx	‖
xx	Loco Yard		

Dover men have all the work on this main line duty with a Bulleid Pacific which could be WC or BB class.

Duty No. 432
5P N15 class

	Loco Yard	11.10pm	‖
11.15pm	Dover Marine	11.25pm	V
11.40pm	Folkestone Junction	12. 1am	V
2.17am	Southwark Depot		
	F. shunting 3.0am to 4.0am		
	Southwark Depot	xx	‖
xx	Ewer Street	5.50am	‖
5.56am	Cannon St.	6.20am	P
9.26am	Dover Priory	xx	‖
xx	Loco Yard		

Dover men have one of the last 'King Arthur' turns left and are relieved at Ashford at 12.55am by Ashford men. Dover men come back onto the engine at 8.32am at Ashford and complete the duty.

Duty No. 433
7P/5F BB class

	Loco Yard	8.23am	‖
xx	Dover Priory	8.59am	P
11.35am	Charing Cross O/R	12. 8pm	E
12.17pm	Rotherhithe Road	xx	‖
xx	Hither Green Loco	4. 5pm	‖
4.13pm	Grove Park (forms 7.20pm)	6.30pm	E
6.56pm	Charing Cross	7.32pm	P
9.59pm	Folkestone Junction	xx	‖
xx	Dover Loco		

Ramsgate men take over from Dover men at Dover Priory at 8.30am and are relieved at Ashford at 9.55am by B'Arms men who have come down on duty No. 100. The B'Arms men work to Rotherhithe Road before being relieved by Hither Green men who work the engine until 7.42pm at London Bridge. B'Arms men work the engine from London Bridge until relieved by Ashford men at Ashford who work the engine to Dover Loco.

Duty No. 434
7P/5F WC class

	Loco Yard	10.30am	‖
xx	Dover Priory	11. 6am	P
1.35pm	Charing Cross (S.R.E.) runs via LB	1.54pm	‖
2.14pm	Ewer Street	3.37pm	‖
3.50pm	Charing Cross (via Dover)	4.10pm	P
6.50pm	Margate	xx	‖
xx	Ramsgate Loco	8.30pm	‖
8.47pm	Margate	9.28pm	P
10.31pm	Dover Priory	xx	‖
xx	Loco Yard		

Dover men have all the work which includes having to shunt at Charing Cross to release the engine and a layover at Ewer Street loco sidings. The duty finishes with the 9.28pm mails from Margate. Two sets of Dover men used.

Duty No. 435
5P N15 class

	Loco Yard	6.10am	‖
	Dover Priory	6.50am	P
7.31am	Ashford	7.56am	P
9.44am	Cannon St.	xx	‖
xx	Ewer St.	11.29am	‖
11.39am	Charing Cross	11.48am	P
1.53pm	Ashford	2.35pm	P
3.41pm	Ramsgate (turn on Loco)	5.17pm	P
8.42pm	Charing Cross	9.17pm	‖
9.27pm	Ewer St.	11.10pm	‖

(Continued)

xx	London Bridge (via Redhill)	11.50pm	P
3. 8am	Dover Priory	3.30am	V
3.35am	Dover Marine	xx	‖
xx	Loco Yard		

Dover men have the engine to Ashford where Ashford men take over at 7.55am. Ashford men have the rest of the duty which finishes off with the night postal (complete with sorting vans) at 11.50pm from London Bridge via Redhill. Four sets of Ashford men are involved.

Duty No. 436 NOT USED

Duty No. 437
3P L1 class

	Loco Yard (with 430)	6.50am	‖
xx	Dover Marine (A/R)	7. 8am	P
9.10am	Victoria	xx	‖
xx	Stewarts Lane Loco	6.27pm	‖
6.32pm	Victoria (off 4.58pm D.P.)	6.52pm	E
7. 2pm	Stewarts Lane Carr. Sidings	xx	‖
xx	Stewarts Lane Loco	8.35pm	‖
xx	Victoria (A/R)	9. 0pm	P
10.40pm	Dover Marine	xx	‖
xx	Loco Yard		

Dover men have the main line work on this prestige turn which is the up and down "Night Ferry" double headed with duty No. 430. Stewarts Lane men have the engine from 9.40am until 8.50pm.

Duty Nos 438 to 443 NOT USED

Dover still had two 'King Arthur' duties in 1957 including No. 30777 which has become the sole survivor and has been restored to its original Southern livery. *Sir Lamiel*, now part of the National Railway Museum collection and restored to working order by the HLPG, is in use today to work steam specials on BR. The engine is seen leaving Marylebone on 30th December 1986 with a Sunday Stratford-on-Avon, "Shakespeare Express".

Duty No. 437 was worked by a Dover L1 class 4-4-0 which double headed the up and down "Night Ferry". An official BR photograph shows an L1 with a good head of steam about to leave Victoria.

10432. "Night Ferry" for Paris & Brussels. British Railways

Duty No. 444
4MT 2-6-4 tank LMR class

	Loco Yard	5.40am	‖
xx	Dover Priory	6.10am	P
7.53am	Gillingham	xx	‖
xx	Loco Yard (with No. 250)	2.33pm	‖
2.43pm	Rochester	2.54pm	V
2.56pm	Chatham	4.21pm	E
4.23pm	Rochester	4.30pm	‖
4.34pm	Strood	4.55pm	P
6.51pm	Dover Priory	6.53pm	E
6.57pm	Dover Marine		
	C. shunting 7.0pm to 2.0am		
	Dover Marine	2. 0am	‖
2. 5am	Loco Yard		

Dover men work the 6.10am passenger and dispose the loco at Gillingham Loco. Faversham men take over the 2.33pm‖ and come off shed coupled to No. 250 as far as Rochester. Faversham men are relieved at Dover Priory at 6.51pm by Dover men who complete the duty. Two Dover sets used.

Duty Nos 445 to 447 NOT USED

Duty No. 448
4MT 2-6-4 tank LMR class

	Loco Yard	5. 0am	‖
xx	Dover Marine	5.10am	E
5.14am	Dover Priory	5.32am	P
6. 7am	Canterbury East	6.20am	P
7.23am	Folkestone Junction	xx	‖
xx	Folkestone Junction Loco	10. 0am	‖
	steam heat stock and shunt		
	Folkestone Junction	11.50am	E
11.55am	Shorncliffe	12.25pm	P
1.33pm	Minster	2.38pm	P
2.44pm	Deal	3.10pm	P
3.27pm	Minster	3.37pm	P
3.53pm	Deal	4.18pm	P
4.34pm	Minster	4.51pm	P
5.59pm	Shorncliffe	6.38pm	P
6.58pm	Dover Priory	xx	‖
xx	Dover Marine	8.18pm	V
8.25pm	Dover Priory	9.13pm	P
10.10pm	Faversham	10.57pm	P
11.55pm	Dover Priory	12.20am	E
12.35am	Folkestone Junction	xx	‖
xx	Dover Loco		

Dover men have this local passenger and empties working using a LMR 2-6-4 tank, ideal for local passenger workings as turning is avoided using this class of loco. Three sets of Dover men; 4.45am, 12.11pm, and 7.45pm are used.

Duty No. 449
4MT 2-6-4 tank LMR class

	Dover Loco	5.53am	||
6.20am	Deal	7. 5am	P
	(C. shunting 6.35am to 6.55am)		
7.21am	Minster (via Dover & Ashford)	7.34am	P
9.44am	Maidstone East	10.34am	P
12. 2pm	Dover Priory	12.12pm	||
12.17pm	Dover Marine A.N.R. with 364	12.45pm	E
1. 1pm	Folkestone Cent.	1. 7pm	P
1.10pm	Folkestone Junction	3.35pm	||
	(C. shunting 1.50pm to 2.5pm)		
3.40pm	Shorncliffe	4.17pm	P
5.22pm	Minster	5.48pm	P
6. 4pm	Deal	6.39pm	P
7.14pm	Ramsgate	9.20pm	P
9.27pm	Minster	9.37pm	P
10.40pm	Folkestone Junction	11. 0pm	||
11.20pm	Dover Loco		

Dover men have local passenger and shunts including running coupled to 364 from Dover Marine to Folkestone Cent. on the 12.45pm empties. Three sets of Dover men are used; 4.53am, 12.5pm, and 3.52pm.

Duty No. 450
4MT 2-6-4 tank LMR class

	Loco Yard	6.45am	||
6.50am	Dover Marine	7. 0am	E
7. 4am	Dover Priory	7. 7am	P
7.31am	Deal	7.45am	P
7.52am	Sandwich	7.55am	E
8.15am	Ramsgate	10. 5am	||
10.22am	Minster	10.50am	P
	(P/O 8.5am freight ex Ashford)		
11. 6am	Deal	11.24am	P
11.40am	Minster	12.40pm	P
1.23pm	Dover Priory	2.40pm	P
3.16pm	Canterbury East	3.43pm	P
4.20pm	Dover Priory	5. 9pm	P
6.42pm	Chatham		
	C. shunting 6.45pm to 7.30pm		
	Chatham	xx	||
xx	Gillingham Loco	10.25pm	||
11. 5pm	Farningham Rd	12.10am	F
12.45am	Chatham Sidings	1.25am	F
1.50am	Gillingham	2. 0am	||
2.10am	Strood	2.28am	F
4.50am	Snowdown	xx	||
xx	Dover Loco		

An early Dover set start the duty and a late turn set are relieved at 5.21pm at Shepherdswell by Gillingham men who take over and complete the duty. Two Dover sets and three Gillingham sets are involved.

Duty No. 451
4P/5F N class

	Loco Yard	11.50am	||
xx	Dover Marine		
	C. shunting 12.0noon to 1.0pm		
	Dover Marine	xx	||
xx	Dover Town	1.40pm	F
7.12pm	Faversham	xx	||
xx	Loco Yard	8.35pm	||
8.55pm	Sittingbourne		
	F. shunting 9.15pm to 10.55pm		
	Sittingbourne	xx	||
xx	Faversham	12.10am	F
1.15am	Shepherdswell	1.45am	EBV
1.53am	Snowdown	xx	||
xx	Dover Loco		

Faversham men have a share of the work taking over from the Dover crew at 2.30pm at Shepherdswell to work a very slow freight to Faversham which stops off to shunt on the way. Faversham men keep the engine until 11.35pm when Dover men take over and complete the duty.

Dover N class 2-6-0s worked freights to Faversham and Gillingham on duties 451 and 452. D1 class No. 31246 arrives at Faversham on a train from Dover in early BR days with a Maunsell set in red and cream. There are at least ten locomotives in this scene apart from the D1. There are two Ns, one Q1, one H, and a shed full of old SECR types in this very steamy view of Faversham.

Lens of Sutton

Duty No. 452
4P/5F N class

	Loco Yard	5.45pm	‖
xx	Dover Priory (via Rams)	6.25pm	F
2.12am	Gillingham	xx	‖
xx	Loco Yard	3.15am	‖
3.24am	Chatham Sidings	3.55am	F
5.57am	Faversham	xx	‖
xx	Loco Yard	7.15am	‖
xx	Faversham	7.40am	F
9.41am	Deal (turn)	10.20am	F
12.48pm	Ashford Sidings	xx	‖
xx	Loco Yard	2. 0pm	‖
xx	Ashford	2.30pm	V
2.48pm	Shorncliffe	3.35pm	V
3.45pm	Folkestone Cent. (steam heat)	4.30pm	E
4.42pm	Dover Marine	xx	‖
xx	Dover Loco		

Faversham men take over the engine at Dover Priory at 6.22pm, Dover men having prepared the 5.45pm‖. After a slow night freight the Faversham men leave the engine on Gillingham Loco where Hither Green men take over the 3.15am‖ and work until 4.9am. Gillingham men relieve at 4.9am at Gillingham and work to Faversham where Ramsgate men take over at 6.0am. Dover men relieve the Ramsgate men at Deal at 10.15am and complete this duty.

Duty Nos 453 to 455 NOT USED

Duty Nos 456 & 458
D.E. 204 hp shunters Drewry,
two duties for Dover men shunting
Ferry Sidings, Dockyard and Harbour
5.30am to 12.30am and 7.15am to 8.30pm

Duty No. 457 NOT USED

Duty No. 459
2F O1 class

	Dover Loco	5. 0am	‖
5.20am	Shepherdswell		
	F. shunting and trips to Tilmanstone		
	5.25am to 3.45pm Shepherdswell	4.25pm	‖
4.40pm	Dover Priory		
	F. shunting 5.0pm to 6.30pm		
	Dover Priory	6.32pm	‖
6.39pm	Loco Yard		

Dover men have one of the last O1 duties, shunting and working loaded coal out of Tilmanstone Colliery. Faversham men get a quick look in on this duty, from 10.30am until 11.45am. An early and middle turn for Dover men.

Duty No. 460 NOT USED

Duty No. 461
2F O1 class

	Loco Yard	5.45am	‖
xx	Dover Town	6.10am	F
7. 5am	Shepherdswell		
	F. shunting and trips to Tilmanstone		
	Shepherdswell	2.42pm	F
3.12pm	Dover Town	xx	‖
xx	Dover Marine		
	C. shunting 4.10pm to 5.0pm		
	Dover Marine	xx	‖
xx	Dover Loco		

Dover men work this aged O1 class until 12.20pm, when they are relieved by Faversham men who work the engine round to 2.30pm. Dover men return and finish the duty. Two Dover sets, an early, on at 4.15am, and 10.34am.

Duty No. 462 NOT USED

Duty No. 463
2F C class

	Dover Loco	3. 0am	‖
xx	Dover Priory (off 11.50pm LB)	3.23am	P
3.44am	Deal (turn)	5.25am	P
5.49am	Dover Priory	5.51am	E
5.56am	Dover Marine		
	C. shunting 6.0am to 7.30am		
	F. shunting 7.40am to 7.0pm including		
	trips to Harbour and Town Yard		
	Dover Marine	7. 0pm	‖
xx	Loco Yard		

Dover men have some passenger work (including a portion off of the 11.50pm ex London Bridge postal) before shunting at Dover Harbour and Town. An early set (3.30am) and a late set (12.20pm) are utilised.

Duty No. 464 NOT USED

RAMSGATE

Duty No. 467
7P/5F BB class

	Loco Yard	6.10am	‖
xx	Ramsgate	6.29am	P
8.53am	Cannon St. (off 6.45am RM)	9.53am	E
10.15am	Rotherhithe Rd	xx	‖
xx	B'Arms	2.40pm	‖
xx	Rotherhithe Rd (4.44pm CS)	3.13pm	E
3.34pm	Cannon St.	5.14pm	P
7.14pm	Ramsgate	xx	‖
xx	Loco Yard		

Stewarts Lane men relieve the Ramsgate men at Gillingham at 7.58am and work round to Cannon St. at 8.53am when they are relieved by B'Arms men. B'Arms men work the engine until 3.34pm when Ramsgate men take over work and dispose.

Dover had four duties for Class 4 2-6-4 tanks, two duties for N15 class 4-6-0s, and two duties for O1 class 0-6-0s (which worked the East Kent Railway). Here, in this line up O1 class No. 31258 is seen on Dover Loco on Sunday afternoon 3rd May 1959.

Dover had an allocation of four C class 0-6-0s of which No. 31150 was one. The SECR engine was built in November 1902 and withdrawn by BR in October 1961. Duty No. 463 refers.

Duty No. 469
7P/5F BB class

	Ramsgate Loco	6.40am	‖
6.57am	Margate (via Dover)	7.34am	P
10.37am	Charing Cross (via LB & CS)	11.17am	‖
11.40am	Ewer St.	12.36pm	‖
12.48pm	Charing Cross	1. 8pm	P
4. 5pm	Margate	4.55pm	P
5.11pm	Ramsgate	xx	‖
xx	Loco Yard		

Ramsgate men have all the work which includes taking the engine light at 11.17am via London Bridge and Cannon St. to Ewer St. to turn for the 1.8pm ex Charing Cross.

Duty No. 471
7P/5F BB class

	Loco Yard	7. 0am	‖
xx	Ramsgate	7.19am	P
9.19am	Cannon St.	xx	‖
xx	Ewer St.	10.55am	‖
11. 2am	Charing Cross	11. 8am	P
2. 5pm	Ramsgate	2.18pm	‖
xx	Loco Yard	4.45pm	‖
xx	Ramsgate	5. 2pm	P
7. 5pm	Victoria (O/R)	7.26pm	E
7.36pm	Stewarts Lane	xx	‖
xx	Stewarts Lane Loco	9.15pm	‖
9.22pm	Victoria	9.35pm	P
12. 0mdt	Ramsgate	xx	‖
xx	Loco Yard		

Ramsgate men have all the work including travelling 'on rear' from Victoria on the 7.26pm empties. The engine goes onto Ramsgate Loco from 2.5pm to 5.2pm.

'Battle of Britain' class No. 34081 *92 Squadron* having worked up to Victoria on duty No. 471 pushes the stock through the Stewarts Lane washer before returning on the 9.35pm to Ramsgate. This locomotive now nears completion of restoration on the Nene Valley Railway.

Ramsgate 'Battle of Britain' class No. 34075 *264 Squadron* prepares to depart from Folkestone East Sidings on bank holiday Monday 21st May 1956. Ramsgate Bulleid 4-6-2s worked to Victoria via Chatham and Dover on duties 467–475 and were seen on specials on summer weekends. On the left is No. 34048 *Crediton*.

E. Wilmshurst

Duty No. 472
7P/5F BB Class
OFF No. 475

	B'Arms	6.10am	‖
6.21am	Rotherhithe Rd (8.20am HS)	6.40am	E
7. 8am	Charing Cross	9. 8am	P
12. 3pm	Ramsgate	2.10pm	P
2.24pm	Margate	3.25pm	P
6.22pm	Charing Cross (S.R.E.)	6.44pm	‖
6.54pm	Ewer St. (via CS & LB)	8.30pm	‖
8.44pm	Charing Cross	9. 8pm	P
12.10am	Ramsgate	xx	
xx	Loco Yard		

B'Arms men start the duty at 6.10am and take up the empties at 6.40am to Charing Cross before working the 9.8am down to Ashford. Ashford men take over at 10.35am and work to Ramsgate where they are relieved by Ramsgate men who work to Charing Cross at 6.22pm. Ashford men take over at Charing Cross at 6.22pm and take the engine to Ewer St. after shunting to release from Charing Cross platforms. The engine runs 8.30pm‖ via Cannon St. and London Bridge to work the 9.8pm passenger. Ramsgate men finish the duty by relieving at Ashford at 10.35pm.

Duty No. 473
5P V class

	Loco Yard	8.10am	‖
xx	Ramsgate	8.22am	P
10.30am	Victoria Propel	10.40am	E
10.45am	Carriage Sidings	11.35am	E
11.40am	Victoria (bank 12.30pm FH)	12.31pm	‖
12.39pm	Stewarts Lane Loco	7.15pm	‖
xx	Victoria	7.35pm	P
10. 1pm	Ramsgate	xx	‖
xx	Loco Yard		

Stewarts Lane men relieve the Ramsgate men at Victoria at 10.30am and have the engine until 7.30pm (two sets) when Ramsgate men relieve and finish the job off.

Duty No. 474
7P/5F BB class

	Loco Yard	8.30am	‖
8.46am	Margate	9.38am	P
12.28pm	Charing Cross (via CS & LB)	1.17pm	‖
1.46pm	Ewer St.	2.55pm	‖
3. 5pm	Charing Cross	3.10pm	P
6. 8pm	Ramsgate	xx	‖
xx	Loco Yard		

Ramsgate men have all the work including running the 1.17pm‖ from Charing Cross to Ewer St. via Cannon St. and London Bridge to turn.

Duty No. 475
7P/5F BB class

	Loco Yard	11.15am	‖
xx	Ramsgate	11.35am	P
11.49am	Margate	12.39pm	P
3.47pm	Charing Cross	4.17pm	‖
4.36pm	Ewer St.	6. 8pm	‖
6.13pm	Cannon St.	6.24pm	P
8.53pm	Dover Priory (via Redhill)	10.40pm	P
1.26am	Cannon St.	3.40am	V
	(C. shunting 1.30am to 3.0am)		
3.48am	London Bridge	3.56am	‖
4.12am	B'Arms Loco		
	Work No. 472		

Ramsgate men work the engine until 4.0pm at Charing Cross when B'Arms take over and complete the duty. The 10.40pm from Dover Priory to Cannon St. runs via Redhill and the Central District. The engine does not need to turn at the London end of the working as it arrives at Charing Cross and departs from Cannon St. on the 6.24pm.

Duty No. 477
5P V class

	Ramsgate Loco	6.15am	‖
6.30am	Margate	7. 9am	P
10.15am	Cannon St.	11.19am	E
	(10.20am ex Rotherhithe Rd)		
11.27am	Charing Cross (off 8.59am DP)	12. 8pm	E
12.17pm	Rotherhithe Rd	xx	‖
xx	B'Arms Loco	2.40pm	‖
2.51pm	Rotherhithe Rd P/O	3.10pm	E
xx	Surrey Canal Junction O/R	xxpm	E
3.34pm	Cannon St.	4.44pm	P
6.57pm	Ramsgate	7.10pm	‖
7.13pm	Loco Yard		

B'Arms men relieve the Ramsgate men at Ashford at 8.35am and work until 4.35pm at Cannon St. Stewarts Lane men relieve at Cannon St. at 4.35pm and work to Faversham at 5.50pm. Faversham men take over at 5.50pm and complete the duty. The engine 'pulls off' the empties at Rotherhithe Rd at 3.10pm and works them to Cannon St. 'on rear' from Surrey Canal Junction.

Ramsgate had twelve 'Schools' class 4-4-0s for six duties. No. 30912 *Downside* is about to start from Margate with a special on the last day of steam working, 14th June 1959.

R. Joanes

Duty Nos 476, 479 & 480 NOT USED

Duty No. 478
5P V class

	Loco Yard	6.35am	‖
xx	Ramsgate	6.53am	E
7.27am	Herne Bay	8.20am	P
9.56am	Cannon St. (off 7.56am AD)	10.17am	E
10.45am	Rotherhithe Rd	xx	‖
xx	B. Arms Loco	3. 0pm	‖
xx	Rotherhithe Rd (forms 5.5pm HS)	3.30pm	E
3.53pm	Cannon St.	xx	‖
xx	Ewer St.	xx	‖
xx	Cannon St.	6.14pm	P
8.23pm	Ramsgate	8.37pm	‖
xx	Loco Yard		

The first set of Ramsgate men are on at 5.35am, work and are relieved at 8.41am. The first set of Faversham men sign on at 8.15am, relieve Faversham at 8.41am and work to B'Arms loco. Gillingham men off No. 421 relieve at 2.55pm at B'Arms work and are relieved at Cannon St. at 4.35pm B'Arms men off No. 486 take over at Cannon St. work and are relieved at 5.30pm by Ramsgate men off No. 481 who take over at Cannon St. at 5.30pm and work the engine back to Ramsgate where they are relieved by No. 9 P&D men who dispose the engine.

Duty No. 481
5P V class

	Loco Yard	1.35pm	‖
xx	Ramsgate	1.50pm	P
4.12pm	Victoria O/R	4.40pm	E
4.50pm	Stewarts Lane	xx	‖
xx	Stewarts Lane Loco	8. 5pm	‖
8.12pm	Victoria	8.35pm	P
11.12pm	Ramsgate	xx	‖
xx	Loco Yard		

Ramsgate men have the main line work up and down and Stewarts Lane men take over at Victoria at 4.20pm and take the empties 'on rear' to Stewarts Lane and back with the 8.5pm‖.

Duty Nos 482 to 484 NOT USED

Duty No. 485
5P V class

	Loco Yard	8.36am	‖
xx	Ramsgate	8.55am	P
11.34am	Redhill (coupled to No. 293)	11.52am	‖
11.55am	Loco Yard	2.10pm	‖
2.15pm	Redhill (7.35am Birkenhead)	2.38pm	P
4.46pm	Margate (turn on Loco Sdgs)	6.47pm	P
10.40pm	Charing Cross	11.10pm	‖
11.18pm	Cannon St. (via LB)	11.48pm	V
12.35am	Charing Cross	12.40am	E
12.50am	Cannon St.	2.30am	E
	(C. shunting 1.30am to 2.0am)		
2.52am	Rotherhithe Rd	xx	‖
xx	B'Arms Loco		
	stable for No. 486		

Ramsgate men have the engine round to Folkestone Junction at 8.8pm where Ashford men relieve and work until 10.25pm at London Bridge. B'Arms men relieve at London Bridge at 10.25pm and complete the duty. The engine works the first part of the Ramsgate to Birkenhead train as far as Redhill in the morning, turning on Redhill Loco. The train runs in two parts to Ashford and joins up with the Hastings/Brighton portion at Redhill.

Duty No. 486
5P V class
OFF No. 485

	B'Arms Loco	2.15pm	‖
2.40pm	Charing Cross (forms 4.31pm RM)	3. 2pm	E
3.12pm	Cannon St.	5. 5pm	P
6.47pm	Hastings (double headed with 408)	6.55pm	E
6.58pm	Ore	xx	‖
xx	Hastings	8.35pm	P
9.16pm	Ashford	xx	‖
xx	Loco Yard		
	stable for No. 487		

B'Arms men take the 2.15pm‖ to Charing Cross and hand over the engine to St. Leonards men at Cannon St. at 4.20pm who work round to Hastings at 8.0pm. Ashford men take over at 8.0pm and take the engine home.

Duty No. 487
5P V class
stabled off No. 486

	Loco Yard (with 366)	5.10am	‖
xx	Ashford	6.10am	V
6.40am	Shorncliffe		
	C. and F. shunting 6.45am to 7.15am		
	Shorncliffe	7.30am	P
8.34am	Minster	8.50am	P
9. 7am	Deal	9.25am	P
9.41am	Minster	9.50am	‖
10. 0am	Ramsgate Loco	11.10am	‖
xx	Ramsgate	11.30am	P
2.50pm	Charing Cross	xx	‖
xx	Ewer St.	xx	‖
xx	Cannon St.	4.37pm	P
7.13pm	Folkestone Junction	xx	‖
xx	Loco Yard	xx	‖
xx	Folkestone Junction (7.32pm ex CX)	10. 5pm	P
11. 9pm	Ramsgate	xx	‖
xx	Loco Yard		

Ashford men have all the work round to Folkestone Junction where Ramsgate men take over at 8.15pm and complete the job. Two sets of Ashford men are used.

Duty No. 488
3P L class

	Ramsgate Loco	4.15am	‖
4.32am	Margate	5. 8am	P
6. 8am	Canterbury West	6.55am	P
7.25am	Ashford		
	C. shunting 7.25am to 8.30am and turn in loco yard		
	Ashford	9.48am	P
10.30am	Hastings	10.35am	P
11.52am	Tonbridge	12.40pm	P
1.18pm	Redhill	xx	‖
xx	Loco Yard (turn)	xx	‖
xx	Redhill		
	C. shunting 3.0pm to 4.15pm		
	Redhill	5. 5pm	P
5.46pm	Tonbridge	7.15pm	P
8. 4pm	Ashford	8.21pm	P
9.43pm	Margate	10.25pm	‖
10.40pm	Ramsgate Loco		

Ramsgate men start the duty and are relieved at Ashford at 9.25am by B'Arms men who turn the engine and get it ready for the 9.48am. St. Leonards men come on at 9.40am and work round to Tonbridge. Tonbridge men step onto the footplate at 12.40pm and work over to Redhill and back to be relieved at Tonbridge at 7.15pm by Ramsgate men who finish the duty.

L class No. 31779 works an up stopping train through the Kentish orchards, near Newington on Saturday 13th June 1959, just before the line was electrified. Ramsgate had five L class 4-4-0s for three duties.

Duty No. 489
3P L class

	Loco Yard	4.15am	‖
xx	Ramsgate	4.38pm	P
6.22am	Chatham	6.36am	E
6.38am	Rochester	6.47am	‖
7. 0am	Gillingham Loco	8.50am	‖
9. 2am	Chatham	9.38am	P
11.11am	Dover Priory	11.15am	‖
11.20am	Dover Marine		
	C. shunting 11.30am to 12.0 noon		
	Dover Marine	12. 0pm	‖
12.15pm	Dover Priory	1. 5pm	P
2. 2pm	Faversham	xx	‖
xx	Loco Yard	3.55pm	‖
xx	Faversham	4.11pm	P
5.18pm	Ramsgate	5.36pm	P
6.47pm	Ashford		
	C. shunting 6.50pm to 7.50pm		
	Ashford	9.35pm	P
10.54pm	Margate	11.15pm	‖
11.33pm	Ramsgate Loco		

Ramsgate men start with the 4.15am‖ off shed for which they have signed on at 3.15am to prepare, they are then relieved at Faversham at 5.41am by Faversham men who work to Gillingham Loco. Faversham men start the 8.50am‖ and work to Faversham where they are relieved at 10.15am by Dover men who take the engine as far as Faversham at 2.2pm. Another Faversham set comes onto the engine at 2.2pm and work to Ramsgate where they are relieved at 5.25pm. Ramsgate men sign on at 5.5pm, relieve at 5.25pm, work and complete the duty.

Duty No. 490
3P L class

	Loco Yard	6.50am	‖
xx	Ramsgate	7. 6am	P
8.41am	Gillingham	xx	‖
xx	Loco Yard	9.25am	‖
xx	Gillingham	9.45am	E
9.55am	Strood	10.30am	P
11.19am	Faversham		
	C. shunting 11.20am to 1.0pm		
	Faversham	1.13pm	P
2.10pm	Dover Priory	xx	‖
xx	Dover Loco	3.30pm	‖
xx	Dover Priory	4.18pm	P
5.16pm	Faversham		
	C. shunting 5.20pm to 6.40pm		
	Faversham	xx	‖
xx	Loco Yard	7.45pm	‖
xx	Faversham	8. 5pm	P
9. 5pm	Ramsgate	xx	‖
xx	Loco Yard		

Gillingham men work the 6.50am‖ and are relieved at 9.25am by Dover men who work until 11.50am. Faversham men come on to the engine at 11.50am and shunt until 12.5pm. Dover men relieve at 12.5pm and work until 5.50pm. Faversham men relieve at 5.50pm, work until 7.0pm and are relieved by Ramsgate men who finish the duty. The Faversham men working on the engine from 11.50am to 12.5pm must be a record for the shortest time that a driver and fireman spend on an engine.

Duty No. 491 NOT USED

Duty No. 492
2MT Ivatt 2-6-2T
OFF No. 493

	Loco Yard	4.40am	‖
xx	Margate	5.30am	P
6.54am	Ashford	7.14am	P
7.50am	Maidstone East	8.28am	P
9. 7am	Ashford	9.42am	P
11. 4am	Margate	xx	‖
xx	Ramsgate Loco	2. 0pm	‖
	(coupled to No. 91)		
2.17pm	Margate		
	C. shunting 2.20pm to 2.35pm		
	Margate	3.15pm	P
4.43pm	Ashford	5. 4pm	P
5.43pm	Maidstone East	6.35pm	P

(*Continued*)

Ramsgate had five BR Standard Class 2 2-6-2 tanks in the 84000 series for three duties for local passenger work. No. 84024, an Ashford engine, leaves Aylesham Halt on an up train on bank holiday Monday 30th March 1959 with BR Mark I stock in red and cream colours.

(Duty No. 492 continued)

7.17pm	Ashford		
	C. shunting 7.20pm to 8.45pm		
	Ashford	8.53pm	P
9.40pm	Hastings	xx	||
xx	St. Leonards Loco		
	Work No. 493		

Ramsgate men have the work until 7.20pm when St. Leonards men take over and finish the duty. Two sets of Ramsgate men are used, an early at 4.25am and a late at 1.45pm.

Duty No. 493
2MT Ivatt 2-6-2T
stabled off No. 492

	St. Leonards Loco	9.43am	||
9.52am	Hastings	10.10am	P
10.54am	Ashford	11. 3am	P
11.43am	Maidstone East	12.28pm	P
2.18pm	Ramsgate	xx	||
xx	Loco Yard		

St. Leonards men start the engine off shed but Ashford men take over at 9.55am and work to Ashford. Ramsgate men relieve at Ashford at 11.0am and complete the duty.

Duty No. 494
2MT Ivatt 2-6-2T

	Ramsgate Loco	6.40am	||
xx	Margate		
	C. shunting 6.55am to 7.45am		
	Margate	8.10am	P
9.36am	Ashford		
	C. shunting 9.40am to 10.30am		
	Ashford	10.50am	P
11.49am	Hastings	11.55am	||
12. 2pm	St. Leonards Loco (with 408)	12.41pm	||
12.50pm	Hastings		
	F. and C. shunting 1.0pm to 2.30pm		
	Hastings	3.20pm	P
4. 8pm	Ashford	4.29pm	P
5. 9pm	Maidstone East	5.58pm	P
6.37pm	Ashford	6.43pm	P
7.48pm	Ramsgate	xx	||
xx	Loco Yard		

Ashford men take over from Ramsgate men at 10.50am and work the engine until 11.50am. St. Leonards men take over at Hastings at 11.50am and work until 4.25pm at Ashford where Ashford men take over and finish the duty.

Duty Nos 495 & 497 NOT USED

Duty No. 496
2F C class

	Loco Yard	5.15am	‖
xx	Ramsgate		
	C. shunting 5.30am to 8.15pm		
	Ramsgate	8.15pm	‖
xx	Loco Yard		

An early and late turn set of Ramsgate men work the carriage shunt and station pilot.

Duty No. 498
2F C class

	Ramsgate Loco	4.30am	‖
4.42am	Minster	5.48am	F
7. 3am	Walmer	8.25am	F
8.35am	Deal		
	F. shunting 8.35am to 1.0pm		
	Deal	1. 0pm	‖
1.26pm	Ramsgate Loco	2.50pm	‖
xx	Ramsgate		
	F. shunting 3.0pm to 10.0pm		
	Ramsgate	xx	‖
xx	Loco Yard		

Ramsgate men work local freights and shunts with three sets, 3.45am, 6.59am, and 2.35pm.

Duty No. 499
2F C class

	Loco Yard	5. 0am	‖
xx	Ramsgate	5.40am	F
6.28am	Margate Goods		
	F. and C. shunting 6.40am to 10.30am		
	Margate Goods	10.50am	‖
11. 9am	Ramsgate Loco	2.54pm	‖
3.10pm	Margate		
	F. shunting 3.15pm to 5.15pm		
	Margate	5.55pm	F
6.22pm	Ramsgate	xx	‖
xx	Loco Yard		

Ramsgate men work local freights and shunts and take the engine back light to Ramsgate Loco to change over from early to late turn.

Ramsgate had three C class duties (Nos 496, 498 & 499) to work freights and local shunts. No. 31004 works a ballast train between Herne Bay and Margate in February 1953, where a mile of track was washed away in floods.
Lens of Sutton

FOREIGN ENGINE WORKINGS

Central District and South Western District engines work over the London East District, see relevant workings. The London East District share Stewarts Lane and Bricklayers Arms depots with the Central District so the engine workings are closely linked, although the men belong to either one district or the other. Eastern Region engines and men work inter-regional transfers from East Goods, Ferme Park and Temple Mills to Hither Green and Herne Hill, a total of 22 workings of freight and van traffic supplemented by extras in the winter. London Midland Region engines and men work Willesden, Brent and Hendon transfer freights to Hither Green, Bricklayers Arms, and Herne Hill, a total of 22 workings. Western Region (Old Oak) engines and men work six transfer trips to Stewarts Lane and South Lambeth (the ex-GWR goods depot) with 87xx class 0-6-0PTs. Western Region engines are too out of gauge to stray any further on the London East District.

The South Eastern Division had numerous freight and trip workings from the LMR and ER regions which were worked by own engines and men. A LMR 2F 0-6-0 tank works bunker first through Elephant & Castle station (before the roof collapsed in 1947) with a transfer freight for Hither Green.

Lens of Sutton

CENTRAL DISTRICT

(12hr clock used in 1960 workings)

STEWARTS LANE

Duty No. 501
4P/5F N class

	Stewarts Lane Loco	12. 0pm	‖
xx	Battersea Yard		
	F. shunting 12.10pm to 12.40pm		
	Battersea Yard	1. 5pm	F
2.57pm	Three Bridges Yard	xx	‖
xx	Loco Yard	10.35pm	‖
xx	Three Bridges	10.48pm	V
12. 2mdt	Victoria	12.20am	‖
12.28am	Stewarts Lane Loco		
	Work No. 508		

Redhill men work the 12.0pm‖ and are relieved by Three Bridges men at Redhill South Yard at 2.12pm. Three Bridges men have the rest of the work.

Duty No. 502
4MT 2-6-4T LMR class

	Stewarts Lane Loco	6.15am	‖
6.35am	Victoria (C)		
	C. shunting 6.45am to 8.15am		
	Victoria	xx	‖
xx	Carr. Sidings (9.31am Nhaven)	9.10am	E
9.12am	Victoria	xx	‖
xx	Carriage Sidings	9.48am	E
9.57am	Victoria	xx	‖
xx	Loco Sidings	10.25am	‖
xx	Victoria (via Eridge)	10.38am	P

(*Continued*)

Stewarts Lane had a Class 4 2-6-4 tank duty which worked to Brighton and back. An unusual working occurred on 13th May 1963 when a member of the class hauled the Bluebell Railway's Chesham set to Neasden for the Metropolitan Centenary exhibition. The train is seen at East Croydon on the up working.

12.41pm	Brighton (propel)	xx	E
xx	Carriage Sidings	xx	‖
xx	Loco Yard	2. 0pm	Coal Empties
2. 5pm	Top Yard	xx	‖
xx	Carriage Sidings		
	C. shunting 2.15pm to 3.0pm		
	Brighton	xx	‖
xx	Brighton Loco	4.49pm	‖
5.36pm	Angmering	6.12pm	V
9.53pm	Victoria	10. 3pm	‖
10.13pm	Stewarts Lane Loco		

Stewarts Lane men start the duty but Brighton men take over at Victoria at 10.5am and work the rest of the duty until relieved by Stewarts Lane men at Hove at 8.0pm. Stewarts Lane men finish the duty after 8.0pm. The engine propels its own empties at Brighton after 12.41pm and collects the loco coal empties from the Loco Yard.

Duty No. 503
4MT BR 4-6-0 class

	Stewarts Lane Loco	5.43am	‖
6. 2am	Victoria (via E. Grin)	6.29am	P
8.36am	Tunbridge Wells West	xx	E
xx	Carriage Sidings	xx	‖
xx	Tunbridge Wells West	9.30am	Coal
xx	Loco Yard	9.55am	‖
xx	Tunbridge Wells West		
	C. shunting 10.0am to 10.30am		
	Tunbridge Wells West	11. 6am	‖
	(via Eridge & Ashurst)		
11.31am	Tunbridge Wells West Loco	1.25pm	‖
xx	Tunbridge Wells West	1.47pm	P
3.32pm	Victoria (propel)	3.40pm	E
xx	Carriage Sidings	xx	‖
xx	Loco Sidings	5.30pm	‖
xx	Victoria (via E.Grin)	5.49pm	P
7.33pm	Groombridge	8. 3pm	‖
	(turn via Eridge & Ashurst)		
8.23pm	Tunbridge Wells West	9.20pm	P
10.45pm	Victoria	11.40pm	‖
11.50pm	Stewarts Lane Loco		

Stewarts Lane men start the duty and are relieved at Tunbridge Wells West at 8.50am by Tunbridge Wells West men who have the engine until 4.20pm when Stewarts Lane men come back to finish the duty. The engine has to collect the 9.30am coal from the yard (now Sainsburys) and turn twice via Eridge and Ashurst during the course of its duty.

Stewarts Lane had an allocation of BR Standard Class 4 4-6-0s which worked Victoria to Tunbridge Wells trains. The engines were always turned out for the Lingfield race specials and No. 75074 is seen pulling away from East Croydon, complete with a Pullman on 5th July 1963.

Duty Nos 504 to 507 NOT USED

Duty No. 508
4P/5F N class
OFF No. 501

	Loco Yard	3.10am	‖
xx	Battersea Yard	3.45am	F
5.32am	Three Bridges Yard	xx	‖
xx	Loco Yard	6.45am	‖
xx	Three Bridges	7. 6am	V
7.10am	Crawley	8.26am	‖
8.34am	Three Bridges Yard	8.52am	F
1. 5pm	Norwood Yard	1.40pm	F
2. 6pm	New Cross Gate	xx	‖
xx	B'Arms Loco	9. 5pm	‖
9.10pm	B'Arms (J. Sect)	9.28pm	F
12.18am	Brighton Top Yard	xx	‖
xx	Loco Yard	1.40am	‖
xx	Brighton Top Yard	2. 0am	F
3.55am	Battersea Yard	xx	‖
xx	Stewarts Lane Loco		
	Work No. 501		

Stewarts Lane men work the 3.10am‖ off shed and leave the engine at Three Bridges Loco. Three Bridges men work the 6.45am‖ as far as Salfords at 10.50am. Redhill men take over at Salfords at 10.50am and work to B'Arms. B'Arms men work the 9.5pm‖ off shed and are relieved at Haywards Heath at 11.20pm by Three Bridges men who work until 2.35am at Three Bridges. Stewarts Lane men come on to the engine at 2.35am and take the engine home.

Duty No. 509
4P/5F N class

	Stewarts Lane Loco	12. 0pm	‖
xx	Battersea Yard (via C.P.)	12.30pm	F
1. 9pm	Norwood Down Yard	1.30pm	F
xx	Norwood Up Yard	2.43pm	F
3.17pm	Battersea Yard	xx	‖
xx	Stewarts Lane Loco	10.50pm	‖
xx	Battersea Yard	11.18pm	F
1. 0am	Three Bridges	2. 0am	F
3. 5am	Brighton Top Yard	xx	‖
xx	Loco Yard		
	Work No. 511		

Stewarts Lane men have the work round to Three Bridges (two sets). Brighton men use the engine from 1.20am and after bringing the freight into Top Yard at 3.5am run the engine light at 3.56am to Hove and back to convey the men off No. 775 duty.

Stewarts Lane N class 2-6-0s worked freight trains on the main line and empty stock to Victoria. No. 31814 is seen working the annual tour of the weedkilling train at East Croydon on 25th March 1964, by which time the engine had been transferred to the South Western Division.

Duty No. 510
4P/5F N class

	Loco Yard	3.45am	‖
xx	Battersea Yard (via C.P.)	4.15am	F
5. 3am	Norwood Yard	6.20am	F
7. 8am	Battersea Yard	xx	‖
xx	Stewarts Lane Loco	9. 5am	‖
9.24am	Victoria (off 8.24am F. Row)	9.52am	E
10. 8am	Eardley		
	C. shunting 10.10am to 3.10pm		
	Eardley (for 5.9pm T.W.W.)	4.42pm	E
4.56pm	Victoria	xx	‖
xx	Carriage Sidings (6.10pm Bton)	5.52pm	E
5.54pm	Victoria	xx	‖
xx	Stewarts Lane Loco		

Stewarts Lane men (two sets) have all the work which includes a transfer freight to Norwood Yard and back, empty stock working at Victoria and shunting at the carriage sidings at Eardley near Streatham (now a housing estate).

Duty No. 511
4P/5F N class
OFF No. 509

	Brighton Loco	6. 0am	‖
6. 9am	Hove	6.22am	F
7.52am	Worthing Ctl		
	C. and F. shunting 7.55am to 10.5am incl. trip to Bognor		
	Worthing Ctl	2.18pm	‖
2.26pm	Goring	2.54pm	F
3. 0pm	Angmering	3.48pm	F
7. 0pm	Hove	7.15pm	‖
7.24pm	Brighton Loco	12.10am	‖
xx	Top Yard	12.30am	F
1.30am	Three Bridges Yard	1.45am	F
3.14am	Battersea Yard	xx	‖
xx	Stewarts Lane Loco		
	Work No. 509		

Brighton men (three sets) work the engine on West Sussex freights including a shunting stint at Bognor and Angmering. Stewarts Lane men take over at Three Bridges at 1.35am and complete the duty.

W class No. 31917 is seen at Clapham Junction on 26th June 1951 on a Battersea to Norwood transfer freight, with re-signalling being carried out in the background. Duty No. 514 refers.

Brian Morrison

W class 2-6-4 tanks worked Norwood to Battersea freights on duties 513–514 but on Saturday 20th July 1963 a member of the class, No. 31918, was seen working passenger empties into London Bridge. W class engines were not allowed to work passenger trains, a relic of the 1927 Sevenoaks accident when a K class 2-6-4 tank was derailed.

J. Smallwood

Duty No. 512 NOT USED

Duty No. 513
6F W class
OFF No. 514

	Stewarts Lane Loco	11. 0am	‖
xx	Battersea Yard (via C.P.)	11.30am	F
12. 9pm	Norwood Down Yard (via Sel)	1.30pm	F
2.18pm	Battersea Yard	xx	‖
xx	Stewarts Lane Loco	7.25pm	‖
xx	Battersea Yard (via C.P.)	7.55pm	F
8.36pm	Norwood Down Yard	xx	‖
xx	Norwood Up Yard (via Sel)	9.12pm	F
9.48pm	Battersea Yard	xx	‖
xx	Stewarts Lane Loco	11.15pm	‖
xx	Battersea Yard	11.45pm	F
12.32am	Norwood Down Yard	1.15am	F
1.25am	Norwood Up Yard (via Sel)	1.45am	F
2.22am	Battersea Yard	2.35am	‖
2.45am	Stewarts Lane Loco	4.15am	‖
xx	Battersea Yard (via C.P.)	4.49am	F
5.40am	Norwood Yard	5.50am	‖
5.55am	Norwood Loco		
	Work No. 514		

Stewarts Lane men (two sets) have the work until 9.48pm. Norwood men relieve, work the 11.15pm‖ and finish the duty. An interesting trip working to Lillie Bridge at 5.45pm was run on Mondays, Wednesdays, and Fridays from Battersea Yard with Stewarts Lane men.

Duty No. 514
6F W. class
OFF No. 513

	Norwood Loco	9.35am	‖
xx	Norwood Down Yard	9.50am	F
10.14am	Wallington	10.53am	‖
11. 6am	Norwood Up Yard (via Sel)	11.43am	F
12.18pm	Battersea Yard (via C.P.)	1.30pm	F
2. 9pm	Norwood Down Yard	2.35pm	F
2.57pm	Waddon Marsh	3.30pm	‖
3.50pm	Norwood Loco	12. 5am	‖

(Continued)

12.15am	Norwood Up Yard	12.30am	F
	(via Sel, West London Line and Gospel Oak)		
2.30am	Ferme Park	4. 0am	F
5.55am	Battersea Yard	6.10am	‖
6.20am	Stewarts Lane Loco		
	Work No. 513		

Norwood men (two sets) have all the work which includes local freights and an inter-regional transfer night working to Ferme Park Eastern Region. The train runs via Selhurst, West London line, Willesden Junction, Gospel Oak, and the T & H line to Ferme Park via Harringay West Junction.

Duty Nos 515 to 530 NOT USED

BRICKLAYERS ARMS

Duty No. 531
7P/5F WC class

	B'Arms Loco	2.38am	‖
1.56am	London Bridge	3.27am	P
5.33am	Eastbourne	xx	‖
xx	Loco Yard	7.55am	‖
xx	Eastbourne	8.16am	P
8.38am	Hailsham	8.44am	P
9. 0am	Eastbourne	xx	‖
xx	Loco Yard	5.15pm	‖
xx	Eastbourne Yard	6.15pm	F
7.42pm	Lewes East Sidings	8. 7pm	‖
8.19pm	Newhaven Yard	10. 2pm	F
	(D/H from Three Bridges with 690)		
12.58am	Norwood No. 1 Up Goods	1.50am	F
2.25am	B'Arms Goods	xx	‖
xx	B'Arms Loco		

Brighton men work the 2.38am‖ off shed and the night newspaper train to Eastbourne. The engine does a filling in turn to Hailsham and back and double heads with a Q class 0-6-0 from Three Bridges to Norwood Up Goods on the 10.2pm ex Newhaven. Three Bridges men work the engine from 7.45pm at Lewes and Horsham men have the engine from 11.33pm to B'Arms Loco. The B'Arms 'West Countries' are shared with the South Eastern Division working.

Bricklayers Arms Class 4 2-6-4 tanks roamed around the Central Division. No. 80084 is seen on duty No. 533, working the 12.45pm Eastbourne to Tunbridge Wells West at Rotherfield.

Duty No. *532* NOT USED

Duty No. *533*

4MT 2-6-4 tank LMR class

	B'Arms Loco	3.55am	‖
4.12am	New Cross Gate (bank)	4.35am	F
4.50am	Forest Hill	xx	‖
xx	B'Arms Loco	7.30am	‖
xx	London Bridge (via E. Grin)	8. 1am	P
9.59am	Tunbridge Wells West	10.39am	P
12. 0pm	Eastbourne	12.45pm	P
2. 4pm	Tunbridge Wells West	xx	‖
xx	Loco Yard	3.25pm	‖
xx	Tun Wells West (via E. Grin)	3.47pm	P
5.11pm	East Croydon	5.27pm	E
5.46pm	London Bridge		
	C. shunting 5.50pm to 7.30pm		
	London Bridge (off 5.6 TWW)	7.39pm	E
7.45pm	New Cross Gate		
	C. & F. shunting 7.50pm to 9.0pm		
	New Cross Gate	9.15pm	F
9.30pm	B'Arms (bank)	10.55pm	F
11.28pm	Forest Hill	11.32pm	‖
11.39pm	New Cross Gate (bank)	12.36am	F
12.46am	Forest Hill	12.48am	‖
12.57am	New Cross Gate (bank)	1.30am	F
1.43am	Forest Hill	1.45am	‖
1.53am	New Cross Gate (bank)	2.30am	F
2.43am	Forest Hill	2.48am	‖
3.10am	B'Arms Loco		

B'Arms men do a stint of night freight banking from New Cross Gate to Forest Hill before working the 8.1am passenger as far as Norwood Junction where they are relieved at 8.18am by Three Bridges men who work round to Tunbridge Wells West. Tunbridge Wells West men relieve at 10.20am and work the engine until relieved at East Grinstead at 4.23pm by Three Bridges men who work round to London Bridge at 5.46pm. B'Arms men finish the duty after relieving the Three Bridges men at 5.46pm at London Bridge. The engine is in continuous use for 24 hours if the 'Q' van train runs at 6.20am from Victoria to New Cross Gate which is rostered for this engine.

Duty No. 533, again with 80084, running into Mayfield with a Tunbridge Wells West to Eastbourne train. The branch closed to passengers on 14th June 1965.

New Cross Gate was the principal shed in the London area for the LBSCR and in its heyday had 90 engines allocated. The shed was run down in the 1930s with the opening of Norwood Junction and when it closed in 1948 the engines duties were diverted to Bricklayers Arms and Norwood. Seen here in the 1930s is C3 0-6-0 No. 2304 of a class of ten engines introduced in 1906. This was the first of the class to be withdrawn in July 1936. On the right is a B4 class 4-4-0, No. 2047, built in June 1901 and withdrawn on July 1939.

Lens of Sutton

New Cross Gate middle shed in Southern Railway days with E4 class 0-6-2 tank No. 2468 in unlined black. The E4 was built in May 1898 and was one of the last to be withdrawn in January 1963.

Lens of Sutton

Duty No. 539
4P/5F N class

	B'Arms Loco	11.40pm	‖
xx	B'Arms (J. Sect)	12. 1am	F
3.33am	Lewes	4.15am	F
4.55am	Eastbourne	xx	‖
xx	Loco Yard		
	Work No. 541		

Bricklayers Arms men work the 11.40pm‖ off shed and the 12.1am freight to Three Bridges being relieved at 2.15am where Newhaven men take over and complete the duty.

Duty No. 540
4P/5F N class
OFF No. 541

	B'Arms Loco	12.35pm	‖
xx	B'Arms	1. 5pm	F
1.56pm	Wadddon Marsh	2.23pm	‖
2.54pm	B'Arms (B. Sect)	3. 5pm	F
3.45pm	Norwood Down Yard		
	Work Trips Down To Up Yard		
	Norwood No 1 Up Goods	6.35pm	F
6.39pm	Norwood Up Yard	6.58pm	F
7.25pm	New Cross Gate	8.32pm	F
	F. shunting 7.30pm to 8.30pm		
8.45pm	B'Arms (bank)	9.28pm	F
9.52pm	Forest Hill	9.56pm	‖
10.18pm	B'Arms	10.55pm	F
11.52pm	Waddon Marsh	12.30am	F
12.46am	Norwood Up Yard	1. 0am	‖
1.26am	B'Arms Loco		

B'Arms men have local freight banking and trip working at Norwood Yards. Two sets are utilised.

Duty No. 541
4P/5F N class
OFF No. 539

	Eastbourne Loco	7.30am	‖
7.45am	Polegate	9. 5am	F
10.29am	Horam	11.17am	F
12.12pm	Polegate	12.23pm	‖
12.39pm	Eastbourne Loco	4.45pm	‖
xx	Eastbourne	5.10pm	F
6.40pm	Lewes	7.23pm	F
7.50pm	Newhaven Yard	xx	‖
xx	Newhaven Loco	12. 5am	‖
12.22am	Lewes East Sidings	12.45am	F
5.17am	B'Arms	xx	‖
xx	B'Arms Loco		

Eastbourne men work the 4.45pm‖ until 5.27pm at Polegate where they are relieved by Three Bridges men who work the engine until 7.0pm at Lewes. Brighton men work from Lewes at 7.0pm and dispose the engine at Newhaven Loco. Newhaven men come on and work the 12.5am‖ and are relieved by Three Bridges men at 2.0am who stay on the engine until B'Arms men take over at 2.50am and work the engine home. Eastbourne men start the duty at 7.30am‖.

Duty No. 542 NOT USED

Duty No. 543
4P/5F N class

	B'Arms Loco	9.50am	‖
xx	B'Arms (B. Sect)	10.21am	F
11.13am	Norwood Down Yard	12. 5pm	F
12.27pm	Waddon Marsh		
	F. shunting 1.0pm to 3.15pm		
	Waddon Marsh	3.23pm	F
3.34pm	Norwood Up Yard	xx	‖
xx	Norwood Loco	7.15pm	‖
xx	Norwood Yard	7.48pm	F
10. 6pm	Three Bridges Yard	xx	‖
xx	Loco Yard (turn)	11.25pm	‖
xx	Three Bridges		
	C. shunting 11.30pm to 12.30am		

(Continued)

	Three Bridges Yard	2. 8am	‖
2.58am	Norwood Up Yard	3.20am	‖
3.22am	Norwood Junction stn	3.25am	‖
3.32am	East Croydon	3.35am	‖
3.45am	Norwood Up Yard	4.23am	F
5.31am	B'Arms (L. Sect)	xx	‖
xx	Loco Yard		

B'Arms men have the engine and dispose it at Norwood Loco. Norwood men start the 7.15pm‖ and are relieved at Three Bridges at 12.25am by B'Arms men who take over and finish the duty. The engine works a taxi service by conveying men from Three Bridges to Norwood Junction and the driver for the East Croydon shunter at 3.25am‖ for duty 607.

Duty Nos 544 to 548 & 550 NOT USED

Duty No. 549
2F C2X class
OFF No. 552

	B'Arms Loco	2. 0am	‖
2.12am	New Cross Gate	2.30am	F
2.55am	Norwood Yard	3.50am	F
8.14am	Tattenham Corner	8.55am	F
9.55am	Purley	10.20am	F
10.40am	Caterham	12.10pm	F
2.46pm	Norwood Up Yard	xx	‖
xx	Norwood Loco		
	stable for No. 552		

B'Arms men work the night freight to Tattenham Corner with Norwood men relieving at 8.30am to work the Caterham branch. The Norwood men finish the duty with the 12.10pm Caterham to Norwood Up Yard.

Duty No. 551
2F C2X class

	B'Arms Loco	3. 0am	‖
xx	B'Arms (B. Sect)	3.30am	F
4.40am	Norwood Down Yard	xx	‖
xx	Norwood No 1 Up Goods	5.45am	F
5.50am	Norwood Up Yard	6.40am	F
6.59am	Streatham Common	9.45am	F
10.10am	Battersea Yard	10.48am	‖
11. 9am	Streatham Common (via T.H.)	11.25am	F
3.24am	New Cross Gate	4.30pm	F
4.35pm	Deptford Wharf	5.30pm	F
5.35pm	New Cross Gate	5.45pm	‖
6. 0pm	B'Arms (L. Sect)		
	F. shunting and trips 6.0pm to 10.0pm		
	B'Arms (J. Sect) bank	10.37pm	F
11. 8pm	Forest Hill	11.14pm	‖
11.29pm	B'Arms Loco		

B'Arms have all the work on this local goods working and shunting duty. Three sets of men are utilised.

Duty No. 552
2F C2X class
stabled off No. 549

	Norwood Loco	12.20am	‖
xx	Norwood Down Yard	12.50am	F
1. 0am	Norwood Up Yard	1.35am	F
2.12am	B'Arms	xx	‖
xx	Loco Yard	6.15am	‖
6.27am	New Cross Gate		
	F. shunting 6.30am to 9.45am		
	New Cross Gate	9.52am	‖
10.10am	B'Arms Loco	9.40pm	‖
xx	B'Arms L. Sect (bank)	10. 5pm	F
10.30pm	Forest Hill	10.31pm	‖
10.38pm	New Cross Gate		
	C. shunting 10.40pm to 11.25pm		
	New Cross Gate (bank)	12. 9am	F
12.19am	Forest Hill	12.23am	‖
12.45am	B'Arms Loco		
	Work No. 549		

B'Arms men have all the work on night freight and banking up Forest Hill bank. Three sets involved. The engine stays on shed during the daytime from 10.10am until 9.40pm.

Bricklayers Arms N class 2-6-0s worked main line freight on both Central and South Eastern districts. No. 31875 in Southern Railway unlined goods black but with BR number in SR style, is seen at Stewarts Lane in early BR days. Built in August 1925 No. 31875 was withdrawn in August 1964.

Lens of Sutton

Bricklayers Arms had three duties for C2X class 0-6-0s (549-552) which worked suburban freights and shunting. When New Cross Gate closed in 1948 the ex-LBSCR engines were sent to Bricklayers Arms. The shed was originally a South Eastern Railway depot and was closed in 1962. C2X class No. 32434 was the Marsh rebuild of the C2 class with a C3 boiler and is seen at Merton Park on a filming special.

Brian Morrison

NORWOOD

Duty No. 581
4F Q class

	Norwood Loco	3.30am	‖
xx	Norwood Yard	4. 0am	F
5.15am	Reigate	6.30am	F
10.50am	Guildford	11.33am	F
11.45am	Shalford		
	F. shunting 11.50am to 12.15pm		
	Shalford	12.20pm	F
12.36pm	Guildford	xx	‖
xx	Guildford Loco	2. 0pm	‖
2.20pm	Woking	2.45pm	F
4. 9pm	Redhill	xx	‖
xx	Loco Yard	9.45pm	‖
xx	Redhill Up Yard	10. 5pm	F
11. 5pm	Norwood Yard	xx	‖
xx	Loco Yard		

Redhill men work round to Reigate where they are relieved by Guildford men at 6.9am. Guildford men work the engine until the return from Woking at 4.9pm where they dispose the engine and home pass on the 5.31pm to Guildford. Redhill men work the 9.45pm‖ off shed and complete the duty.

Duty No. 582
4F Q class

	Norwood Loco	4.50am	‖
xx	Norwood Yard	5.20am	F
8.35am	Groombridge	9. 8am	‖
9.14am	Tunbridge Wells West Loco	4.55pm	‖
xx	Tunbridge Wells West		
	C. shunting 5.0pm to 5.20pm		
	Tunbridge Wells West	5.29pm	‖
5.41pm	Ashurst	6. 8pm	P
6.19pm	Tunbridge Wells West	6.40pm	‖
7. 0pm	Crowborough	7.17pm	F
9.52pm	Norwood Yard	xx	‖
xx	Loco Yard		

Norwood men work round to Tunbridge Wells West and leave the loco in the shed to be prepared by Tunbridge Wells men for the 4.55pm‖. Norwood men take over at 5.20pm and finish the duty.

A distinguished visitor to Norwood Junction shed on 11th May 1958 was *City of Truro* which had worked to East Croydon on a railtour. Norwood had two duties (581 & 582) for Q class 0-6-0s and six members of the class to work them. No. 30533 of this class is on the right.

Duty No. 582 shows a Q class working to Groombridge and back. The Southern antecedent to the Q class working was the C2X. C2X No. 2444 is seen near Hever on the 5.20am ex-Norwood Yard goods on a summer's morning.

S. C. Nash

Duty Nos 583 & 585 NOT USED

Duty No. 584
6F W class

	Norwood Loco	9.45am	Coal empties
9.52am	Norwood Down Yard	10.10am	F
xx	Norwood Up Yard (via Sel)	10.43am	F
11.35am	Old Oak Common (via C.P.)	1.20pm	F
3. 3pm	Norwood Down Yard	3.30pm	F
xx	Norwood Up Yard	4. 0pm	F
xx	Norwood Down Yard	xx	‖
xx	Norwood Loco	7.20pm	‖
xx	Norwood Up Yard	7.50pm	F
xx	Norwood Down Yard	8.33pm	F
8.55pm	Waddon Marsh	9.23pm	F
10. 5pm	Battersea Yard	10.15pm	‖
10.50pm	Norwood Up Yard (via Sel)	11.23pm	F
1. 5am	Willesden	xx	‖
xx	Sudbury Sidings (via C.P.)	3.50am	F
5.19am	Norwood Yard	xx	
xx	Loco Yard		

Norwood men have all the work which starts with the W class taking the loco coal empties out of the shed yard before inter-regional transfer trips to Old Oak and Willesden. Three sets are used.

Duty No. 586
6F W class

	Loco Yard	5.10am	‖
xx	Norwood Yard	5.30am	F
7.34am	Epsom Goods		
	F. shunting 8.30am to 11.15am		
	Epsom Goods	11.32am	F
12. 6pm	Norwood Up Yard	xx	‖
xx	Loco Yard	10.30pm	‖
10.37pm	East Croydon (via Sel)	11. 8pm	F
11.48pm	Battersea Yard (via C.P.)	12.45am	F
1.31am	Norwood Yard	xx	‖
xx	Norwood Loco		

Norwood men work local goods and shunts with a long layover in the afternoon on Norwood Loco. W class 2-6-4 tanks were not permitted to work passenger trains. Two sets of men are used.

114

Norwood had three W class 2-6-4T duties which worked inter-regional transfer freights and local trip workings. No. 31921 is seen plodding up Forest Hill bank near Honor Oak Park on 1st March 1963. The engine was withdrawn the same year, in October.

Duty No. 587
6F W class

	Norwood Loco	5.30am	‖
5.40am	Norwood Yard (via Sel)	6. 0am	F
7.55am	Willesden	9.40am	F
11.30am	Norwood Down Yard	xx	‖
xx	Norwood Loco	7.15pm	‖
7.29pm	East Croydon	8.35pm	F
8.51pm	Norwood Up Yard	8.55pm	F
9. 0pm	Norwood Down Yard	9.10pm	‖
9.15pm	Norwood Up Yard	10.13pm	F
11.18pm	Old Oak Common (via C.P.)	12.50am	F
2. 0am	Norwood Yard	xx	‖
xx	Norwood Loco		

Norwood men work inter-regional transfer freights to Willesden and Old Oak Common, the engine spends most of the daytime on shed. An early and late turn set of Norwood men cover the duty.

Duty No. 588
2F C2X class

	Norwood Loco	7. 0pm	‖
7.12pm	Waddon Marsh	7.40pm	V
7.53pm	Crystal Palace	8.10pm	V
8.23pm	East Croydon	9.45pm	V
10.43pm	London Bridge	10.58pm	‖
11. 6pm	New Cross Gate	11.30pm	V
11.37pm	London Bridge	12.20am	V
12.28am	New Cross Gate	1.30am	F
2. 3am	Norwood Up Yard	2.47am	F

(Continued)

3.13am	New Cross Gate (bank)	4.10am	F
4.25am	Forest Hill	4.30am	‖
4.40am	Norwood Yard	5.35am	F
5.49am	Forest Hill	7.13am	F
	(F. shunting 6.0am to 7.0am)		
7.44am	Norwood Down Yard	10.20am	F
xx	Norwood Up Yard	xx	‖
xx	Norwood Loco		

Norwood men work local freight and van trains including banking and shunting at Forest Hill Goods (now a car park). Two sets of Norwood men are used.

Duty No. 589
2F C2X class

	Loco Yard	4.10am	‖
xx	Norwood Down Yard		
	F. shunting 4.15am to 6.30am		
	Norwood Down Yard	7. 5am	F
10.15am	East Grinstead		
	F. shunting 10.5am to 12.10pm		
	East Grinstead	12.40pm	F
2.26pm	Oxted	6. 5pm	F
8.12pm	Norwood Yard	xx	‖
xx	Norwood Loco		

Norwood men work the East Grinstead goods and are relieved at 12.15pm. Three Bridges men take over at 12.15pm and work the 12.40pm freight to Oxted. Norwood men relieve at 2.26pm, shunt at Upper Warlingham and work the 6.5pm freight home.

Duty No. 590
2F C2X class

	Loco Yard	1.40am	‖
xx	Norwood Down Yard	2. 5am	F
2.28am	East Croydon		
	F. shunting 2.30am to 3.30am		
	East Croydon	3.35am	‖
3.48am	Norwood Loco	4.25am	‖
xx	Norwood Yard	4.55am	F
8.50am	Banstead	10.10am	F
10.21am	Sutton	11. 4am	‖
11.10am	Wallington	12.22pm	F
1.36pm	Norwood Up Yard	xx	‖
xx	Norwood Loco	3. 7pm	‖
3.21pm	Wallington	4.12pm	F
4.21pm	Sutton		
	F. shunting 4.25pm to 7.10pm		
	Sutton	7.14pm	F
7.37pm	Norwood Up Yard	xx	‖
xx	Loco Yard		

Norwood men have all the work with local freight and shunting. Three sets of men are used, 12.55am, 4.30am, and 11.25am.

Duty No. 591
2F C2X class

	Loco Yard (with 594)	3. 0am	‖
xx	Norwood Yard	3.55am	F
6. 0am	Dorking North	7. 5am	‖
7.15am	Leatherhead		
	F. shunting 7.15am to 10.30am		
	Leatherhead	11.10am	F
12.35am	Guildford	xx	‖
xx	Loco Yard	4.35pm	‖
xx	Guildford	5. 0pm	F
5.40pm	Leatherhead	6.20pm	EBV
6.32pm	Epsom Goods	7.15pm	F
8. 8pm	Leatherhead	8.33pm	‖
8.43pm	Dorking North	9.50pm	F
11.25pm	Norwood Yard	xx	‖
xx	Norwood Loco		

Norwood men work round to 9.5am at Leatherhead where they are relieved by Guildford men who work the engine until 5.35pm when a late set of Norwood men take over work and dispose.

Duty No. 592 NOT USED

Norwood C2X class 0-6-0s were replaced by Moguls of the U1 and U classes. No. 31807, a U class 2-6-0, was allocated to Norwood Loco in 1962 to replace the U1s. The engine was built as a K class 2-6-4 tank in November 1926, converted to a 2-6-0 in 1928 and withdrawn by BR in January 1964. The engine is seen working empty stock through Three Bridges on 23rd February 1963.

The E4 class 0-6-2Ts had a reprieve in the spring of 1963, and one member of the class was sent to Norwood where it worked empty stock and shunts at London Bridge, where it is seen pulling off empty stock on 9th March 1963. The engine was withdrawn soon afterwards in May.

Norwood Junction shed (75C) had an allocation of W class 2-6-4 tanks to work transfer trips to other regions in the London area as well as local freights. Here, No. 31919 works such a train from Norwood Yard, with a Billinton E6 class 0-6-2T. No. 31919 was built in 1935 and was withdrawn in November 1963.

Brian Morrison

Duty No. 593
2F C2X
OFF No. 594

	Stewarts Lane Loco	5.50am	‖
xx	Battersea Yard	6.18am	F
12.28pm	Norwood Up Yard	xx	F
xx	Norwood Down Yard	xx	‖
xx	Loco Yard	2.45pm	‖
xx	Norwood Yard	3.10pm	F
3.20pm	Thornton Heath	4.40pm	F
4.48pm	Streatham Common		
	F. shunting 4.50pm to 6.20pm		
	Streatham Common	6.25pm	F
6.29pm	Streatham	7.22pm	F
8.46pm	Norwood Yard	8.55pm	F
xx	Norwood Down Yard	xx	‖
xx	Norwood Loco		

Stewarts Lane men work local transfer freights in the morning and Norwood men in the afternoon, starting with the 2.45pm‖.

Duty No. 594
2F C2X class

	Norwood Loco (with 591)	3. 0am	‖
xx	Norwood Yard	3.15am	F
5.30am	Streatham	6. 5am	‖
6.10am	Eardley		
	C. shunting 7.50am to 9.50am		
	Eardley (via Streatham)	9.55am	‖
10.28am	Wimbledon	11.20am	F
11.55am	Haydons Road	12.45pm	F
12.50pm	Wimbledon West Yard (M.W.F.O.)	1.22pm	F
1.41pm	St. Helier	2.25pm	F
2.33pm	Wimbledon West Yard		
	F. shunting 2.35pm to 3.0pm		
	Wimbledon West Yard	3.32pm	‖
	(Continued)		

3.53pm	Eardley		
	Q. shunting 3.55pm to 5.0pm		
	Eardley (for 5.49pm Groom)	5.19pm	E
5.36pm	Victoria		
	C. shunting 5.40pm to 6.30pm		
	Carriage Sdgs (for 7.8pm T.W.W.)	6.53pm	E
6.55pm	Victoria		
	C. shunting 8.15pm to 1.0am		
	Victoria	1. 0am	‖
xx	Stewarts Lane Loco		
	stable for No. 593		

Norwood men work on the engine until 2.50pm (two sets) when they are relieved at Wimbledon by Stewarts Lane men who finish the duty.

Duty No. 595
2F C2X class

	Norwood Loco	5.45am	‖
xx	Norwood Yard	6.15am	F
6.35am	Coulsdon North		
	F. shunting 6.40am to 8.0am		
	Coulsdon North	10.15am	F
10.50am	Norwood Up Yard	11. 0am	F
xx	Norwood Down Yard	xx	‖
xx	Norwood Up Yard	12. 0pm	F
xx	Norwood Down Yard	12.20pm	F
1.35pm	Hackbridge	2.25pm	F
2.34pm	Mitcham		
	CCE & F. shunting 3.15pm to 7.15pm		
	Mitcham	7.59pm	‖
8. 9pm	Wimbledon West Yard	8.27pm	F
9.22pm	Norwood Yard	xx	‖
xx	Norwood Loco		

Norwood men work local freights and shunts. Three sets of men are used.

Duty No. 596 NOT USED

Diesel electric shunters 204hp and 350hp based at Norwood for maintenance purposes.

Duty No.				
597	Norwood Down Yard and trips	24 hrs	350hp	DSL
598 & 599	NOT USED	-	-	
600	Nine Elms Goods Shunt	24 hrs	204hp	DSL
601	Wimbledon West Yard shunts	24 hrs	204hp	DSL
602	New Cross Gate shunts and trips 6.0am to 3.55am		350hp	DSL
603	New Cross Gate shunts and trips 7.0am to 5.0am		350hp	DSL
604	Clapham Junction shunts and trips	24 hrs	350hp	DSL
605	Clapham Junction shunts and trips	24 hrs	350hp	DSL
606	South Lambeth shunts and trips 7.15am to 5.30am		350hp	DSL
607	East Croydon shunts and trips 3.45am to 12.15am		204hp	DSL
608	Battersea Yard shunts and trips	24 hrs	350hp	DSL
609	Redhill shunts and trips	24 hrs	350hp	DSL
610	Redhill shunts and trips	24 hrs	350hp	DSL
611	Norwood Yard shunts and trips	24 hrs	350hp	DSL
612	Norwood Yard shunts and trips	24 hrs	350hp	DSL
613	Norwood Yard shunts and trips	24 hrs	350hp	DSL
614	Norwood Yard shunts and trips	24 hrs	350hp	DSL
615	Norwood Yard shunts and trips	24 hrs	350hp	DSL
616	Nine Elms shunts and trips	24 hrs	350hp	DSL
617	Nine Elms shunts and trips	24 hrs	350hp	DSL
618	Nine Elms shunts and trips	24 hrs	350hp	DSL
619	NOT USED			

REDHILL

Duty No. 620
5P V class
OFF No. 621

	Reading South Loco	6.50am	‖
xx	Reading South	7.27am	P
9.12am	Redhill	9.14am	P
9.49am	London Bridge	10.30am	E
10.37am	New X Gate (via Old Kt Rd Jcn)	10.53am	E
11.21am	Eardley	11.56am	E
12.25pm	New Cross Gate (with 675)	1.18pm	‖

(Continued)

(Duty No. 620 continued)

1.30pm	B'Arms Loco (with 675)	4.10pm	‖
4.23pm	New Cross Gate (O/R)	5. 7pm	E
5.17pm	London Bridge	5.25pm	P
6. 0pm	Redhill	6. 3pm	P
7.59pm	Reading South	xx	‖
xx	Loco Yard	9.14pm	‖
xx	Reading South	9.34pm	P
11.25pm	Redhill		
	C. shunting 11.25pm to 12.30am		
	Redhill	12.30am	‖
xx	Loco Yard		
	Work No. 621		

Redhill men relieve the Reading men at Guildford at 8.20am and work round to London Bridge at 9.50am. B'Arms men come onto the engine at 9.50am, work and dispose at B'Arms. Redhill men work the 4.10pm‖ off shed and are relieved by Reading men at 6.1pm at Redhill who finish the job. This Redhill schools worked the through 'parliamentary' train to and from Reading to London Bridge.

Duty No. 621
5P V class
OFF No. 620

	Redhill Loco	5. 0am	‖
xx	Redhill		
	C. shunting 5.35am to 6.5am		
	Redhill	6.10am	E
6.30am	Edenbridge	6.58am	P
7.17am	Redhill	7.48am	P
9.32am	Reading South		
	C. shunting 10.0am to 10.45am		
	Reading South	xx	‖
xx	Loco Yard	1.20pm	‖
1.25pm	Reading South	1.50pm	P
3.41pm	Redhill	4.10pm	‖
4.13pm	Loco Yard	4.20pm	‖
4.40pm	Redhill South Goods		
	F. shunting 5.0pm to 6.30pm		
	Redhill South Goods	7.10pm	F
7.24pm	Redhill Up Yard	xx	‖
xx	Loco Yard	9.25pm	‖
xx	Redhill	9.37pm	P
11.38pm	Reading South	xx	‖
xx	Loco Yard		
	Work No. 620		

Redhill men have all the work until the engine is taken over by Reading men at 9.25pm who finish the duty. The duty starts off with a local passenger from Edenbridge and has some trip working from Redhill South Goods.

'Schools' class No. 30911 *Dover* is seen near Shalford Junction with the 1.50pm Reading to Redhill on 18th May 1962, on duty No. 621.

Duty No. 622
4P/5F N class
stabled off No. 633

	Location		
	Reading Loco	6.40am	‖
xx	Reading South		
	C. shunting 6.50am to 8.10am		
	Reading South	8.20am	P
10. 5am	Redhill (with 736)	10.20am	‖
10.23am	Redhill Loco	5.55pm	‖
xx	Redhill	6. 9pm	P
6.46pm	Tonbridge	6.48pm	P
7. 6pm	Tunbridge Wells West	7.40pm	P
7.55pm	Tonbridge	xx	‖
xx	Loco Yard	9.25pm	‖
xx	Tonbridge	9.45pm	P
10.22pm	Redhill	xx	‖
xx	Loco Yard		

Reading men work the engine until 10.23am. Redhill men work the 5.55pm‖ off shed and complete the duty.

Duty No. 623
4P/5F N class
OFF No. 627

	Location		
	Redhill Loco	12.50am	F
xx	Redhill Up Yard	1.10am	F
4. 5am	Woking	4.50am	F
5. 6am	Guildford		
	C. shunting 5.30am to 7.15am		
	Guildford	7.15am	‖
7.20am	Loco Yard	8.40am	‖
xx	Guildford	9. 0am	F
12.48pm	Reading Yard	xx	‖
xx	Loco Yard	11. 0pm	‖
xx	Reading South		
	C. shunting 11.15pm to 12.30am		
	Reading South	12.30am	‖
xx	Reading Spur	12.50am	F
	(8.40pm Moreton Cutting)		
3.16am	Redhill	xx	‖
xx	Loco Yard		
	Work No. 635		

Redhill men start the duty with the 12.50am coal empties off of the loco to Up Yard and work the engine to Guildford to be relieved at 7.20am. Reading men work the 8.40am‖ and dispose. Guildford men work the 11.0pm‖ and are relieved at 2.5am at Guildford by Redhill men who work and dispose.

Duty No. 624
4P/5F N class

	Location		
	Loco Yard	2. 0am	‖
xx	Redhill Up Yard	2.25am	F
4.25am	Hove	5.15am	‖
5.20am	Preston Park	5.33am	F
5.38am	Top Yard	5.50am	‖
5.55am	Brighton Loco	8.15am	‖
xx	Brighton		
	C. shunting 8.20am to 9.30am		
	Brighton	9.41am	V
2. 0pm	London Bridge	2.25pm	‖
2.40pm	B'Arms Loco	11.22pm	‖
12.21am	Redhill Loco		

Brighton men start the 2.0am‖ which has been prepared by Redhill No. 1 P & D men and work the engine back to Brighton. Brighton men (2nd set) work until 1.0pm at New Cross Gate when they are relieved by B'Arms men who take the engine home. Redhill men work the 11.22pm‖ B'Arms to Redhill Loco. Brighton men work a 7.40am empties from Hove to Lovers Walk on Wednesday and Thursdays. The 11.22pm‖ from B'Arms to Redhill balances the working and could be useful for special traffic purposes.

Duty Nos 625 to 626 NOT USED

Duty No. 627
4P/5F N class
OFF No. 629

	Location		
	Loco Yard	4. 0am	‖
	Redhill (1.30am ex Snodland)	4.20am	F
7.10am	Reading Spur	xx	‖
xx	Reading Loco	8.35am	‖
xx	Reading Spur (2.5am ex Didcot)	9.11am	F
12.12pm	Redhill Up Yard	xx	‖
xx	Redhill Loco	4.50pm	‖
xx	Redhill	5. 4pm	P
6.55pm	Reading South	7. 0pm	‖
7.5pm	Reading Loco	7.35pm	‖
xx	Reading Spur Junction (3.25pm ex Moreton Cutting)	8. 3pm	F
11. 0pm	Redhill	xx	‖
xx	Redhill Loco		
	Work No. 623		

Guildford men start the duty with the 4.0am‖ and are relieved at Guildford at 5.40am. An early turn set of Guildford men relieve at 5.40am and work until 11.0am when Redhill men take over and finish the duty. A late turn Redhill set sign on at 3.50pm to work the 4.50pm‖ and complete the duty.

Duty No. 628 NOT USED

Duty No. 629
4P/5F N class

	Location		
	Loco Yard	7.50am	‖
xx	Redhill (Ton Sidings)	8.12am	F
8.17am	Redhill Up Yard	xx	‖
xx	Redhill Loco Yard	11.10am	‖
xx	Redhill Up Yard	11.49am	F
2.52pm	Reading South	xx	‖
xx	Reading Spur	4.10pm	F
4.20pm	Reading West Junction	xx	‖
xx	Reading Loco	6.30pm	‖
xx	Reading South	7. 4pm	F
12.43am	Redhill Up Yard	xx	‖
xx	Redhill Loco		
	Work No. 627		

Redhill men work round to 11.10am including shunting coal empties on the loco shed at 9.40am. Reading men relieve at 11.10am and work round to Reading Spur where they are relieved by Guildford men at 3.45pm who finish the duty (two sets).

Duty No. 630
4P/5F N class

	Location		
	Loco Yard	6.15am	‖
xx	Redhill	6.42am	P
7.17am	Tonbridge	8.12am	P
8.30am	Tunbridge Wells West C. shunting 8.35am to 9.15am		
	Tunbridge Wells West	9.40am	V
9.55am	Tonbridge	xx	‖
xx	Loco Yard	11.45am	‖
xx	Tonbridge	12.10pm	P
1.41pm	Brighton	xx	‖
xx	Loco Yard	3.40pm	‖
xx	Brighton	3.55pm	P
5.32pm	Tonbridge	5.45pm	P
6.22pm	Redhill	xx	‖
xx	Redhill Down Yard F. shunting 6.30pm to 8.30pm		
	Redhill Down Yard	xx	‖
xx	Loco Yard	10.50pm	‖
xx	Redhill	11.10pm	P
11.50pm	Tonbridge	xx	‖
xx	Loco Yard		

Tonbridge men work round to Brighton (two sets) including working the 9.40am vans tender first from Tunbridge Wells West to Tonbridge. Brighton men bring the 3.40pm‖ out into the station and Tonbridge men take over at 3.50pm to be relieved at Redhill at 7.0pm by Redhill men who finish the duty.

Duty Nos 631 & 632 NOT USED

A Mogul is seen at Betchworth as No. 31618, a Redhill U class, heads the 12.24pm Woking to New Cross Gate stone train on 22nd November 1963. This engine was going to be a K class 2-6-4 tank but was built as a Mogul in 1928 and withdrawn in 1964. The engine can be seen today working on the Bluebell Railway.

Duty No. 633
4P/5F N class

	Loco Yard	5.20am	‖
xx	Redhill	6. 0am	P
7.56am	Reading South		
	C. shunting 8.30am to 10.0am		
	Reading South	10. 0am	‖
xx	Loco Yard	10.45am	‖
xx	Reading South	11. 5am	P
12.46pm	Redhill	xx	‖
xx	Loco Yard	5.15pm	‖
xx	Redhill	5.40pm	P
5.59pm	Edenbridge	6.37pm	E
6.53pm	Tonbridge	xx	‖
xx	Loco Yard	8.10pm	‖
xx	Tonbridge	8.34pm	P
9.13pm	Redhill	xx	‖
xx	Redhill Loco	11.15pm	‖
xx	Redhill Up Yard	11.40pm	F
2.46am	Reading Spur	3. 6am	F
3.16am	Reading W. Junction	xx	‖
xx	Reading Loco		

Work No. 622

Redhill men have the work until 1.0am at Guildford when they are relieved by Reading men who complete the duty. Three sets of Redhill men are used. A curious working is the 5.40pm Redhill to Edenbridge which then continues at 6.37pm empty to Tonbridge. Why not advertise the train and run it straight through as a stopping passenger?

Duty Nos 634, 637, 638 & 641 to 645 NOT USED

Duty No. 635
4P/5F N class
OFF No. 623

	Loco Yard	7.10am	‖
xx	Redhill	7.27am	P
8. 4am	Tonbridge	9.10am	P
10.37am	Brighton	xx	‖
xx	Top Table (turn)	xx	‖
xx	Brighton	11.55am	P
1.27pm	Tonbridge	2.15pm	P
2.51pm	Redhill	xx	‖
xx	Redhill Loco	5.15pm	‖
xx	Redhill	5.31pm	P
7.19pm	Reading South	xx	‖
xx	Loco Yard	8.50pm	‖
xx	Reading South	9.40pm	F
12. 8pm	Redhill	xx	‖
xx	Loco Yard		

Redhill men are relieved at Tonbridge at 8.40am by Brighton men who have the engine until 1.30pm when Tonbridge men come on the engine and work to Redhill Loco. Redhill men start the 5.15pm‖ and finish the duty.

Duty No. 636
4P/5F N class

	Loco Yard	1.25pm	‖
xx	Redhill Up Yard	1.47pm	F
	(9.42am ex Hoo Junction)		
3.56pm	Reading Spur	xx	‖
xx	Reading Loco	5.50pm	‖
xx	Reading South		
	C. shunting 5.55pm to 6.45pm		
	Reading South	6.52pm	P
8.48pm	Redhill	xx	‖
xx	Redhill Loco		

Redhill men have all the work but have the engine prepared and disposed at Redhill Loco.

Duty No. 639
6F S15 class

	Redhill Loco	4.30am	‖
xx	Redhill (1.15am ex Hoo Junction)	4.50am	F
6.24am	Woking	6.50am	‖
7. 5am	Guildford Loco	7.55am	‖
xx	Guildford		
	C. shunting 8.0am to 8.45am		
	Guildford	8.55am	‖
9. 8am	Shalford (2.35am ex Ashford)	9.35am	F
10.17am	Woking	11.48am	F
1.13pm	Redhill	xx	‖
xx	Loco Yard	3.30pm	‖
xx	Redhill	4. 4pm	P
5.48pm	Reading South	xx	‖
xx	Reading Loco	7.30pm	‖
xx	Reading South	7.50pm	P
9.46pm	Redhill	xx	‖
xx	Redhill Loco		

Redhill men work to Guildford Loco. Guildford men work from 7.55am until 9.15am at Shalford where Redhill men come on and complete the duty. The 2.35am ex Ashford has been recessed at Shalford until 9.35am. Three sets of Redhill men and an early set of Guildford men are utilised.

Duty No. 640
6F S15 class

	Redhill Loco	1.45am	‖
xx	Redhill Up Yard (6.20pm ex Dover)	2.10am	F
4.50am	Reading Spur	xx	‖
xx	Reading Loco	4.30pm	‖
xx	Reading Spur	5.15pm	F
	(12.10pm ex Moreton)		
8. 9pm	Redhill	xx	‖
xx	Redhill Loco		

Reading men have all the work which includes taking over Western Region freights at Reading Spur (the wartime connection) which originate from Moreton Cutting near Didcot. Two sets of Reading men are used.

Duty No. 646
4P/5F N class

	Redhill Loco	4.10am	‖
xx	Redhill Down Yard	4.30am	F
5.17am	Tonbridge West Yard	xx	‖
xx	Loco Yard	6.45am	‖
xx	Tonbridge	7.16am	P
7.54am	Redhill	8.30am	P
8.47am	Dorking Town	9.16am	P
9.33am	Redhill	xx	‖
xx	Redhill Up Yard	10. 7am	F
10.12am	Redhill South Yard	10.40am	F
1.42pm	Three Bridges Yard	2. 3pm	‖
2.20pm	Haywards Heath		
	F. shunting 2.20pm to 5.0pm		
	Haywards Heath	5. 2pm	F
5.27pm	Three Bridges Yard	xx	‖
xx	Three Bridges Loco	12.10am	‖
xx	Three Bridges Yard	12.35am	F
1. 0am	Redhill	xx	‖
xx	Redhill Loco		

Redhill men work round to Salfords where they are relieved at 10.50am by Three Bridges men who work round to Three Bridges Loco. Brighton men work the 12.10am‖ and finish the duty.

Duty No. 647
2F C2X class

	Loco Yard	10.15pm	‖
xx	Redhill		
	C. shunting 10.20pm to 10.50pm		
	Redhill	xx	‖
xx	Up Yard	12. 8am	F
1. 7am	Betchworth	1.35am	F
3. 3am	Redhill Up Yard	xx	‖
xx	Redhill		
	C. shunting 3.50am to 4.30am		
	Redhill	5.10am	F
5.15am	Redhill South Yard		
	F. shunting 5.15am to 11.45am		
	Redhill South Yard	12.17pm	F
12.35pm	Redhill Up Yard	xx	‖
xx	Loco Yard		

Redhill men have all the work which is trip working and local freights including the loco coal working. Three sets are used.

Duty Nos 648 to 654 NOT USED

TUNBRIDGE WELLS WEST

Duty No. 655
4MT 2-6-4T BR Standard

	Loco Yard	6.34am	‖
xx	Tunbridge Wells West	7.12am	P
8.42am	Victoria (propel)	9.14am	E
9.16am	Carriage Sidings	xx	‖
xx	Loco Sidings	9.50am	‖
xx	Victoria (via E.G.)	10. 8am	P
11.59am	Tunbridge Wells West	xx	‖
xx	Loco Yard	1.10pm	‖
xx	Tunbridge Wells West	1.39pm	P
3. 0pm	Eastbourne	xx	‖
xx	Loco Yard	4.35pm	‖
xx	Eastbourne	4.47pm	P
6.10pm	Tunbridge Wells West	6.55pm	P
8.37pm	Eastbourne	xx	‖
xx	Loco Yard		

Tunbridge Wells West men start the duty and work round to Eastbourne Loco Yard. Eastbourne men work the 4.35pm‖ and are relieved at Tunbridge Wells West at 6.45pm by Tunbridge Wells men who change over at Eastbourne at 8.37pm with Eastbourne men who dispose the engine. Three sets of Tunbridge Wells men are used.

Redhill with L class No. 31760 on the 12.4pm to Tonbridge on 11th October 1958. On the left can be seen the three-road engine shed with a C2X, Mogul, and a Standard '76000' class.

Redhill duty No. 647 involved shunting and trip working for a C2X class 0-6-0. No. 32448 is seen on 25th June 1951, south of Redhill collecting empty wagons.

Brian Morrison

Redhill Loco in 1964 with a most interesting line up. The B1 (No. 61313) came over on a pigeon special, the "Black 5" (No. 44951) on an excursion, and the 'Manor' (No. 7808 *Cookham Manor*) was a regular working from Reading. On the left is Q class No. 30543 and a BR Standard Class 4 2-6-4T.

P. Abbot

The changing scene on the "Cuckoo Line". I3 class 4-4-2T No. 32090 is seen on 3rd June 1950 entering Rotherfield with the then timed 1.50pm Tunbridge Wells to Eastbourne. This approximates to 1.39pm ex-Tunbridge Wells after the regular interval service was introduced in the 1950s. Duty No. 655 would be the 1960 equivalent.

S. C. Nash

Duty No. 656
4MT 2-6-4T BR Standard

	Loco Yard (with 670)	5.50am	‖
xx	Tunbridge Wells West (A.N.R.)	6.12am	E
6.18am	Groombridge	7.55am	P
9.13am	London Bridge (off 7.19am Bton)	9.37am	E
9.45am	New Cross Gate	10.16am	‖
10.30am	B'Arms Loco	2.40pm	‖
2.51pm	New Cross Gate	3.18pm	E
3.25pm	London Bridge (S.R.E.)	4.20pm	P
5.20pm	East Grinstead	5.37pm	‖
6. 0pm	Oxted (via E.G.)	6.54pm	P
7.56pm	Tunbridge Wells West	xx	‖
xx	Loco Yard		

B'Arms men relieve the Tunbridge Wells men at London Bridge at 9.13am, and work and prepare the 2.40pm‖. Stewarts Lane men work the 2.40pm‖ and are relieved at 7.18pm at East Grinstead. Tunbridge Wells men take over at 7.18pm, work and dispose. The 6.12am empties are double headed to Groombridge.

Duty No. 657 NOT USED

Duty No. 658
4MT 2-6-4T BR Standard
stabled off No. 655

	Eastbourne Loco	9.20am	‖
xx	Eastbourne	9.45am	P
11 .7am	Tun Wells West (via E.G.)	11.47am	P
1.33pm	Victoria	xx	‖
xx	Loco Sidings	2.50pm	‖
xx	Victoria (via E.G.)	3. 8pm	P
4.59pm	Tunbridge Wells West	5.41pm	P
7. 3pm	Eastbourne	xx	‖
xx	Eastbourne Loco	8.25pm	‖
xx	Eastbourne	9.45pm	P
	(C. shunting 8.40pm to 9.5pm)		
10.51pm	Eridge	11. 6pm	E
11.15pm	Tunbridge Wells West	xx	‖
xx	Loco Yard		

Tunbridge Wells West men relieve the Eastbourne shed enginemen at 9.10am and work the engine to 3.25pm at East Croydon where Norwood men come on and work the engine until 5.0pm at Tunbridge Wells West. Eastbourne men take over at 5.0pm and work to Eastbourne. Tunbridge Wells West men relieve at 8.37pm, work and dispose.

Hellingly, once the junction for the private electric railway to Hellingly hospital, which had a short ½-mile branch off to the left, sees a Class 4 2-6-4 tank, No. 80141 arrive with an Eastbourne-Tunbridge Wells train. The line closed to passenger traffic on 14th June 1965, a few days after the picture was taken.

Hailsham on 4th June 1965, with Class 4 tank No. 80142 ready to depart on an Eastbourne train. The section north of Hailsham closed on 4th June 1965 but passenger services for Hailsham to Eastbourne lasted until 9th September 1968. Duties Nos 655-667 refer.

Rotherfield in the final days with an up train for Tunbridge Wells behind Class 4 2-6-4 tank No. 80142, seen arriving on 4th June 1965 – a few days before this picturesque station was closed to all traffic.

Duty No. 659
4MT 2-6-4T BR Standard

	Loco Yard	8. 0am	‖
xx	Tun Wells West (via E.G.)	8.26am	P
10. 6am	London Bridge (off 8.47am T.W.W.)	10.55am	E
11. 3am	New Cross Gate	11.33am	‖
11.46am	B'Arms Loco	3.12pm	‖
3.30pm	New X Gate (for 4.40pm Bton)	3.48pm	E
3.55pm	London Bridge	5.20pm	P
6.44pm	Tunbridge Wells West		
	C. shunting 6.50pm to 8.15pm		
	Tunbridge Wells West	xx	‖
xx	Loco Yard		

B'Arms men relieve the Tunbridge Wells West men at London Bridge at 10.15am and work round to 4.15pm being relieved at London Bridge by Tunbridge Wells West men who take the engine home. Brighton men work on the engine from 6.45pm to 7.20pm but Tunbridge Wells West men dispose.

Duty No. 664
4MT 2-6-4T BR Standard

	Loco Yard	6.15am	‖
xx	Tun Wells West (via E.G.)	7. 3am	P
9. 0am	London Bridge (off 7.55am Groom)	9.21am	E
9.28am	New Cross Gate	9.53am	‖
10. 6am	Norwood Down Yard	10.30am	F
10.55am	Wallington	11.28am	‖
11.49am	Norwood Loco	1.12pm	‖
1.22pm	East Croydon		
	C. shunting 1.30pm to 3.00pm		
	East Croydon	3.44pm	P
4.37pm	East Grinstead	5.26pm	P
6.38pm	Victoria	xx	‖
xx	Loco Sidings	7.50pm	‖
xx	Victoria (via E.G.)	8. 8pm	P
9.59pm	Tunbridge Wells West	xx	‖
xx	Loco Yard		

B'Arms men take over at 6.35am the engine having been prepared by Tunbridge Wells West men. Three Bridges men take over from the B'Arms men at London Bridge at 9.0am. Norwood men relieve the Three Bridges men at 10.4am at Norwood Junction and take the engine back to Norwood Loco after the Wallington freight. B'Arms men start the 1.12pm‖ and work round to East Grinstead at 4.49pm. Tunbridge Wells West men take over at 4.49pm at East Grinstead and finish the duty.

Duty No. 665 NOT USED

Duty No. 666
4MT 2-6-4T BR Standard
stabled off No. 667

	Eastbourne Loco	6.15am	‖
xx	Eastbourne	6.41am	P
7.59am	Tunbridge Wells West	8.40am	P
10. 1am	Eastbourne	xx	‖
xx	Loco Yard	11.10am	‖
xx	Eastbourne	11.45am	P
1. 4pm	Tunbridge Wells West		
	C. shunting 1.10pm to 2.30pm		
	Tunbridge Wells West	2.39pm	P
4. 0pm	Eastbourne	xx	‖
xx	Loco Yard	5.35pm	‖
xx	Eastbourne	6. 0pm	P
7.24pm	Tunbridge Wells West	xx	‖
xx	Loco Yard		

Eastbourne men work the engine until 5.35pm (two sets) when Tunbridge Wells West men take over and complete the duty which is to work the late lamented "Cuckoo Line" closed on 14 June 1965.

Duty No. 667
4MT 2-6-4T BR Standard

	Loco Yard	7.10am	‖
xx	Tunbridge Wells West	7.30am	P
7.40am	Eridge	8.15am	P
8.48am	Tonbridge	8.59am	P
9.37am	Redhill		
	C. shunting 9.45am to 10.35am		
	Redhill	xx	‖
xx	Loco Yard	1.55pm	‖
xx	Redhill	2.11pm	P
2.48pm	Tonbridge	4.10pm	P
6. 3pm	Eastbourne	xx	‖
xx	Loco Yard	7.20pm	‖
7.23pm	Eastbourne	7.38pm	P
9. 4pm	Tunbridge Wells West	9.39pm	P
11. 0pm	Eastbourne	xx	‖
xx	Loco Yard		
	stable for No. 666		

Redhill men relieve the Tunbridge Wells West men at Tonbridge at 8.55am who work and dispose the engine on Redhill Loco. Tonbridge men work the 1.55pm‖ off shed and are relieved at Tonbridge at 3.30pm by Eastbourne men who finish the duty.

Mayfield on 4th June 1965 with Tunbridge Wells Class 4 2-6-4T No. 80142 arriving, and the signalman holding the staff for the fireman. This perfect LBSCR station came complete with a stationmaster's house and subway. Duty No. 666 refers.

Heyday of the Southern Railway in the 1930s with B4 class 4-4-0 No. 2067 rolling into Oxted with a Victoria to Tunbridge Wells evening train. The engine has the duty 667 of the time which is in the Tunbridge Wells series. No. 2067 was built September 1901, rebuilt in October 1923 and withdrawn in September 1951. Note the D1 class 0-4-2T waiting in the bay.

Lens of Sutton

Duty No. 668
1P H class P & P fitted

	Loco Yard	5.25am	‖
xx	Tunbridge Wells West	5.38am	E
6. 4am	Forest Row	6.22am	P
6.48am	Three Bridges	7.27am	P
	work push and pull trains to East Grinstead until		
10.41am	Three Bridges	xx	‖
xx	Loco Yard	3.30pm	‖
xx	Three Bridges	3.52pm	P
4. 8pm	East Grinstead	4.27pm	P
4.41pm	Three Bridges	5. 8pm	P
5.59pm	Tunbridge Wells West	6.15pm	‖
xx	Loco Yard	7.45pm	‖
xx	Tunbridge Wells West	8. 0pm	P
8.37pm	Oxted	9. 4pm	P
9.38pm	Tunbridge Wells West	xx	‖
xx	Loco Yard		

Tunbridge Wells West men start the duty and are relieved at Forest Row at 6.5am by Three Bridges men who work the East Grinstead push and pull until 5.0pm when Tunbridge Wells West men take over and complete the duty.

Duty No. 669
1P H class P & P fitted

	Loco Yard	5.40am	‖
xx	Tunbridge Wells West	6. 6am	P
6.41am	Oxted	7.34am	P
	work push and pull trains Oxted to Tun Wells West until		
3.37pm	Oxted	4. 4pm	P
4.55pm	Tonbridge	5.22pm	P
6.37pm	Oxted	7.24pm	P
8. 1pm	Tunbridge Wells West	xx	‖
xx	Loco Yard		

Tunbridge Wells West men have all the work over the now closed Ashurst Junction to Groombridge and Tunbridge Wells West line. Two sets are used; 5.25am, and 1.30pm.

Hartfield station with M7 0-4-4T No. 30055 on 17th May 1963 working the 5.8pm Three Bridges to Tunbridge Wells West, duty No. 668. The M7s were brought in briefly to replace scrapped H class 0-4-4s but were not very popular with the fitters or locomen owing to the inaccessibility of the lubricating points. The station still exists as a private dwelling and the trackbed is a footpath, the line having closed on 2nd January 1967.

LBSCR splendour at Tunbridge Wells West with Billinton E5 class No. 585 *Crowborough* resplendent in Brighton livery and brass fittings. The engine was built in December 1903 and survived until May 1954 under BR. D. E. Marsh had the engine converted to a 2-4-2T until 1909. The station buildings survive as a Beefeater restaurant.

Tunbridge Wells had an allocation of H class 0-4-4 tanks to work the Three Bridges, Oxted and Uckfield lines. H class No. 31310 waits at Tonbridge on duty No. 668, the Saturday version of 669, 5.22pm Tonbridge to Oxted. Photograph taken on 30th April 1960.

E. Wilmshurst

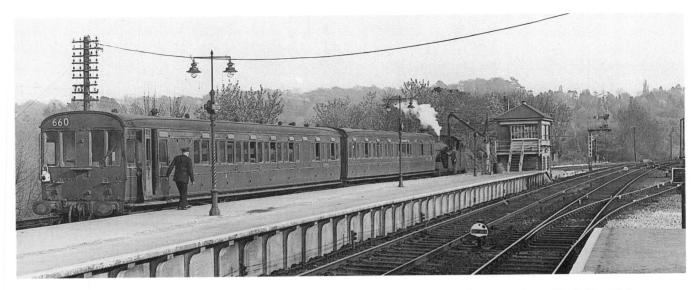

H class No. 31162 is seen in the bay at Oxted on 18th April 1961 taking water before returning to Tunbridge Wells West on duty No. 669.

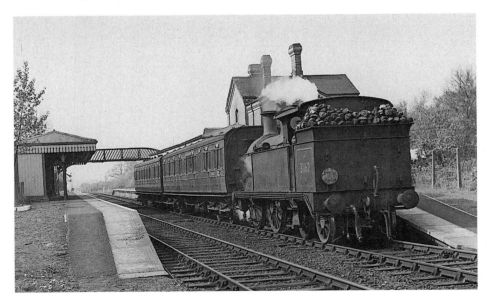

A flashback to pre-war Southern Railway days when duty No. 669 was worked by the classic Stroudley D1 class 0-4-2 tanks. No. 2254 waits in the bay at Groombridge with Brighton "balloon" coaches.

Lens of Sutton

Duty No. 669, with H class No. 31162, making a brief pause at Hever before moving on to Tunbridge Wells West with a two-coach set of ex-SECR stock. The station survives but has been 'modernised' by Network SouthEast.

Duty No. 670

1P H class P & P fitted

	Loco Yard (coupled to 656)	5.50am	||
xx	Tun Wells West (with 656)	6.12am	E
6.18am	Groombridge	6.24am	E
6.47am	Uckfield	7.20am	P
8. 8am	Oxted	8.22am	P
	work push and pull trains to T.W.W. until		
7.37pm	Oxted	8. 4pm	P
8.38pm	Tunbridge Wells West		
	C. shunting 8.45am to 10.45am		
	Tunbridge Wells West	xx	||
xx	Loco Yard		

Tunbridge Wells West men have the work which includes working the 6.12am empties double headed with No. 656. First set is on at 5.5am, second set is on at 12.40pm.

Duty No. 671

1P H class P & P fitted

	Loco Yard	7.10am	||
xx	Tun Wells West (via E.G.)	7.42am	P
8.36am	Oxted	9. 4am	P
	work push and pull trains to T.W.W. until		
9.46pm	Oxted	10. 4pm	P
10.38pm	Tunbridge Wells West	xx	||
xx	Loco Yard		

Tunbridge Wells West men have all the work on the push and pull trains from Oxted to Tunbridge Wells and Tonbridge via Grove Junction which closed on 8th July 1985. Three sets of men involved.

THREE BRIDGES

Duty No. 674

4MT 2-6-4T BR Standard

OFF No. 675

	Eastbourne Loco	5.15am	||
xx	Eastbourne	5.38am	P
6.22am	Heathfield	6.35am	P
7.21am	Eastbourne	7.58am	P
9.28am	Tun Wells West (via E.G.)	10.47am	P
12.33pm	Victoria	xx	||
xx	Loco Sidings	1.50pm	||
xx	Victoria (via E.G.)	2. 8pm	P
3.59pm	Tunbridge Wells West	4.47pm	P
5.41pm	Three Bridges	xx	||
xx	Loco Yard		

Eastbourne men work round until 10.30am at Tunbridge Wells West when they are relieved by Three Bridges men who complete the duty. Ashurst Junction to Three Bridges closed on 2nd January 1967, and the route is now mainly a footpath and bridleway.

Duty No. 675

4MT 2-6-4T BR Standard

	Loco Yard (with 692)	4.15am	||
xx	Three Bridges A.N.R.	4.45am	F
5.18am	East Grinstead	6.34am	P
7.43am	London Bridge (off 7.0am ex F. Row)	8.33am	E
8.40am	New Cross Gate		
	shunt and pull off stock		
	New Cross Gate	10.35am	V
10.43am	London Bridge		
	C. shunting 11.0am to 12.30pm		
	London Bridge	1. 2pm	V
1. 9pm	New Cross Gate (with 620)	1.18pm	||
1.30pm	B'Arms Loco (with 620)	4.10pm	||
4.23pm	New X Gate (for 5.25pm Rdg)	5. 7pm	E
5.17pm	London Bridge	6.15pm	P
7.36pm	Tunbridge Wells West	xx	||
xx	Loco Yard (coal)	8.20pm	||

(Continued)

(*Duty No. 675 continued*)

xx	Tunbridge Wells West	8.39pm	P
10. 0pm	Eastbourne	10.45pm	P
11. 1pm	Hailsham	11.18pm	P
11.33pm	Eastbourne	xx	‖
xx	Loco Yard		

Three Bridges men work the 4.15am‖ including a double header from Three Bridges to East Grinstead at 4.45am and are relieved at London Bridge at 8.10am by B'Arms men. B'Arms men work the engine from 8.10am until 5.20pm when Tunbridge Wells West men take over. Eastbourne men relieve at Tunbridge Wells West at 8.15pm, after the engine has been coaled, and work and dispose.

Duty No. 676
4MT 2-6-4T BR Standard

	Loco Yard	4.55am	‖
xx	Three Bridges Yard	5.13am	F
5.18am	Three Bridges	5.20am	F
6. 8am	East Grinstead	7.41am	P
8.45am	London Bridge (off 7.8am T.W.W.)	9.11am	E
9.18am	New Cross Gate	9.42am	E
9.54am	Rotherhithe Rd	xx	‖
xx	B'Arms Loco	2.35pm	‖
2.51pm	London Bridge		
	C. shunting 3.0pm to 3.40pm (inc. p/o 3.18pm NXG)		
	London Bridge	5.37pm	P
6.45pm	East Grinstead	7.26pm	P
8.33pm	Victoria	xx	‖
xx	Loco Sidings	9.20pm	‖
xx	Victoria	9.31pm	V
11. 8pm	Three Bridges	xx	‖
xx	Loco Yard		

Three Bridges men work the engine to B'Arms Loco and home pass. B'Arms men take the 2.35pm‖ and work to London Bridge to be relieved at 5.10pm. Three Bridges men take over at 5.10pm and complete the duty.

Three Bridges had a duty for a Class 4 4-6-0 which involved a visit to Victoria and return with the 3.50pm Victoria to Brighton via Eridge. The train is seen passing Cowden behind No. 75075 on 18th April 1961 as duty No. 677.

Duty No. 677
4MT 4-6-0 BR Standard

	Three Bridges Loco	6.40am	‖
xx	Three Bridges (tender first)	7. 7am	P
7.31am	Forest Row	8.24am	P
9.38am	Victoria	10.16am	‖
10.26am	Stewarts Lane Loco	3.10pm	‖
3.35pm	Victoria (via Eridge)	3.50pm	P
5.48pm	Brighton	xx	‖
xx	Loco Yard (turn)	7. 0pm	‖
xx	Brighton	7.14pm	P
8.28pm	Horsham (7.29pm ex Chic.)	9.54pm	V
10.35pm	Three Bridges	xx	‖
xx	Loco Yard		

An interesting mixed bag of work for a BR Standard Class 4, 4-6-0. Three Bridges men start with the 6.40am and work the 7.7am to Forest Row tender first to be relieved at Victoria at 10.15am by Stewarts Lane men who work a local coal trip to Victoria on Mondays and Fridays. Tunbridge Wells West men work the 3.10pm‖ and leave the engine at Brighton. Brighton men take the 7.0pm‖ off shed and work round to Three Bridges Loco.

Duty No. 678
4MT 2-6-4T BR Standard

	Loco Yard	3.15am	‖
xx	Three Bridges Yard	3.45am	F
6.11am	Norwood Up Yard	6.30am	F
xx	Down Yard	xx	‖
xx	Norwood Loco	8.57am	‖
xx	Norwood Down Yard	9.12am	F
9.34am	Waddon Marsh		
	F. shunting 9.40am to 12.15pm		
	Waddon Marsh	1.32pm	F
2. 4pm	Norwood Yard	xx	‖
xx	Norwood Loco	4.12pm	‖
4.22pm	East Croydon (off 4.20pm LB)	4.44pm	F
5.51pm	Tunbridge Wells West	xx	‖
xx	Loco Yard	7. 5pm	‖
xx	Tun Wells West (via E.G.)	7.47pm	P
9.33pm	Victoria	xx	‖
xx	Loco Sidings	10.40pm	‖
xx	Victoria	11.38pm	P
12.56pm	East Grinstead	1. 5am	‖
1.21am	Three Bridges Loco		

Three Bridges men work round to Norwood Loco. Norwood men work the 8.57am‖ to Waddon Marsh including a trip to Beddington Lane to shunt CCE sidings if required. Tonbridge men work the 4.12pm‖ to Tunbridge Wells West at 6.0pm where they are relieved by Tunbridge Wells West men who work to East Grinstead and home pass. Stewarts Lane men take over at East Grinstead at 8.22pm and finish the duty.

Three Bridges' Class 4 tanks worked to Tunbridge Wells, Eastbourne and London, via Oxted on duties 674–678. A member of the class is seen leaving Heathfield on an Eastbourne to Tunbridge Wells train on 4th June 1965. This was the now closed "Cuckoo Line".

Duty No. 679
1P H class P & P fitted

	Loco Yard	5.50am	‖
xx	Three Bridges	6.10am	P
6.26am	East Grinstead	7.27am	P
	work push & pull trains until		
10.41pm	Three Bridges	xx	‖
xx	Loco Yard		

Three Bridges men work the push and pull trains to East Grinstead and back all day which involves three sets of men, at 5.5am, 1.21pm, and 3.21pm.

Duty Nos 680 to 683 NOT USED

Duty No. 684
4P/5F K class

	Three Bridges Loco	9.45pm	‖
xx	Three Bridges Yard	10.12pm	F
12.17am	Willesden (S.W. Sidings)	xx	‖
xx	Loco Yard	xx	‖
xx	Willesden	2.30am	F
4.50am	Three Bridges Yard	5.50am	F
10.42am	Hove		
	F. shunting 10.50am to 12.20pm		
	Hove	12.33pm	F
4.18pm	Three Bridges Yard	xx	‖
xx‖	Three Bridges Loco		

Three Bridges men work the night freight to Willesden and the morning train to Hove. Horsham men work on the engine from Hove at 11.15am and complete the duty.

Duty No. 685
4P/5F K class
OFF No. 691

	Three Bridges Loco	3.45am	‖
xx	Three Bridges Yard	4.10am	F
4.55am	Merstham	5. 5am	‖
5.32am	Norwood Up Yard	5.40am	F
5.45am	Norwood Down Yard	6.25am	F
6.39am	East Croydon	7.10am	‖
7.16am	Norwood Yard	7.53am	F
9.24am	Gipsy Hill	10.25am	F
11. 2am	Norwood Yard	11.45am	Coal
11.53am	Norwood Loco	12.45pm	‖
xx	Norwood Yard (via Sel & T.H.)	1.10pm	F
1.50pm	Herne Hill S.S.	2. 9pm	‖
2.36pm	Norwood Loco	7.10pm	‖
xx	Norwood Up Yard	7.41pm	F
8.12pm	B'Arms	xx	‖
xx	B'Arms Loco		
	Work No. 686		

B'Arms men work the 3.45am‖ to Norwood Junction at 5.28am. Norwood men relieve at 5.28am at Norwood Junction station and have the engine until 11.53am including the 11.45am coal trip into the shed with loco coal. B'Arms men take over the engine at 7.10pm and complete the duty.

Duty No. 686
4P/5F K class
OFF No. 685

	B'Arms Loco	10.15pm	‖
xx	B'Arms J. Sect	10.37pm	F
12.16am	Three Bridges	12.50am	F
3.39am	Chichester (1.30am Bton)	4.35am	F
5.56am	Eastleigh Yard	6.50am	F
7. 0am	Town Yard	xx	‖
xx	Eastleigh Loco	9.30am	‖
xx	Eastleigh	10. 3am	F
11. 0am	Fratton Yard	11.10am	‖
xx	Fratton Loco		
	stable for No. 691		

B'Arms men are relieved at Three Bridges at 12.45am by Horsham men who work to Chichester. Fratton men complete the duty after 3.55am.

Duty No. 687 NOT USED

Rowfant on 16th March 1958 with H class No. 31530 propelling on the Three Bridges to East Grinstead branch passenger. The staff has been collected by the guard and the crew wait patiently for the photographer to get back on the train. Duty No. 679 worked this line which closed on 2nd January 1967.

Three Bridges Loco with H, K, Q1, and 4MT tanks on shed on 20th January 1963. Three K class duties (684–686) operated from Three Bridges which involved main line freights. No K class 2-6-0s were preserved and all were withdrawn by December 1962. No. 32353 is seen on 20th January 1963 awaiting departure to the breaker's yard.

Duty No. 688
2F C2X class

	Loco Yard	12.25am	‖
xx	Three Bridges Yard		
	F. shunting 12.30am to 4.30am		
	Three Bridges Yard	5. 5am	F
6.51am	Brighton Top Yard	7. 5am	‖
xx	Brighton Loco	8.30am	‖
8.41am	Hove (via Steyning)	9. 2am	F
1.45pm	Three Bridges Yard	2. 0pm	F
2. 7pm	Crawley New Yard	3.15pm	F
3.22pm	Three Bridges Yard	xx	‖
xx	Three Bridges Loco		

Three Bridges men work the 12.25am‖ and leave the engine in Brighton Loco. Brighton men work the 8.30am‖ off shed and complete the duty.

Duty No. 689
4P/5F K class

	Three Bridges Loco	6.25am	‖
xx	Up Yard		
	F. shunting 6.30am to 7.30am		
	Three Bridges	7.56am	F
8.56am	Lewes	10. 9am	F
11.32am	Eastbourne	xx	‖
xx	Loco Yard	4.25pm	‖
4.28pm	Eastbourne	4.59pm	P
5.12pm	Hailsham	5.20pm	P
5.26pm	Polegate	5.34pm	P
5.40pm	Hailsham	6. 0pm	P
6. 6pm	Polegate	6.40pm	P
6.46pm	Hailsham	7. 6pm	P
7.12pm	Polegate	7.27pm	E
7.35pm	Eastbourne	xx	‖
xx	Loco Yard	1.30am	‖
xx	Eastbourne	1.50am	F
2.35am	Lewes E. Sdgs (1.55am ex NH)	3.53am	F
5. 4am	Three Bridges	xx	‖
xx	Loco Yard		

Three Bridges men work round to Polegate at 11.5am where they are relieved by Eastbourne men who have the rest of the work including the Hailsham passenger turns. Eastbourne use three sets of men.

Three Bridges had Q class 0-6-0s to work West Sussex freights. Two spick and span members of the class are seen double heading a railtour away from Havant on 3rd November 1963. Nos 30531 and 30543 were members of a small class of 20, introduced in 1938. One member of the class survives, No. 30541 now on the Bluebell Railway.

Duty No. 690
4F Q class

	Three Bridges Loco	11.30pm	‖
xx	Three Bridges A.N.R. (with 531)	12. 3am	F
12.58am	Norwood No 1 Up Goods	1.20am	F
1.42am	New Cross Gate		
	F. shunting 3.15am to 4.15am		
	New Cross Gate	4.35am	F
5.58am	Three Bridges Yard	6.10am	‖
6.35am	Horsham		
	F. shunting 6.55am to 8.20am		
	Horsham	8.33am	F
11.27am	Littlehampton		
	F. shunting 11.30am to 2.15pm		
	Littlehampton	2.35pm	F
3.33pm	Chichester	4.34pm	F
4.48pm	Barnham	5.32pm	F
5.47pm	Chichester	7.27pm	V
9.28pm	Horsham	9.30pm	‖
9.54pm	Three Bridges Loco		

Three Bridges have the work round to 6.35am at Horsham. The engine has double headed the 12.3am night freight from Three Bridges to Norwood No. 1 Up Goods with duty No. 531 a 'West Country' class. Horsham men come onto the engine at 6.35am and are relieved by Bognor men at Arundel at 10.54am, who are relieved by Horsham men at Barnham at 5.2pm. Three Bridges men come on at 7.45pm at Barnham and complete the duty.

Duty No. 691
4P/5F K class
OFF No. 686

	Fratton Loco	3.20am	‖
3.55am	Chichester	4.15am	F
4.30am	Barnham		
	F. shunting 4.30am to 5.45am		
	Barnham	5.50am	F
6. 0am	Bognor Regis		
	F. shunting 6.0am to 8.15am		
	Bognor Regis	9.11am	F
9.35am	Barnham	10.37am	‖
10.48am	Chichester		
	F. shunting 11.0am to 12.45pm		
	Chichester	1.30pm	‖
1.53pm	Bognor Regis		
	F. shunting 2.0pm to 4.0pm		
	Bognor Regis	5. 0pm	F
7.55pm	Three Bridges Yard	xx	‖
xx	Three Bridges Loco		
	Work No. 685		

Fratton men are relieved at 3.55am at Chichester by Horsham men who work to Bognor to be relieved at Bognor at 7.45am by Bognor men who finish the duty. Two sets of Bognor men are used an early, at 7.30am, and a late at 3.0pm.

Duty No. 692
2F C2X class

	Loco Yard (with 675)	4.15am	‖
xx	Three Bridges (with 675)	4.45am	F
7.10am	Groombridge	7.20am	‖
7.27am	Tun Wells West Loco	11.55am	‖
xx	Tunbridge Wells West		
	C. and F. shunting 12.00noon to 1.20pm		
	Tunbridge Wells West	2. 6pm	‖
2.30pm	Forest Row	2.50pm	F
4.14pm	Three Bridges Yard	xx	‖
xx	Loco Yard	6.12pm	‖
6.18pm	Crawley		
	F. shunting 6.20pm to 8.40pm		
	Crawley	9.10pm	F
9.20pm	Three Bridges	xx	‖
xx	Loco Yard		

Three Bridges men start off with a double header on the 4.45am freight to East Grinstead (No. 675 4MT tank). Tunbridge Wells West men relieve at Forest Row at 6.5am, work until 4.34pm (two sets). Three Bridges men come on at 6.12pm and work the rest of the duty.

An idyllic country scene with C2X class 0-6-0 No. 32523 at Rowfant on an East Grinstead to Three Bridges freight. The C2Xs were all withdrawn by 1962 and replaced by Moguls reallocated from other divisions. The C2X was the Marsh rebuild of the Billinton C2 of 1908 with a C3 class boiler. None of the class survived into preservation. Rowfant station buildings survive however, and the old trackbed is now a public footpath.

Brian Morrison

Duty No. 693
2P/2F E4 class
OFF No. 694

	Horsham Loco	7. 5am	‖
xx	Horsham	7.25am	P
10.20am	Midhurst	11.30am	F
3.12pm	Horsham	xx	‖
xx	Horsham Loco	6.17pm	‖
6.37pm	Crawley	7. 8pm	V
7.13pm	Three Bridges	xx	‖
xx	Three Bridges Loco		

Horsham men have the Midhurst Goods with an LBSCR E4 class 0-6-2 tank. The line closed from Midhurst on 2nd October 1964 (back to Petworth).

Duty No. 694
2P/2F E4 class

	Three Bridges Loco	1.20am	‖
xx	Three Bridges Yard	1.50am	F
2.28am	Horsham	3.30am	‖
3.58am	Three Bridges Loco	5.10am	‖
xx	Three Bridges	5.30am	F
8.42am	Horsham	9. 6am	F
10.48am	Holmwood	11.45am	F
12.57pm	Horsham		
	F. shunting 1.20pm to 3.45pm		
	Horsham	xx	‖
xx	Horsham Loco	4.55pm	‖
xx	Horsham	5.35pm	E
6.55pm	Brighton	8.30pm	P
9.32pm	Horsham	xx	‖
xx	Horsham Loco		
	Work No. 693		

Three Bridges men work round to Crawley where they are relieved by Horsham men at 8.5am. Horsham men have the rest of the work which includes the Holmwood freight on Mondays, Wednesdays and Fridays and the Warnham freight on Tuesdays and Thursdays. Two sets of Horsham men are supplied an early and a late.

Three Bridges Loco on 23rd June 1935 with a nice selection of motive power. Left to right, H class No. 1264, C2 No. 2531, D3 No. 2383, E4s Nos 2493, 2518 and D1 No. 2235. The E4 0-6-2 tanks worked at Three Bridges until 1963 and were used on local goods and shunts. Duties 693 and 694 refer.

H. N. James

Duty No. 693 was the Midhurst goods working stabled out at Horsham. E4 0-6-2T No. 32469 is seen at Petworth (now a private house) on the return working from Midhurst on 14th April 1960.

BRIGHTON

Duty Nos 695 to 729 NOT USED

Duty No. 730
7P/5F WC class

	Brighton Loco	9.25am	‖
xx	Brighton	9.40am	P
12. 9pm	Bournemouth Ctl	xx	‖
xx	Bournemouth Loco	1.20pm	‖
xx	Bournemouth West Sdgs (propel)	xx	E
xx	Bournemouth West	1.50pm	P
4.54pm	Brighton (off 11.0am Ply)	5.37pm	E
5.42pm	Hove	xx	‖
xx	Brighton Loco		

Brighton men have all the work and have to propel the empty stock in from the sidings at Bournemouth West. The duty only operates until 28th October and from 1st May.

Duty No. 731
7P/5F WC class

	Brighton Loco	10.45am	‖
xx	Brighton	11. 0am	P
1.31pm	Salisbury	xx	‖
xx	Loco Yard	2.30pm	‖
xx	Salisbury (11.0am ex Ply)	2.55pm	P
5.24pm	Brighton	xx	‖
xx	Brighton Loco	9.10pm	‖
xx	Brighton	9.32pm	F
11.55pm	Norwood Yard	xx	‖
xx	Norwood Loco	2. 0am	‖
xx	London Bridge	3.20am	P
4.32am	Brighton	xx	‖
xx	Brighton Loco		

Brighton men have all the work on the Salisbury working by day and the newspapers at night.

Brighton had an allocation of 'West Country' class 4-6-2s including No. 34039 *Boscastle* seen here chuntering away from Southampton Central with the 11am Plymouth to Brighton on 8th March 1958. Brighton men worked the train as far as Salisbury on duty No. 731. *Boscastle* was rebuilt in 1959 and withdrawn in 1965 but can be seen today in rebuilt form working on the Great Central Railway.

The Brighton to Plymouth was worked by H2 class Atlantics before the arrival of 'West Countries'. No. 32424 is seen passing Chichester West box in the early fifties still with the "Southern" lettering on the tender.

Duty No. 732
7P/5F WC class

	Brighton Loco	11.15am	‖
xx	Brighton	11.30am	P
1.58pm	Salisbury	xx	‖
xx	Salisbury Loco	3.25pm	‖
xx	Salisbury (1.0pm ex Cardiff)	3.53pm	P
6.24pm	Brighton	xx	‖
xx	Brighton Loco (with 733)	10.40pm	‖
xx	Brighton	11.18pm	V
	(double headed to E. Croy)		
1.31am	London Bridge S.R.E.	1.45am	‖
2. 3am	B'Arms Loco (with 733)	4.30am	‖
4.52am	London Bridge	5.32am	V
7.42am	Brighton	8.20am	E
xx	Carriage Sidings	xx	‖
xx	Loco Yard		

Brighton men work the 11.15am‖ to Salisbury and back. Brighton men take the 10.40pm‖ off shed and double head the 11.18pm vans with duty No. 733 to be relieved at Three Bridges at 11.57pm. Three Bridges men take over at 11.57pm and have the engine until relieved by Brighton men at 8.15am.

Duty No. 733
7P/5F WC class

	Loco Yard	1.30pm	‖
xx	Brighton (via Eridge)	1.55pm	P
3.59pm	Victoria (propel)	4.12pm	E
xx	Carriage Sdgs	4.14pm	‖
4.23pm	Stewarts Lane Loco	5.38pm	‖
5.56pm	Victoria (via Eridge)	6.10pm	P
8.11pm	Brighton	xx	‖
xx	Loco Yard (with 732)	10.40pm	‖
xx	Brighton (A.N.R.)	11.18pm	V
12.47am	East Croydon	12.53am	‖
1.18am	B'Arms Loco (with 732)	4.30am	‖
4.52am	London Bridge	5. 8am	P
7. 2am	Horsham	7.16am	P
8.24am	Brighton	xx	‖
xx	Top Yard (via P. Pk)	9. 1am	F
9.24am	Hove (forms 11.30am Plymouth)	11. 5am	E
11.11am	Brighton	xx	‖
xx	Loco Yard		

Brighton men have all the work on a Brighton to Victoria and back including the difficult 6.10pm ex Victoria, a notoriously bad time keeper. The 11.18pm vans at night is double headed with another 'West Country' class (duty No. 732) as far as East Croydon. On three days of the week the 11.5am empties from Hove run in from Lovers Walk sidings for the 11.30am Plymouth.

Duty No. 734
4MT 2-6-4T BR Standard
stabled off No. 741

	Loco Yard	6. 5am	‖
xx	Tunbridge Wells West	6.25am	P
7.49am	Eastbourne	8.43am	P
10. 5am	Tunbridge Wells West	xx	‖
xx	Loco Yard	10.55am	‖
xx	Tunbridge Wells West	11.10am	P
11.25am	Tonbridge (10.55am Bton)	12.40pm	P
1.18pm	Redhill	1.26pm	‖
xx	Redhill Loco	6.10pm	‖
xx	Redhill	6.30pm	P
6.57pm	Penshurst	7. 0pm	E
7.22pm	Tunbridge Wells Ctl	7.24pm	P
8.41pm	Brighton	xx	‖
xx	Loco Yard		

Tunbridge Wells West men work the 6.5am‖ and are relieved at 11.8am by Tonbridge men who stay on the engine until 11.25am, (17 minutes – almost a record). Another Tonbridge crew relieve at 11.25am and work to Redhill Loco where they dispose the engine. Redhill men prepare the 6.10pm for Tonbridge men who work and dispose.

Duty No. 735
4MT 2-6-4T BR Standard
OFF No. 745

	Eastbourne Loco	5.55am	‖
xx	Eastbourne		
	C. shunting 6.0am to 7.0am		
	Eastbourne	7.31am	P
8.49am	Tunbridge Wells West	9.41am	P
11. 0am	Eastbourne	xx	‖
xx	Loco Yard	2.35pm	‖
xx	Eastbourne	2.45pm	P
4. 4pm	Tunbridge Wells West	xx	‖
xx	Loco Yard	5.15pm	‖
xx	Tunbridge Wells West	5.35pm	P
6.41pm	Brighton	xx	‖
xx	Top Table	7.41pm	‖
xx	Brighton	7.55pm	P
9.29pm	Tonbridge	10.10pm	P
11.45pm	Brighton S.R.E.	xx	‖
xx	Top Yard (via P. Pk)	1.30am	F
2.20am	Shoreham	2.55am	‖
3. 9am	Brighton Loco		

Eastbourne men work round to Tunbridge Wells West at 4.4pm. Tunbridge Wells West men work the 5.15pm‖ off shed for Tonbridge men who come on to the engine at 5.33pm and work to Brighton at 6.55pm. Brighton men relieve at 6.55pm and complete the duty.

Duty No. 736
4MT 2-6-4T BR Standard

	Loco Yard	7.30am	‖
xx	Brighton	7.55am	P
9.25am	Tonbridge	9.32am	P
10.10am	Redhill (with 622)	10.20am	‖
10.23am	Loco Yard	11.58am	‖
xx	Redhill	12. 4pm	P
12.42pm	Tonbridge	1.10pm	P
2.41pm	Brighton		
	C. shunting 2.50pm to 3.50pm		
	Brighton	3.50pm	‖
xx	Loco Yard	5. 5pm	‖
xx	Brighton	5.25pm	V
5.27pm	Top Yard	5.41pm	V
9.35pm	New Cross Gate	10.40pm	V
12.50am	Brighton	xx	‖
xx	Loco Yard		

Brighton men start the duty until relieved at 9.7am at Tunbridge Wells West by Tonbridge men who work round to Brighton where they are relieved at 3.40pm by Brighton men who finish the duty.

Brighton Class 4 tanks on duties 734–746 worked the Tunbridge Wells lines. No. 80138 is seen at Tunbridge Wells West (now Sainsburys' car park) in the spring of 1960 awaiting departure. An H class 0-4-4 tank can be seen on the left. Photograph taken on 21st February 1960.

Brighton locomotives worked to Eastbourne via Tunbridge Wells West. No. 80013 is seen at Heathfield on the "Cuckoo Line", closed on 14th June 1965. Duties 734–746 apply.

Duty No. 736 takes Class 4 2-6-4 tank No. 80012 on a through train, the 7.55am from Brighton to Redhill via Tonbridge. The engine returned on the 12.4pm to Tonbridge and the 1.10pm Tonbridge to Brighton before working to New Cross Gate and back. No. 80012 is seen leaving Redhill on 15th January 1959.

Duty No. 737
4MT 2-6-4T BR Standard

	Brighton Loco		‖
	Brighton Loco	6.15am	‖
xx	Brighton	6.58am	P
8. 6am	Tunbridge Wells West	9.24am	P
10.44am	Victoria (propel)	11.10am	E
xx	Carriage Sidings	xx	‖
xx	Loco Sidings	11.50am	‖
xx	Victoria	12. 8pm	P
1.59pm	Tunbridge Wells West	xx	‖
xx	Loco Yard	3.50pm	‖
xx	Tunbridge Wells West		
	C. shunting 4.0pm to 5.0pm		
	Tun Wells West (via E.G.)	5. 6pm	P
7.19pm	London Bridge	7.41pm	‖
7.48pm	New Cross Gate	9. 0pm	E
9.12pm	Rotherhithe Road	xx	‖
xx	B'Arms (L. Sect)	10. 5pm	F
10.43pm	Norwood Down Yard	xx	‖
xx	Norwood Loco		
	stable for No. 743		

Brighton men are relieved at Tunbridge Wells West at 9.20am by Stewarts Lane men who work to Victoria where they are relieved by Tunbridge Wells West men at 10.45am. Tunbridge Wells West men work round to East Grinstead where they are relieved at 5.44pm by B'Arms men who finish the duty.

Duty No. 738
4MT 2-6-4T BR Standard

	Loco Yard	4.35am	‖
4.37am	Brighton	4.55am	V
5.19am	Worthing Ctl	6. 5am	‖
6.15am	Shoreham	6.30am	F
6.42am	Beeding	7. 8am	‖
7.12am	Steyning	7.35am	P
8. 2am	Brighton		
	C. shunting 8.10am to 9.40am		
	Brighton	10.55am	P

(Continued)

12.27pm	Tonbridge		
	C. shunting 1.40pm to 2.30pm		
	Tonbridge	3.10pm	P
4. 4pm	Brighton	xx	‖
xx	Carriage Sdgs. (propel)	6.41pm	E
xx	Brighton	6.55pm	P
8.59pm	Victoria (propel)	9. 6pm	E
xx	Carriage Sidings	xx	‖
xx	Loco Yard	9.50pm	‖
xx	Victoria (via E.G.)	10. 8pm	P
12. 0mdt	Tunbridge Wells West	xx	‖
xx	Loco Yard		
	stable for No. 745		

Brighton men start the 4.35am‖, work and are relieved at Brighton at 10.40am by Tonbridge men who are relieved at Tonbridge at 2.54pm. Brighton men come onto the engine at 2.54pm and are relieved at 6.50pm by Tunbridge Wells West men who finish the duty.

Duty No. 739
4MT 2-6-4T BR Standard

	Loco Yard	7.30am	‖
xx	Carriage Sdgs (propel)	7.45am	E
xx	Brighton (via Eridge)	8.20am	P
10.20am	Victoria	xx	‖
xx	Carriage Sidings		
	C. shunting 11.0am to 11.35am		
	Carriage Sidings	xx	‖
xx	Loco Yard	12.50pm	‖
xx	Victoria (via E.G.)	1. 8pm	P
2.59pm	Tunbridge Wells West	3.30pm	P
5. 0pm	Eastbourne	xx	‖
xx	Loco Yard	6.15pm	‖
xx	Eastbourne	6.43pm	P
8.25pm	Tonbridge	9.10pm	P
10.41pm	Brighton	xx	‖
xx	Loco Yard		

Brighton men start the duty and work until Tunbridge Wells West men take over at Victoria at 1.5pm. Tunbridge Wells West men work the loco until 5.0pm at Eastbourne when Eastbourne men take over and work to Tunbridge Wells West at 8.7pm. Brighton men relieve at Tunbridge Wells West at 8.7pm, work and dispose.

Brighton Class 4 2-6-4 tanks worked up the Steyning line to Horsham and back. No. 80152 is seen working bunker first at Southwater with a Maunsell three set. The line closed to passengers on 7th March 1966.

Duty No. 740

4MT 2-6-4T BR Standard

	Loco Yard	6. 5am	‖
xx	Top Yard (propel)	6.15am	E
xx	Brighton (via Eridge)	7.17am	P
9.28am	London Bridge (off 7.27am Rdg)	9.56am	E
10. 2am	New Cross Gate	10.16am	‖
xx	B'Arms Loco	11.55am	‖
xx	Rotherhithe Rd	12.25pm	E
12.51pm	New Cross Gate	xx	‖
xx	Loco Sidings	3. 0pm	‖
xx	New Cross Gate (for 4.20pm E.G.)	3.33pm	E
3.40pm	London Bridge (via Eridge)	4.40pm	P
6.54pm	Brighton	xx	‖
xx	Loco Yard		

Brighton men work to 7.5am on this engine when they are relieved by Newhaven men who work to London Bridge to be relieved by B'Arms men at 9.45am. B'Arms men work the engine until 3.15pm at New Cross Gate when Brighton men take over and complete the duty. New Cross Gate Loco was closed but the sidings and turntable were still intact.

Duty No. 741

4MT 2-6-4T BR Standard

	Loco Yard	5.30am	‖
xx	Brighton	6. 5am	P
7.27am	Tonbridge	8.23am	P
9. 2am	Redhill	10.18am	P
10.53am	Tonbridge	11.10am	P
1. 0pm	Eastbourne	1.45pm	P
3.25pm	Tonbridge	xx	‖
xx	Loco Yard	4.45pm	‖
xx	Tonbridge	5.11pm	P
5.30pm	Tunbridge Wells West	5.55pm	P
6.52pm	Horam	7.18pm	P
7.37pm	Polegate	7.50pm	E
7.57pm	Eastbourne	8.45pm	P
10. 4pm	Tunbridge Wells West	xx	‖
xx	Loco Yard		
	stable for No. 734		

Brighton men are relieved at Tonbridge at 8.20am by Tonbridge men who work round to 11.29am at Tunbridge Wells West when Eastbourne men take over. Tonbridge men come back at 3.25pm and work until 5.30pm when they are relieved by Tunbridge Wells West men who complete the duty. Plenty of running around the now closed branch lines of East Sussex.

The N class 2-6-0s replaced the Ks at Brighton after the former had been withdrawn in December 1962. No. 31833 is seen leaving East Croydon on 21st December 1963 with the 9.45am Bricklayers Arms to Brighton Christmas parcels train. No. 31833 was a Woolwich built engine and was completed at Ashford in 1924, being withdrawn by BR on February 1964.

Duty No. 742
4MT 2-6-4T BR Standard

	Loco Yard	6.30am	‖
xx	Top Yard (propel)	6.50am	E
xx	Brighton (via Eridge)	7.35am	P
9.47am	Victoria (propel)	9.55am	E
xx	Carriage Sidings	xx	‖
xx	Loco Sidings	10.50am	‖
xx	Victoria (via E.G.)	11. 8am	P
12.59pm	Tunbridge Wells West	2.47pm	P
4.47pm	Victoria (propel)	4.55pm	E
xx	Carriage Sidings	xx	‖
xx	Loco Sidings	xx	‖
xx	Victoria	6.48pm	P
8. 5pm	East Grinstead	8.55pm	‖
9.46pm	Tunbridge Wells West Loco		
	stable for No. 744		

Brighton men are relieved at Victoria at 9.47am by Tunbridge Wells West men who finish the job. Two sets of Tunbridge Wells West men are used.

Duty No. 743
4MT 2-6-4T BR Standard
OFF No. 737

	Norwood Loco	12.45am	‖
12.54am	East Croydon	1.13am	V
1.40am	Victoria		
	C. shunting & trips 2.0am to 4.0am		
	Victoria (via Eridge)	5.20am	V
8.36am	Eastbourne	xx	‖
xx	Loco Yard	10.10am	‖
xx	Eastbourne	10.45am	P
12. 4pm	Tunbridge Wells West	12.39pm	P
2. 0pm	Eastbourne	xx	‖
xx	Loco Yard	3.35pm	‖
xx	Eastbourne	3.45pm	P
5. 4pm	Tun Wells West (via E.G.)	5.47pm	P
7.33pm	Victoria	xx	‖
xx	Loco Sidings	8.50pm	‖
xx	Victoria (via E.G.)	9. 8pm	P
10.59pm	Tunbridge Wells West		
	C. shunting 11.0pm to 12.0mdt		
	Tunbridge Wells West	xx	‖
xx	Loco Yard		
	stable for No. 746		

Norwood men work the 12.45am‖ and work the engine to Victoria where they are relieved at 5.0am. Stewarts Lane men take over at 5.0am, work and are relieved at Eridge at 6.46am by Tunbridge Wells West men who take the engine to Eastbourne Loco. Eastbourne men start with the 10.10am‖ and work the engine until 3.35pm when they are relieved by Tunbridge Wells West men who finish the duty.

Duty No. 744
4MT 2-6-4T BR Standard
OFF No. 742

	Tunbridge Wells West	5.15am	‖
6. 4am	Forest Row	7. 0am	P
8.16am	London Bridge (off 7.41am E.G.)	8.53am	E
9. 0am	New Cross Gate	9.17am	‖
9.27am	B'Arms Loco	9.50am	Coal
xx	B'Arms (N. Sect) bank	10.21am	F
11. 0am	Forest Hill	11. 7am	‖
xx	New Cross Gate	1.39pm	V
	(C. shunting 1.10pm to 1.30pm)		
4. 8pm	Brighton	xx	‖
xx	Loco Yard	5.24pm	‖
xx	Brighton	5.55pm	P
7.29pm	Tonbridge	8.10pm	P
9.41am	Brighton		
	C. shunting 9.50pm to 10.55pm		
	Brighton	xx	‖
xx	Loco Yard		

Tunbridge Wells West men start the 5.15am‖ and work the engine until 8.50am at London Bridge where B'Arms men take over until 1.30pm. Brighton men relieve at 1.30pm and take the engine home.

Duty No. 745
4MT 2-6-4T BR Standard
OFF No. 738

	Loco Yard	6. 0am	‖
xx	Tunbridge Wells West	6.39am	P
8. 5am	Victoria (propel)	8.13am	E
xx	Carriage Sidings	xx	‖
xx	Loco Sidings	8.50am	‖
xx	Victoria (via E.G.)	9. 9am	P
10.59am	Tunbridge Wells West		
	C. shunting 11.0am to 11.25am		
	Tun Wells West (via E.G.)	12.47pm	P
2.33pm	Victoria	xx	‖
xx	Loco Sidings	4.50pm	‖
xx	Victoria (via E.G.)	5. 9pm	P
6.59pm	Tunbridge Wells West	7.39pm	P
9. 0pm	Eastbourne	10. 0pm	V
11.16pm	Haywards Heath	12.40am	V
1.44am	Eastbourne		
	C. shunting 1.50am to 2.20am		
	Eastbourne	xx	‖
xx	Loco Yard		
	stable for No. 735		

Tunbridge Wells West men work to 7.0pm (two sets). Eastbourne men take over at 7.0pm and finish the duty. The standard passenger service was nine minutes past the hour from Victoria to Tunbridge Wells West via East Grinstead.

Duty No. 746
4MT 2-6-4T BR Standard
OFF No. 743

	Loco Yard	8.30am	‖
xx	Tun Wells West (via E.G.)	8.47am	P
10.39am	London Bridge	10.55am	E
11. 3am	New Cross Gate		O/R
	F. shunting 11.30am to 1.0pm		
	New Cross Gate	1.15pm	‖
	B'Arms (B. Sect) bank	3. 5pm	F
3.31pm	Forest Hill	3.32pm	‖
3.41pm	New X Gate (for 5.20pm T.W.W.)	4.45pm	E
4.52pm	London Bridge	6.31pm	P
7.50pm	Forest Row	8.35pm	‖
9.23pm	Three Bridges Loco	11. 5pm	‖
xx	Three Bridges (9.31pm ex Vic)	11.24pm	V
11.37pm	Haywards Heath (off 9.28 B.A.)	12.15am	F
12.44am	Hove	1.20am	‖
xx	Brighton Loco		

Stewarts Lane men work the 8.30am‖ and are relieved at London Bridge at 10.45am by B'Arms men who work to 6.0pm at London Bridge. Three Bridges men come on to the engine at 6.0pm work and dispose. Brighton men work the 11.5pm‖ off shed and take the engine home. The engine travels 'on rear' of the 10.55am empties from London Bridge.

Duty No. 747
1P H class P & P fitted

	Loco Yard	5.45am	‖
xx	Brighton	6.28am	P
7.32am	Horsham	8.15am	P
9.21am	Brighton		
	shunt Pullman shops 9.30am to 11.30am		
	C. shunting 11.30am to 11.55am		
	Brighton	xx	‖
xx	Loco Yard	1.15pm	‖
xx	Brighton	1.30pm	P
2.32pm	Horsham	3.19pm	P
4.21pm	Brighton	4.30pm	P
5.32pm	Horsham	7.12pm	P
8.14pm	Guildford	8.34pm	P
9.25pm	Horsham	xx	‖
xx	Loco Yard		
	stable for No. 748		

Brighton men do shunts in the Pullman works (building still standing) and trips up the Steyning branch to Horsham which closed on 7th March 1966. Horsham men relieve at 5.50pm for a turn over the Guildford branch which closed on 14th June 1965.

Brighton had H class 0-4-4 tanks to work the Brighton to Horsham and Horsham to Guildford passenger trains on duties 747–752. No. 31279 and crew wait to cross at Cranleigh on 8th August 1959.

Duty No. 748
1P H class P & P fitted
stabled off No. 747

	Horsham Loco	3.50am	‖
4.15am	Three Bridges	4.35am	V
4.53am	Horsham	5.30am	V
5.52am	Pulborough	6.14am	‖
6.39am	Horsham	7.55am	P
8.42am	Guildford	9.22am	P
10.11am	Horsham	12. 9pm	P
1. 6pm	Guildford	1.34pm	P
2.22pm	Horsham	4.19pm	P
5.21pm	Brighton	5.30pm	P
6.34pm	Horsham	7.19pm	P
8.21pm	Brighton	xx	‖
xx	Loco Yard		

Horsham men (two sets) work the push and pull in the morning being relieved at 6.34pm by Brighton men who complete the duty.

Baynards, with its immaculate flower beds full of dahlias, was a favourite stopping off point for visitors. Ivatt No. 41294 is seen on 5th June 1965 with a Horsham train, just prior to closure.

Rudgwick, the next station down the line from Baynards, is seen on 10th June 1965 with Ivatt 2-6-2 tank No. 41299. The Ivatt tanks ousted the SECR H class 0-4-4Ts and worked the line until closure on 14th June 1965.

H classes cross at Cranleigh on 8th August 1959 on the picturesque Horsham to Guildford branch, closed on 14th June 1965. Brighton engines stabled at Horsham Loco on duties Nos 747, 749 and 751.

The H class replaced the M7s which had replaced the D3s. D3 No. 32380 which was a Billinton 0-4-4 tank of 1892, reboilered by Marsh, is seen at Guildford about to propel to Horsham with a two-coach set of LBSCR stock in the early fifties.

Lens of Sutton

Duty No. 749
1P H class P & P fitted

	Loco Yard	5.40am	‖
xx	Brighton		
	C. shunting 5.45am to 6.30am		
	Brighton	8. 0am	P
9. 3am	Horsham	9.19am	P
10.21am	Brighton	10.30am	P
11.32am	Horsham	12.19pm	P
1.21pm	Brighton	3.30pm	P
4.32pm	Horsham	4.53pm	P
5.47pm	Guildford	6. 5pm	P
6.59pm	Horsham	xx	‖
xx	Loco Yard		
	stable for No. 750		

Brighton men (two sets) have all the work on the Steyning and Guildford, branches now public footpaths and bridleways.

Duty No. 750
1P H class P & P fitted
stabled off No. 749

	Horsham Loco	5.50am	‖
xx	Horsham	6.17am	P
7.21am	Brighton	7.28am	P
8.32am	Horsham	10.19am	P
11.21am	Brighton	11.37am	P
12.44pm	Horsham	1.19pm	P
2.21pm	Brighton	2.30pm	P
3.32pm	Horsham	xx	‖
xx	Loco Yard	5.40pm	‖
xx	Horsham	6.17pm	P
7.10pm	Guildford	7.34pm	P
8.17pm	Horsham	9.19pm	E
10.21pm	Brighton	10.30pm	P
11. 2pm	Steyning	11. 5pm	E
11.31pm	Brighton	xx	‖
xx	Loco Yard		

Horsham men work the engine until 1.15pm when Brighton men take over and finish the duty.

Slinfold, the last station on the Guildford to Horsham line on 5th June 1965, shortly before closure. The rustic station has been demolished and the line is now a footpath. Ivatt 2-6-2 No. 41294 is in charge.

Duty No. 751
1P H class P & P fitted

	Loco Yard	9. 0am	‖
xx	Brighton	9.30am	P
10.32am	Horsham	11.19am	P
12.21pm	Brighton	12.30pm	P
1.32pm	Horsham	2.19pm	P
3.21pm	Brighton	xx	‖
xx	Loco Yard	4.55pm	‖
xx	Brighton		
	C. shunting 5.0pm to 5.40pm		
	Brighton	6.13pm	P
7.18pm	Horsham	8.19pm	P
9.21pm	Brighton	9.30pm	P
10.32pm	Horsham	xx	‖
xx	Loco Yard		
	stable for No. 752		

Brighton men (two sets) work round to Brighton at 9.21pm when Horsham men take over and complete the duty.

Duty No. 752
1P H class P & P fitted
OFF No. 751

	Horsham Loco	6. 0am	‖
xx	Horsham	6.46am	P
7.35am	Guildford	8. 4am	P
8.54am	Horsham	9.30am	P
10.14am	Guildford	10.34am	P
11.22am	Horsham	xx	‖
xx	Loco Yard	2.50pm	‖
xx	Horsham	3. 9pm	P
4. 6pm	Guildford	5. 4pm	P
5.49pm	Horsham	6.26pm	P
7.27pm	Brighton	xx	‖
xx	Loco Yard		

Horsham men (two sets) have all the work and take the engine off shed at 6.0am‖. Horsham Loco was a half round-house and the lost branch lines are now footpaths and bridleways known as the Downs Link.

Duty No. 755
2P/2F E4 class

	Brighton Loco	5.55am	‖
6.26am	Haywards Heath	7.22am	V
8.15am	Eastbourne		
	C. shunting 8.30am to 10.0am		
	Eastbourne	11. 5am	‖
11.19am	Polegate		
	C & W. shunting 11.20am to 12.20pm		
	Polegate	12.25pm	‖
12.34pm	Eastbourne	1.11pm	P
1.27pm	Hailsham	2. 7pm	P
2.22pm	Eastbourne	3. 5pm	F
5.36pm	Lewes East Sidings	8.30pm	F
9. 3pm	Brighton Top Yard	xx	‖
xx	Brighton Loco		

Brighton men work the 5.55am‖ to Haywards Heath and are relieved by Eastbourne men at 6.26am who have the engine until 7.5pm at Lewes (two sets) where they are relieved by Three Bridges men who stay on the engine until 7.45pm. Brighton men take over at 7.45pm and complete the duty.

Duty No. 756
4P/5F K class

	Brighton Loco (via P. Pk)	9.40am	‖
9.53am	Hove (for 11.0 Cardiff)	10.21am	E
10.26am	Brighton	xx	‖
xx	Top Yard	11.32am	F
12.18pm	Lancing		
	F. shunting 1.30pm to 3.30pm		
	Lancing	3.35pm	F
3.55pm	Hove	4.25pm	‖
4.30pm	Portslade		
	F. shunting 5.0pm to 6.30pm		
	Portslade (via P. Pk)	6.33pm	F
7.18pm	Brighton Top Yard	7.30pm	F
xx	Brighton stn	xx	‖
xx	Brighton Loco	10.35pm	‖
10.44pm	Hove Yard	11.20pm	F
2.10am	Norwood Yard	xx	‖
xx	Norwood Loco	4. 0am	‖

(Continued)

Brighton had five K class duties for main line freight working. No. 32338 was the second of the class of 17 to be built and is seen at Brighton in ex-works condition. This engine was built in December 1913 and withdrawn in December 1962.

4.10am	Norwood Yard	4.30am	F
5.22am	Redhill Goods	xx	‖
xx	Up Yard	6.15am	F
8.20am	Brighton	xx	‖
xx	Brighton Loco		

Brighton men (two sets) work the duty until Three Bridges at 1.5am when Norwood men take over and work home to Norwood Loco where the 4.0am‖ is prepared. Brighton men take over the 4.0am‖ and complete the duty.

Duty No. 757
4P/5F K class

	Brighton Loco	11.52am	‖
12. 1pm	Holland Road	1.24pm	F
1.30pm	Hove	2. 0pm	F
2.22pm	Beeding	3.45pm	F
4. 7pm	Hove	5. 1pm	‖
5.25pm	West Worthing		
	C. shunting 5.25pm to 5.40pm		
	West Worthing	5.55pm	‖
6.12pm	Lancing	6.53pm	V
6.58pm	Shoreham	8.10pm	‖
8.19pm	Beeding	8.50pm	F
9. 2pm	Shoreham	9.32pm	F
10.45pm	Chichester (turn)	11.50pm	F
1. 8am	Preston Park	2.10am	‖
2.58am	Three Bridges Loco	4.55am	‖
xx	Three Bridges Yard	5.40am	F
6. 5am	Haywards Heath	6.43am	F
6.56am	Horstead Keynes	7.22am	F
10. 5am	Lewes East Sidings	10.30am	‖
10.53am	Brighton Loco		

Brighton men start off the duty and work the engine round to Hove at 4.35pm where they are relieved by Bognor men. Bognor men work round to 11.10pm at Chichester and are relieved after turning on the Chichester triangle. Horsham men relieve the Bognor men at 11.10pm and work the engine back to Three Bridges Loco at 2.58am where it is prepared for the 4.55am‖. Eastbourne men take the 5.40am freight to Haywards Heath and Brighton men take over at Haywards Heath and complete the duty from 6.30am. The Horstead Keynes freight is booked to run Mondays, Wednesdays and Fridays.

Duty No. 758 NOT USED

Duty No. 759
4P/5F K class

	Brighton Loco	10. 0pm	‖
10.10pm	Hove	10.30pm	F
12.48am	Norwood Yard	1. 0am	‖
1.15am	Norwood Loco	2.40am	‖
2.45am	Norwood Yard	3. 5am	F
5.30am	Hove	6.42am	F
6.50am	Portslade		
	F. shunting 7.0am to 8.10am		
	Portslade	8.25am	‖
8.31am	Hove	9. 5am	E
9.10am	Brighton	9.41am	‖
xx	Top Yard	10. 5am	Coal
10.15am	Brighton Loco	12. 5pm	‖
12.14pm	Hove (via P. Pk)	1.16pm	F
1.37pm	Brighton Top Yard	xx	‖
xx	Loco Yard		

Brighton men (two sets) have the work which includes the night freight to Norwood Yard and back and loco coal into Brighton shed.

Duty No. 760
2P/2F E4 class

	Newhaven Loco	5.55am	‖
xx	Newhaven Middle Yard		
	F. and C. shunting 6.0am to 6.0pm		
	Newhaven	6. 0pm	‖
xx	Newhaven Loco		

An early and late turn set of Newhaven men shunt the yard. 1st set on at 5.40am, 2nd set on at 1.10pm. Shed enginemen prepare and dispose.

Duty No. 761 NOT USED

Duty No. 762
4P/5F K class

	Brighton Loco	2. 0am	‖
xx	Brighton Top Yard	2.30am	F
3.15am	Lewes East Sidings		
	F. shunting 3.15am to 4.15am		
	Lewes East Siding	5. 5am	F
9.41am	Hastings	10.30am	F
10.42am	Galley Hill Sidings	11. 0am	F
11. 5am	St. Leonards W.M.		
	F. shunting 11.5am to 12.5pm		
	St. Leonards W.M.	xx	‖
xx	Loco Yard	1.15pm	‖
xx	Rye	2.30pm	F
3.55pm	Hastings		
	F. shunting 4.0pm to 6.45pm		
	Hastings	6.50pm	F
10. 2pm	Brighton Top Yard (via P. Pk)	10.45pm	F
11.10pm	Hove	11.38pm	‖
xx	Brighton Loco		

Brighton men work round to Polegate where they are relieved at 5.39am by Eastbourne men who work to St. Leonards. St. Leonards men relieve at 9.15am and work round to Hastings where Ashford men take over at 4.35pm. Newhaven men relieve the Ashford men at Hastings at 5.20pm and work until 8.39pm where they are relieved at Lewes by Brighton men who take the engine home.

Duty No. 763
2P/2F E4 class

	Brighton Loco	6.32am	‖
6.45am	Hove	7. 1am	F
7. 6am	Holland Road	xx	‖
xx	Top Yard	7.40am	F
9.15am	Falmer	10.13am	F
11.15am	Brighton Top Yard	11.32am	F
11.51am	Kemp Town		
	F. shunting 11.55am to 1.20pm		
	Kemp Town	1.29pm	F
1.54pm	Brighton Top Yard		
	F. shunting 1.55pm to 2.50pm		
	Brighton Top Yard	xx	‖
xx	Brighton Loco	4. 3pm	‖
4.27pm	Lancing (A/R)	5.31pm	P
5.56pm	Brighton	6.22pm	‖
6.34pm	Kingston Wharf (via P. Pk)	7.29pm	F
8.43pm	Brighton Top Yard	8.55pm	F
xx	Brighton	xx	‖
xx	Brighton Loco		
	Work No. 766		

Brighton men (two sets) work local freight and trip workings including the freight-only Kemp Town branch and the 5.31pm "Lancing Belle" which is double headed.

Duty No. 764 NOT USED

Duty No. 765
4P/5F K class

	Loco Yard	3.15am	‖
xx	Brighton Top Yard	3.40am	F
7.52am	Tun Wells West (via Ashurst)	8. 9am	‖
9.2am	Tunbridge Wells West		
	F. shunting 9.5am to 10.35am		
	Tunbridge Wells West	11.53am	F
4.13pm	Lewes East Sidings	4.20pm	‖
4.35pm	Newhaven Loco	8.50pm	‖
xx	Newhaven	9. 8pm	V
9.22pm	Lewes East Sidings	10.35pm	F
11.10pm	Newhaven	11.45pm	F
12.40am	Brighton Top Yard	xx	‖
xx	Brighton Loco		

Brighton men are relieved at Tunbridge Wells West at 8.5am by Tunbridge Wells West men who turn the engine on the triangle via Ashurst and Eridge. Brighton men relieve at 9.15am and work to Buxted where Newhaven men take over and finish the duty.

Brighton had several E4 duties for working local freights and shunts including the "Lancing Belle" which was the staff train from Lancing to Brighton for the carriage works staff. E4 class No. 32485 is seen on Brighton shed. It was built in 1899 and named *Ashington* by the LBSCR but withdrawn by BR in December 1957.

Lens of Sutton

Duty No. 766
2P/2F E4 class

	Loco Yard	2.35am	‖
2.40am	Top Yard (via P. Pk)	3. 0am	F
3.21am	Hove	4.15am	F
4.56am	Worthing Ctl		
	F. shunting 5.0am to 8.15am		
	Worthing Ctl	8.25am	F
9. 0am	Angmering	9.35am	‖
9.46am	Littlehampton	10.14am	‖
10.39am	Chichester	11.13am	V
1.27pm	Brighton	xx	‖
xx	Loco Yard	3.25pm	‖
xx	Brighton	3.59pm	P
5. 0pm	Horsham	5.19pm	P
6.21pm	Brighton (off 1.0pm Cardiff)	6.49pm	E
6.55pm	Hove	8. 3pm	‖
8.26pm	West Worthing		
	F. shunting 8.30pm to 9.50pm		
	West Worthing	9.55pm	F
10. 5pm	Worthing Ctl		
	F. shunting 10.10pm to 12.15am		
	Worthing Ctl	1.15am	F
1.45am	Hove	1.50am	‖
2. 0am	Brighton Loco		
	Work No. 763		

Brighton men work local freights and trips with a passenger working up the now closed Steyning line. Three sets are utilized.

Duty No. 767
2P/2F E4 class

	Brighton Loco	6.17am	‖
6.23am	Holland Road (propel)	6.58am	E
7. 2am	Brighton	7.10am	P
7.33am	Lancing		
	C. & W. shunting 7.45am to 5.0pm		
	Lancing (double headed)	5.31pm	P
5.56pm	Brighton (propel)	6. 0pm	E
6. 6pm	Holland Road	6.38pm	‖
6.41pm	Brighton Loco		

Brighton men have the "Lancing Belle", the workers' train that runs daily from Lancing to Brighton, with two E4 class 0-6-2 tanks. An early 5.32am, and a late 12.9pm, turn set are used.

Duty No. 768
0P A1X class

	Newhaven Loco	7.20am	‖
xx	Newhaven		
	Steam heat & C. & W. and Marine stores shunting		
	Newhaven	3.45pm	‖
xx	Newhaven Loco		

Newhaven men use an A1X class 0-6-0 tank for steam heating and shunting. One set only on at 6.35am.

Duty No. 769
0P A1X class

	Brighton Loco	8.45am	‖
xx	Brighton Works		
	F. shunting 9.0am to 5.45pm		
	Brighton Works	5.45pm	Trip
xx	Top Yard	6.15pm	‖
xx	Loco Yard		

Brighton men shunt the works and make trips to Top Yard as required. The regular engine was an A1X painted in Stroudley livery and numbered 377S. An early set on at 8.0am and a late set on at 2.0pm are utilised.

Duty Nos 770 to 779
Diesel electric shunters 204hp and 350hp based at Brighton for maintenance

Duty No.		
770	350hp	12.20am to 12.0mdt Lewes shunts & trips
771	350hp	5.0am to 12.0mdt Newhaven shunts & trips
772		NOT USED
773	350hp	24 hrs shunt Three Bridges shunts & trips
774	350hp	5.35am to 3.50am Three Bridges shunts & trips
775	350hp	2.0pm to 10.50am Brighton shunts & trips
776	350hp	24 hrs Top & Lower Yards shunts & trips
777	204hp	24 hrs Top & Lower Yards shunts & trips
778	204hp	7.30am to 5.50pm Kingston Wharf shunts & trips
779	204hp	5.0am to 8.45pm Eastbourne shunts & trips

Duty No. 780
P or A1X
Brighton Loco shunter
8.0am to 3.0pm

The Loco Yard shed shunter has one set of men on duty at 7.35am and they work any spare engine, usually a P or A1X, but a B4 class 0-4-0T could be used.

ELECTRIC LOCO DUTIES

The Central District had three loco duties for the Bulleid/Raworth Co + Co third rail electrics numbered 20001 to 20003.

Duty No. 1
7P/5F 20001 class

	New Cross Gate	11. 8pm	‖
11.15pm	B'Arms J. Sect	11.45pm	E
2. 0am	Lewes East	3.10am	F
4.49am	Norwood No. 1 Up Goods	5.16am	‖
5.46am	Victoria		
	Berth		
	Victoria	8.51am	P
10. 5am	Newhaven Hbr	10.58am	‖
12.14pm	Norwood Down Yard	1. 5pm	F
3.21pm	Lewes	3.40pm	‖
3.51pm	Newhaven Hbr	4.41pm	P
5.27pm	Victoria (propel)	5.45pm	E
5.50pm	Carr Rd North	7.12pm	‖
7.50pm	New Cross Gate		
	Berth		

Newhaven men have all the work which includes the up and down Newhaven boat trains. A light run at 10.58am from Newhaven to Norwood was useful for special freights and engineers trains.

The Brighton Works shunter was an A1X, formerly No. 2635, which was repainted in 1947 in the Stroudley livery and numbered 377S. The engine was trundled out on railtours from time to time and is seen here in Purley goods yard in August 1956 with youthful admirers and a SECR birdcage set. The engine worked a special to Caterham to celebrate the centenary of the line. Built in 1878 and formerly No. 35 *Morden* the engine was cut up by BR in September 1963. Duty No. 769 applies.

Brighton had a shed shunter rostered for duty No. 780 which was shown for an A1X but in 1956 was worked by a B4 0-4-0T No. 30083. This ex-LSWR engine, dating from 1908, was built for dock shunting but was made redundant after the USA tanks took over at Southampton.

The Marsh Atlantics worked the Newhaven to Victoria boat trains to the very end and were popular with Newhaven men. No. 2424 *Beachy Head* is seen at Victoria in Southern Railway days awaiting departure with oil lamp headcode for night working. The last H2 ran a special from Victoria to Brighton on 13th April 1958. Electric locomotives took over the Newhaven boat train work – see E.L. duties 1 to 3.

Lens of Sutton

Duty No. 2
7P/5F 20001 class

	Horsham	3.45pm	F
5. 3pm	Norwood No. 1 Up Goods	5.55pm	‖
	(via C. Pal)		
6.40pm	Norwood Down Yard	7.15pm	F
8. 8pm	Three Bridges Yard	9.48pm	F
11.36pm	Polegate	11.55pm	F
12.52am	Haywards Heath	1. 7am	F
1.36am	Preston Park	1.50am	F
1.58am	Hove	2.50am	F
3.52am	Chichester Yard	4.30am	F
6.12am	Three Bridges Yard	6.28am	‖
6.50am	Horsham		
	Berth		

Horsham men have all the work and after working the 3.45pm freight from Horsham run the engine light at 5.55pm via Crystal Palace to keep it out of the way of the evening passenger services. The engine is available from 6.50am to 3.45pm for any special traffic but the problem is that there are only limited electrified sidings for freight trains.

The Central Division of the Region had the three Bulleid electric locomotives which worked the Newhaven boat trains and heavy main line freights. This official photograph shows No. 20001 as built, in malachite green with pantograph extended for demonstration purposes.

SR/National Railway Museum

Duty No. 3

7P/5F 20001 class

	Three Bridges Yard	12.38am	F
2.18am	Chichester	2.20am	‖
3.25am	Three Bridges Yard	3.53am	F
6.17am	Bognor Regis	6.44am	‖
7.16am	Chichester	10.55am	F
11.54am	Hove	12.23pm	‖
1. 0pm	Three Bridges	1.53pm	F
3.59pm	Chichester	9.10pm	F
11. 2pm	Three Bridges Yard		

Horsham men have all the work. The engine has spare time at Chichester in the morning and afternoon for any special traffic on offer.

FOREIGN ENGINE WORKINGS

Eastern and Western Districts' engines work over the Central District. London Midland Region work inter-regional transfers from Willesden to Norwood Yard, out via Crystal Palace, return via Selhurst. There are five booked workings per weekday and one booked working Willesden to East Croydon. Eastern Region have Temple Mills to Norwood Yard, one working at 8.25pm from Temple Mills via Crystal Palace and back via Selhurst. Western Region work the 6.50am Reading South and back with the 11.5am Redhill to Reading rostered for a 43xx class 2-6-0.

The Central Division had numerous transfer trips from other regions and the LMR 8F class was no stranger to Southern metals. On 4th June 1965 8F 2-8-0 No. 48544 works a 21-coach length train through East Croydon with a Newcastle to Hove pigeon special.

SOUTH WESTERN DIVISION

(24hr clock used in 1966 workings)

NINE ELMS

Duty No. 100
4MT 2-6-4T BR Standard

	Nine Elms Loco	0820	||
0850	Clapham Junction	0926	M
1354	Waterloo		
	C. shunting 1400 to 1430		
xx	Waterloo	1434	E
1445	Clapham Junction	1547	E
1556	Waterloo	1637	||
1651	Clapham Junction	1823	E
1833	Waterloo	1908	||
1938	Walton	1958	V
2115	Clapham Junction	2125	||
2140	Nine Elms Loco		

Nine Elms men have all the work (two sets) including unloading the milk tanks at Vauxhall. The duty includes the 1958 vans Walton to Clapham Yard which runs via East Putney. The 1st set is on duty at 0720 and the 2nd set is on at 1420.

Duty No. 101
3MT 2-6-2T BR Standard
OFF No. 102

	Nine Elms Loco	0410	||
0425	Waterloo	0450	E
0500	Clapham Junction	0625	E
0635	Waterloo		
	C. shunting 0635 to 0800		
	Waterloo	0805	E
0815	Clapham Junction	0945	||
0955	Waterloo		
	C. shunting 1035 to 1220		
	Waterloo	1225	E

(Continued)

Nine Elms in the heyday of steam with 'Merchant Navy' class 4-6-2 No. 35004 *Cunard White Star* being disposed after heading the up "Atlantic Coast Express" which was worked through to Waterloo behind an Exmouth Junction engine with Nine Elms men working the engine from Salisbury. A rebuilt version, No. 35020 *Bibby Line* and an ex-LBSCR E4 class 0-6-2 tank are also being attended to.

1236	Clapham Junction		
	C. shunting 1330 to 1430		
	Clapham Junction	1457	E
1507	Waterloo	1538	‖
1548	Clapham Junction	1725	E
1735	Waterloo	1822	‖
1834	Nine Elms Loco	2020	‖
2050	Clapham Junction	2119	E
2129	Waterloo		
	C. shunting 2320 to 2350		
	Work No. 102		

Nine Elms men (three sets) have all the work which includes taking the loco back to Nine Elms for the change over. 1st set on duty at 0630, 2nd on duty at 1100 and 3rd on at 1800.

Duty No. 102
3MT 2-6-2T BR Standard
OFF No. 101

	Waterloo		
	C. shunting 0001 to 0300		
	Waterloo	0300	‖
0311	Clapham Junction	0404	E
0417	Waterloo	0637	M
0647	Clapham Junction	0754	E
0803	Waterloo	0903	E
0913	Clapham Junction	1043	V
1053	Waterloo (S.R.E.)	1213	E
1223	Clapham Junction	1255	‖
1310	Nine Elms Loco	1620	‖
1650	Clapham Junction	1720	E
1729	Waterloo		
	C. shunting 1805 to 1835		
	Waterloo	1910	E
1922	Clapham Junction		
	C. shunting 1945 to 2045		
	Clapham Junction	2113	E
2122	Waterloo (S.R.E.)	2240	E
2252	Clapham Junction	0023	E
0032	Waterloo	0250	‖
0305	Nine Elms Loco		
	Work No. 101		

Nine Elms men (four sets) have all the work on an engine which is nearly in use for 24 hours. 1st set 0001, 2nd set 0705, 3rd set 1530, and 4th set on 2230.

In the final year of operation the Waterloo empties were mainly in the hands of Class 3 2-6-2 tanks numbered in the 82000 series of which Nine Elms had eight left by January 1966. But here, an Ivatt Class 2 type works an empty stock train into Clapham Yard on 14th January 1967 on duty Nos 101-105.

Clan Line was a Stewarts Lane engine and then became a Nine Elms engine until sent to Weymouth when it worked to the end of steam on the South Western Division in 1967. Today, the locomotive has been preserved and has featured on many specials. No. 35028 is seen here on 17th September 1987 on a test run at Andover.

Waterloo empty stock working was in the hands of the ex-LSWR M7 class 0-4-4 tanks until replaced by pannier tanks from the Western Region, which were themselves later replaced by Class 3 2-6-2 Standard tanks in the 82000 series. M7 No. 30123 is seen at Waterloo in March 1962 on a Nine Elms duty.

Duty No. 103
3MT 2-6-2T BR Standard

	Nine Elms Loco	0705	‖
0735	Clapham Junction	0816	P
0824	Kensington (O)	0833	P
0841	Clapham Junction	0846	P
0854	Kensington (O)	0900	P
0908	Clapham Junction		
	C. shunting 0940 to 1125		
	Clapham Junction	1130	‖
1145	Nine Elms Loco	1400	‖
1430	Waterloo	1445	E
1455	Clapham Junction	1537	E
1547	Waterloo S.R.E.	1620	‖
1630	Clapham Junction	1705	E
1714	Waterloo		
	C. shunting 1745 to 0445		
	Waterloo	0515	V
0525	Clapham Junction	xx	‖
xx	Nine Elms Loco		

Nine Elms men (four sets) work this Standard Class 3 2-6-2T round the clock but including the "Kensington Belle" which was still steam worked at the time of the rostering. Nine Elms men on at 0615, 1600, 2020, and 2315.

Duty No. 104 NOT USED

Duty No. 105
3MT 2-6-2T BR Standard

	Nine Elms Loco	0230	‖
0250	Clapham Junction	0319	E
0329	Waterloo		
	C. shunting 0445 to 0700		
	Waterloo	0700	‖
0715	Nine Elms Loco	1040	‖
xx	Nine Elms Goods	1110	F
1152	Stewarts Lane	1312	F
1342	Nine Elms Goods	1400	‖
1410	Clapham Junction	1445	E
1455	Waterloo	1540	‖
1548	Clapham Junction	1615	E
1623	Kensington (O)	1636	P
1646	Clapham Junction	1650	E
1658	Kensington	1706	P
1714	Clapham Junction	1745	‖
1800	Nine Elms Loco	2047	‖
2102	Waterloo	2115	E
2125	Clapham Junction	2230	E
2240	Waterloo	0117	‖
0130	Nine Elms Loco		

Nine Elms men (three sets) have the work which includes the afternoon "Kensington Belle" which was taken off Stewarts Lane after it closed to steam. The Kensington trains run ½-hour later on Mondays and Tuesdays.

Duty No. 106
4MT 2-6-4T BR Standard
OFF No. 107

	Nine Elms	0515	‖
0545	Clapham Junction		
	C. shunting 0545 to 0945		
	Clapham Junction	0945	‖
1020	Feltham Loco		
	stable for No. 107		

Nine Elms men have the work but Feltham men take over at 0930 and take the engine home.

Duty No. 107
4MT 2-6-4T BR Standard
OFF No. 106

	Feltham Loco	0405	‖
xx	Feltham Yard	0435	F
0505	Clapham Junction	0722	E
0731	Waterloo	0815	‖
0826	Clapham Junction	1100	‖
	(C. shunting 0830 to 1055)		
1110	Waterloo	1145	E

(Continued)

1155	Clapham Junction		
	C. shunting 1215 to 1315		
	Clapham Junction	1315	‖
1330	Nine Elms Loco	1700	‖
1727	Clapham Junction	1757	E
1807	Waterloo	1900	V
2007	Staines	2036	V
2257	Waterloo (S.R.E.)	2348	E
2355	Clapham Junction	0035	M
0046	Kensington (O)	0215	V
0226	Clapham Junction	0240	‖
0255	Nine Elms Loco		
	Work No. 106		

Feltham men work on the engine until 0930 when they are relieved by Nine Elms men who finish the duty (two sets).

Duty No. 108
3MT 2-6-2T BR Standard

	Nine Elms Loco	0040	‖
0110	Clapham Junction	0130	M
0621	Waterloo		
	C. shunting 0645 to 0720		
	Waterloo	0728	V
0743	Clapham Junction	0827	E
0837	Waterloo	0953	E
1003	Clapham Junction	1132	E
1141	Waterloo		
	C. shunting 1235 to 1615		
	Waterloo	1624	E
1634	Clapham Junction	1919	V
1929	Waterloo (S.R.E.)	2004	V
1014	Clapham Junction	xx	‖
xx	Waterloo	2056	E
2106	Clapham Junction	2135	‖
2150	Nine Elms Loco		

Nine Elms men (three sets) have all the work which includes the 0130 milk tanks to Vauxhall where they are unloaded en route.

Duty No. 109
4MT 2-6-4T BR Standard
TUES & THURS ONLY

	Nine Elms	0325	‖
xx	Nine Elms Goods	0355	F
0409	Waterloo	0450	F
0500	Nine Elms Goods	xx	‖
xx	Nine Elms Loco		

FRIDAYS ONLY

	Nine Elms Loco	1430	‖
1500	Clapham Junction	1532	E
1542	Waterloo	1637	‖
1647	Clapham Junction	1745	E
1755	Waterloo	1825	‖
1835	Clapham Junction	1914	E
1924	Waterloo	1950	‖
2005	Nine Elms Loco		

Nine Elms men have all the work.

Duty No. 110 NOT USED

Duty No. 111
3MT 2-6-2T BR Standard
Loco shed shunt and coal empties 0001 to 2359

Nine Elms shed engine men work (three sets) 0600, 1400 and 2200.

Duty Nos 112 to 149 NOT USED

Duty Nos 150 to 159
Diesel locomotive rosters.

Class 4 Standard 2-6-4Ts worked from Nine Elms until the end of steam on the Region in July 1967. Like the Class 3 2-6-2 tanks the Standard Class 4s worked empty stock and vans as well as the "Kensington Belle". Photograph taken on 14th January 1967.

Nine Elms Bulleid No. 34090 *Sir Eustace Missenden Southern Railway* crosses Fareham Viaduct with the down "Belle" on 4th November 1962. The train had been diverted via the Portsmouth Direct line as a result of engineering works. By 1967 the "Bournemouth Belle" had become rostered for diesel haulage but there were occasions when the train became steam hauled owing to locomotive failures.

GUILDFORD

Duty No. 161
5MT 4-6-0 BR Standard
OFF No. 165

	Guildford Loco	0330	‖
0353	Woking	0432	V
0527	Basingstoke	xx	‖
xx	Basingstoke Loco	0615	‖
xx	Barton Mill	xx	E
xx	Basingstoke	0727	P
0845	Waterloo	0930	E
0940	Clapham Junction	1040	‖
1053	Waterloo	1140	V
1150	Clapham Junction	1257	E
1306	Waterloo	1410	M
1423	Clapham Junction	1450	‖
1505	Nine Elms Loco (with 461)	1732	‖
1747	Waterloo	1809	P
1928	Basingstoke		
	C. shunting 1930 to 0100		
	Basingstoke	0100	‖
0105	Basingstoke Loco		
	stable for No. 162		

Guildford men start the duty and are relieved at Woking at 0423 by Nine Elms men who are relieved in Basingstoke shed. Basingstoke men take the engine off shed at 0615‖ and are relieved by Eastleigh men at 0700 who work to Waterloo. Nine Elms men come on at Waterloo at 0845, work and dispose. Guildford men work the 1732‖ and have the engine until 1930 when Basingstoke men finish the duty.

Duty No. 162
OFF No. 161
spare at Basingstoke for special traffic
Work No. 163

Duty No 163
5MT 4-6-0 BR Standard
OFF No. 162

	Basingstoke Loco	0545	‖
xx	Barton Mill	xx	E
xx	Basingstoke	0629	P
0751	Waterloo	0839	E
0849	Clapham Junction	0945	‖
1000	Nine Elms Loco		
	Work No. 164		

Basingstoke men are relieved at Waterloo at 0751 by Nine Elms men who finish the duty.

No. 73089 *Maid of Astolat*, a BR Standard Class 5 4-6-0 allocated to Guildford, works one of the last steam trains on the Central Division on 8th January 1966. It is seen approaching Anerley with the 11.24 Woking to New Cross Gate stone train.

Ash loco shed can be seen on the right of Standard Class 4 2-6-4T No. 80137 working a Guildford to Reading train. Ash shed, of the former South Eastern Railway, was closed in 1946 and had been used as a stabling point for engines working the Tongham line.

Duty No. 164
5MT BR Standard
OFF No. 163

	Nine Elms Loco	0305	‖
0320	Waterloo	0340	V
0430	Guildford (0445 Woking)	0510	V
0729	Portsmouth & S'Sea	0836	E
0846	Fratton Yard (turn)	0930	‖
1103	Guildford (via E. Put)	1126	V
1340	Clapham Junction	1415	‖
1430	Nine Elms Loco		
	Work No. 165		

Nine Elms men are relieved at Woking at 0417 by Guildford men who finish the duty (two sets)

Guildford was a stronghold of the ugly Bulleid Q1 class 0-6-0s which worked passenger as well as freight duties. Left to right are Nos 33009, 33020 and 33027.

M. Wilkins

A Q1 on a passenger working, No. 33035, a Guildford engine, approaches North Camp with the 3.20pm Guildford to Reading on 11th May 1963.

Guildford duty No. 182 with N class No. 31819 on 11th May 1963 heading the 4.20pm Reading to Redhill at Wanborough. The N class 2-6-0s had a lot of work on the Reading to Redhill line but by 1966 had been displaced by diesels.

Duty No. 165
5MT 4–6–0 BR Standard
OFF No. 164

	Nine Elms Loco	0651	‖
0706	Waterloo	0718	P
1009	Salisbury	1030	‖
1035	Salisbury Loco	1115	‖
	or as ordered		
xx	Guildford Loco		
	Work No. 161		

Nine Elms men start the 0651‖ and are relieved at Woking by Guildford men at 0755 who complete the duty. A wonderful opportunity for special traffic with a light run from Salisbury to Guildford.

Workhorse of the Southern N class, No. 31811 works a down freight of considerable length past the Worting Junction gantry. The N class 2-6-0s were a versatile class of locomotive and could be seen on all types of work. No. 31811 built in 1920, lasted until July 1965 and worked from Guildford Loco.

No. 73081 *Excalibur* was a Guildford engine in 1966 but had been at Nine Elms until the big engines were transferred. On 25th July 1964 the 4-6-0 is seen with a lightweight 5.15pm Salisbury to Waterloo passing Worting.

Duty Nos 166 to 180 NOT USED

Duty No. 181
4P/5F N class

	Guildford Loco	0630	‖
0652	Woking	0730	P
0817	Basingstoke	xx	‖
xx	Guildford Loco		

Guildford men work this duty, another golden opportunity for special traffic work.

Duty Nos 182 to 183 NOT USED

Heavy freight on the Southern with S15 class 4-6-0 No. 30843 still showing a 72A Exmouth Junction headcode on a down freight, passing Worting on 25th July 1964. The engine was withdrawn soon afterwards.

Class 4 2-6-4 tank No. 80043 displays Guildford duty No. 224 on 18th May 1962 as it saunters into Shalford with a Guildford to Redhill stopping train consisting of Bulleid stock. The elegant station buildings have since been demolished.

The much travelled Class 3 2-6-0 No. 77014 was the only engine of this rare Standard class to be allocated to the Region and was the last engine to be in steam on the Southern. The Mogul worked the last steam train which was a Bournemouth to Weymouth van train on Sunday 9th July 1967. The locomotive, nominally allocated to Guildford in 1966, is seen here working a railtour near Corfe Mullen on 16th October 1966.

M. Wilkins

The 2.10pm Exeter to Waterloo is seen belting past Worting Junction on 25th July 1964 with 'Merchant Navy' class No. 35019 *French Line CGT* in charge.

Duty No. 184
4P/5F N class

	Guildford Loco		0445	‖
0502	Woking		0520	V
0545	Aldershot			
	F. & C. shunting 0555 to 1845			
	Aldershot		1857	V
1918	Guildford		xx	‖
xx	Guildford Loco			

Guildford men (three sets) work this scrappy turn. 1st set on at 0210, 2nd set on at 0805, and 3rd set on at 1245.

Duty Nos 185 to 200 NOT USED

Duty Nos 201 to 229
Diesel rosters.

EASTLEIGH

Duty Nos 230 to 233 NOT USED

Duty No. 234
7P/6F WC class
OFF No. 238

	Eastleigh Loco		0445	‖
xx	Eastleigh Yard		0515	F
0820	Bournemouth Ctl Goods		xx	‖
xx	Bournemouth Loco		0950	‖
1017	Branksome		1052	E
1100	Bournemouth Ctl		1107	P
1417	Waterloo		1507	E
1517	Clapham Junction		1545	‖
1600	Nine Elms Loco			
	stable for No. 235			

Eastleigh men work the engine round to Bournemouth loco and Bournemouth men work the 0950‖ off shed. Nine Elms men take over the engine at 1105 and work it home.

Eastleigh had a large allocation of Class 4 2-6-0s of the BR Standard type in 1966. No. 76033 is seen on the 3.15pm Salisbury to Waterloo in 1964 bearing a Guildford duty number.

Duty No. 235
7P/6F WC class
OFF No. 234

	Nine Elms Loco	0735	‖
0748	Waterloo	0810	P
1139	Weymouth Junction	xx	‖
xx	Weymouth Loco	1550	‖
xx	Weymouth Junction (1600 ex Quay)	1623	P
1945	Waterloo	2043	E
2053	Clapham Junction	2125	‖
2140	Nine Elms Loco		
	Work No. 236		

Nine Elms men are relieved at Bournemouth at 1033 by Weymouth men who work round to Southampton Central at 1751 to be relieved by Eastleigh men who are relieved at Waterloo at 1945. Nine Elms men finish the duty.

Duty No. 236
7P/6F WC class
OFF No. 235

	Nine Elms Loco	0758	‖
0812	Waterloo	0835	P
1252	Weymouth	xx	‖
xx	Weymouth Loco	1745	‖
1750	Weymouth	1815	P
2256	Waterloo	2351	‖
0006	Nine Elms Loco		
	stable for No. 237		

Weymouth men relieve the Nine Elms men at Bournemouth Central at 1129 and have the engine until 1800. Bournemouth men take over the engine at 1800 and work until 1935. Nine Elms men come onto the engine at 1935 and finish the duty.

Duty No. 237
7P/6F WC class
OFF No. 236
spare at Nine Elms Loco
Work No. 238

Duty No. 238
7P/6F WC class
OFF No. 237

	Nine Elms Loco	0215	‖
0231	Waterloo	0245	P
0613	Bournemouth Ctl	xx	‖
xx	Bournemouth Loco	0750	‖
0752	Bournemouth Ctl	0846	P
1210	Waterloo	1322	E
1332	Clapham Junction	1400	‖
1415	Nine Elms	2200	‖
2213	Waterloo	2235	P
0105	Southampton Term.	0146	‖
0200	Eastleigh Loco		
	Work No. 234		

Nine Elms men are relieved at Bournemouth Central at 0615 by Bournemouth men who work round to Waterloo at 1230 (two sets). Nine Elms men relieve at Waterloo at 1230 and work on the engine until 0044 at Eastleigh where Eastleigh men come onto the engine and finish the duty. Two sets of Bournemouth men and two sets of Nine Elms men are used.

Duty No. 239
7P/5F WC class
as ordered by special traffic to Nine Elms

	Nine Elms Loco	1515	‖
1545	Clapham Junction	1612	E
1622	Waterloo	1723	P
2007	Bournemouth Ctl	2015	E
2031	Hamworthy Junction		
	C. shunting 2035 to 2155		
	Hamworthy Junction	2158	‖
2225	Bournemouth Loco (with 254)	2340	‖
0124	Eastleigh Loco		

Nine Elms men work until Southampton Central to be relieved at 1912. An opportunity on this duty to work any up boat trains. Eastleigh men relieve at 1912 and finish the duty.

Class 5 4-6-0 No. 73113 *Lyonnesse*, formerly a Nine Elms engine, is seen here hard at work with a Waterloo to Bournemouth train, climbing the bank from Alton to Medstead on a Sunday diversion. The engine carries an Eastleigh duty number which was allocated to a 'West Country' class. Photograph taken on Sunday 5th June 1966.

One of the last regular steam workings was the 17.23 Fridays only Waterloo to Bournemouth, seen here passing Wandsworth Common on the last Friday before steam finished on 7th July 1967. Motive power is No. 34093 *Saunton*, a Nine Elms engine in 1963 but an Eastleigh allocation in 1966. Nine Elms men worked to Southampton Central on duty No. 239.

Duty No. 240
Spare at Eastleigh Loco for special traffic

Duty Nos 241 to 242 NOT USED

Duty No. 243
7P/5F WC class

	Eastleigh Loco	0400	‖
xx	Eastleigh Yard	0435	F
0550	Basingstoke Up Yard	xx	‖
xx	Basingstoke Loco	0740	‖
0745	Barton Hill	xx	E
xx	Basingstoke	0823	P
0942	Waterloo	1038	E
1048	Clapham Junction	1135	‖
1146	Nine Elms Loco	1625	‖
1637	Waterloo	1709	P
1828	Basingstoke	1906	P
2015	Southampton Term.		
	C. shunting 2015 to 2115		
	Southampton Term.	2115	‖
2125	Eastleigh Loco		

Eastleigh men work round to Basingstoke Loco and are relieved at Basingstoke Loco by Basingstoke men who take the engine out for the 0823 passenger which Nine Elms men work. Nine Elms men have the engine from 1625‖ until 1659 when they are relieved by Eastleigh men who complete the duty.

A reminder of better times on the South Western Division. Nine Elms duty No. 11 was for a 'West Country' which worked a Waterloo to Basingstoke train returning in the evening. To release a light Pacific for other duties during busy summer Saturdays the preserved T9 4-4-0 No. 120 covered the 'West Country' class duty in the summer of 1962. Here, the T9 in LSWR green waits to start from Basingstoke with the 7.40pm to Waterloo on 7th July 1962. The engine was incorrectly painted as it never ran in that condition in LSWR days.

Duty No. 244
7P/6F WC class
OFF No. 245

	Eastleigh Loco	0520	‖
0525	Eastleigh	0548	P
0910	Weymouth	xx	‖
xx	Weymouth Loco	1515	‖
1520	Weymouth	1550	P
1703	Bournemouth Ctl	1713	P
2025	Waterloo	2123	‖
2135	Nine Elms Loco		
	Work No. 245		

Bournemouth men are relieved at 0910 by Weymouth men who work round to Bournemouth at 1710 to be relieved by Eastleigh men (two sets). Eastleigh men work on the engine from 1710 until 1829. Nine Elms men come on the engine at 1829 and work the engine home.

Duty No. 245
7P/6F WC class
OFF No. 244

	Nine Elms Loco		0907	‖
0920	Waterloo		0930	P
1236	Bournemouth Ctl		1242	E
1257	Hamworthy Junction			
	C. shunting 1300 to 1400			
	Hamworthy Junction		1405	‖
1410	Poole	O/R bank	1507	E
1517	Bournemouth Ctl		xx	‖
xx	Bournemouth Loco		1605	‖
1607	Bournemouth Ctl		1628	P
1751	Eastleigh		xx	‖
xx	Eastleigh Loco			
	Work No. 244			

Nine Elms men work the engine up to Waterloo to be relieved at 0920 by Eastleigh men who complete the duty including banking 'on rear' from Poole to Bournemouth Central.

Duty Nos 246 to 248 NOT USED

Duty No. 249
OFF No. 252
7P/6F WC class

	Eastleigh Loco	0618	‖
0625	Eastleigh	0715	P
0859	Waterloo	0932	‖
0944	Nine Elms Loco	1100	‖
1112	Waterloo	1130	P
1432	Bournemouth Ctl	1438	E
1446	Branksome	1502	E
1512	Bournemouth West (propel)	1519	E
1524	Bournemouth West Sidings	1610	E
1615	Branksome	1635	E
1643	Bournemouth Ctl	xx	‖
xx	Bournemouth Loco		
	stable for No. 250		

Eastleigh men work the engine until 1643 when they are relieved at Bournemouth Central by Bournemouth men who dispose the engine. Two sets of Eastleigh men are used, 1st set on at 0603, and 2nd set on at 1209.

Duty No. 250
OFF No. 249
7P/6F WC class

	Bournemouth Loco	1347	‖
1409	Hamworthy Junction	1459	E
1517	Bournemouth Ctl	1523	P
1846	Waterloo	2000	E
2010	Clapham Junction	2040	‖
2055	Nine Elms Loco		
	stable for No. 251		

Bournemouth men work round to Waterloo at 1846 when they are relieved by Nine Elms men who work and dispose.

Duty No. 251
7P/6F WC class
OFF No. 250
Nine Elms Loco spare
Work No. 252

Duty No. 252
7P/6F WC class
OFF No. 251

	Nine Elms Loco	0200	‖
0212	Waterloo (via ELO)	0230	P
0539	Portsmouth Hbr (propel)	0600	E
0610	Fratton	xx	‖
xx	Loco Yard	1105	‖
xx	Fratton	1125	V
1132	Portsmouth & S.S. (LL)	1205	‖
xx	Fratton	1355	V
1410	Portsmouth Hbr	1540	V
1548	Portsmouth & S.S. (LL)		
	C. shunting 1550 to 1630		
	Portsmouth & S.S.	1630	‖
1640	Fratton Loco	1845	‖
xx	Fratton (propel)	1916	E
1926	Portsmouth & S.S.		
	C. shunting 1930 to 2025		
	Portsmouth & S.S.	2125	‖
2130	Cosham		
	F. shunting 2135 to 2235		
	Cosham	2250	F
2302	Fratton	0001	F
0039	Chichester (turn)	0140	F
0242	Eastleigh Yard	xx	‖
xx	Eastleigh Loco		
	Work No. 249		

Nine Elms men work the 0200‖ round to Basingstoke at 0344 to be relieved by Eastleigh men who work to 0431 at Eastleigh. Fratton men relieve at 0431 and complete the duty (three sets). The engine turns on the Chichester triangle between 0039 and 0140.

Duty No. 254
7P/6F WC class
spare at Eastleigh for special traffic

Eastleigh 'Battle of Britain' class No. 34088 *213 Squadron* enjoyed brief fame as a royal engine when at Stewarts Lane and Nine Elms. In this picture the engine is seen in a grubby state working the 16.30 Waterloo to Bournemouth through Weybridge cutting on 5th June 1966.

Duty Nos 253 & 255 to 263 NOT USED

Duty No. 264
5MT 4-6-0 BR Standard

	Eastleigh Loco	0430	‖
0451	Northam Yard	0505	F
0542	Woolston	0603	‖
0610	Northam Yard	0620	F
0625	Southampton Term.	0710	V
0803	Fareham	0902	F
0917	Cosham		
	F. shunting 0920 to 1015		
	Cosham (turn via Portcreek)	1020	‖
1045	Fareham		
	F. shunting 1130 to 1300		
	Fareham	1328	F
1510	Eastleigh Yard	xx	‖
xx	Eastleigh Loco	2010	‖
xx	Eastleigh	2040	V
2307	Waterloo (S.R.E.)	2335	‖
2350	Nine Elms Loco		
	Work No. 265		

Eastleigh men (two sets) work and dispose. Nine Elms men work the 2010‖ and dispose on Nine Elms Loco. The engine is turned at 10.20 via Farlington and Portcreek Junctions.

Duty No. 265
5MT 4-6-0 BR Standard
OFF No. 264

	Nine Elms Loco	0403	‖
0420	Waterloo	0440	P
0550	Woking	0630	P
0840	Salisbury	xx	‖
xx	Salisbury Loco	1925	‖
xx	Salisbury		
	C. shunting 1935 to 2030		
	Salisbury	2039	P
2137	Basingstoke	xx	‖
xx	Basingstoke Loco		
	Work No. 266		

Nine Elms men work the 0403‖ and are relieved at 0730 at Basingstoke. Salisbury men take over at Basingstoke at 0730 and finish the duty (two sets).

Duty No. 266
5MT 4-6-0 BR Standard
OFF No. 265

	Basingstoke Loco	0615	||
xx	Barton Mill	xx	E
xx	Basingstoke	0705	P
0822	Waterloo	0914	||
0926	Nine Elms Loco	1512	||
1542	Clapham Junction	1612	E
1621	Waterloo	1741	P
2016	Salisbury	2040	||
2045	Salisbury Loco		
	Work No. 267		

Nine Elms men work the 0615‖ which has been prepared for them by Basingstoke men. Nine Elms men work the engine until 1901 when they are relieved at Basingstoke by Salisbury men who complete the duty.

Duty No. 267
5MT 4-6-0 BR Standard
OFF No. 266

	Salisbury Loco	1330	||
xx	East Sidings	1402	E
1405	Salisbury (steam heat)	1435	||
xx	Salisbury Loco	1530	||
xx	Salisbury	1600	P
1716	Basingstoke	xx	||
xx	Basingstoke Loco	1915	||
xx	Basingstoke		
	C. shunting 1930 to 0105		
	Basingstoke	xx	||
xx	Basingstoke Loco		

Salisbury men start the 1330‖, work and dispose on Basingstoke Loco. Basingstoke men work the 1915‖ off shed and finish the duty.

Fareham on 4th November 1962 sees a Waterloo to Bournemouth train diverted because of engineers works which occurred for two weekends. Steam hauled passenger trains then ran via the Portsmouth Direct line. Rebuilt 'West Country' No. 34097 *Holsworthy*, displaced from Ramsgate as a result of electrification, negotiates the crossover and heads for Southampton.

Duty No. 268
5MT 4-6-0 BR Standard
OFF No. 267

	Basingstoke Loco	0630	‖
xx	Basingtoke West Yard	0700	F
0844	Eastleigh East Yard	xx	‖
xx	Eastleigh Loco	1330	‖
xx	Eastleigh	1402	P
1527	Bournemouth Ctl	xx	‖
xx	Bournemouth Loco	1620	‖
xx	Bournemouth Ctl	1640	E
1648	Branksome	1717	E
1725	Bournemouth Ctl	1742	P
1857	Eastleigh	xx	‖
xx	Eastleigh Loco		

Work No. 264

Eastleigh men (two sets) have all the work. 1st set is on at 1000, 2nd set is on at 1230.

Duty No. 269 NOT USED

Duty No. 270
4MT 2-6-0 BR Standard
OFF No. 271

	Eastleigh Loco Yard	0325	‖
0335	Eastleigh Yard	0355	F
0459	Fratton Yard	0545	F
0600	Dockyard	0633	F
0643	Fratton Yard	xx	‖
xx	Fratton Loco	1023	‖
xx	Fratton (0850 Elo)	1053	V
1059	Portsmouth & S.S.	1126	E
1136	Fratton	1243	F
1331	Havant	1433	F
1447	Fratton Yard	xx	‖
xx	Carriage Sidings	1545	F
1650	Eastleigh Carr. Sdgs	xx	‖
xx	Eastleigh Loco	2035	‖
xx	Eastleigh Carr. Sdgs	2105	F
2200	Fratton Carr. Sdgs	xx	‖
xx	Fratton Loco		

stable for No. 279

Eastleigh men start the duty at 0325‖ and work round to Fratton at 0545. Fratton men (two sets) work the engine from 0545 until 1650. The afternoon freights take coaching stock into Eastleigh for repair at the works. Eastleigh men relieve at 1650 and work the engine until 2100 when Fratton men take over work and dispose.

Class 5 Standard 4-6-0 No. 73116 *Iseult* heads a train of LMS stock on the 2.15pm Portsmouth Harbour to Cardiff across Bursledon Viaduct on 28th October 1962. This former Nine Elms engine had been re-allocated to Eastleigh in 1966 by which time the Portsmouth to Cardiff trains had been dieselised.

Duty No. 271
4MT 2-6-0 BR Standard

	Eastleigh Loco	2315	‖
xx	Eastleigh		
	C. shunting 2330 to 0140		
	Eastleigh	0157	V
0247	Portsmouth Hbr	0305	E
0313	Fratton Yard	0400	‖
0414	Havant	0455	V
0505	Fratton	0546	E
0605	Fareham	0630	P
0650	Eastleigh	0705	‖
0710	Eastleigh Loco	1020	‖
xx	Eastleigh Yard	1050	F
1145	Winchester City	1210	‖
1238	Eastleigh Loco		

Eastleigh men have all the work (three sets) which on Wednesdays and Fridays includes a trip at 1215 to Micheldever sidings to collect stock for Eastleigh Works for repair.

Duty No. 272
4MT 2-6-0 BR Standard

	Eastleigh Loco	0647	‖
xx	Eastleigh Yard	0717	F
0810	Salisbury East Yard	xx	‖
xx	Salisbury Loco	1115	‖
xx	Salisbury East Yard	1146	F
1301	Eastleigh	xx	‖
xx	Loco Yard		

Eastleigh men have this duty which involves taking the stone empties over to Salisbury. The ballast for the entire Region came from the railway's own quarry at Meldon near Okehampton.

Duty No. 273 NOT USED

Duty No. 274
4MT 4-6-0 BR Standard
OFF No. 277

	Eastleigh Loco	0045	‖
xx	Eastleigh	0115	V
0215	Portsmouth & S.S.	0230	‖
0310	Chichester	0350	F
0424	Fratton Yard	0500	‖
0505	Fratton Loco	0740	‖
0750	Portsmouth & S.S.		
	C. shunting 0755 to 0830		
	Portsmouth & S.S.	0834	V
0839	Portsmouth Hbr	0915	V
0925	Fratton Yard	0945	F
0958	Hilsea	1143	F
1150	Fratton	xx	‖
xx	Fratton Loco	1430	‖
xx	Fratton (propel)	1450	V
1484	Portsmouth & S.S.	1606	V
1609	Fratton	xx	
xx	Fratton Loco	1745	‖
xx	Fratton	1815	V
2004	Southampton Term.	2105	V
2117	Eastleigh	xx	‖
xx	Eastleigh Loco	2230	‖
xx	Eastleigh	2300	V
0009	Portsmouth & S.S. S.R.E.	0015	‖
0020	Fratton (turn)	0118	F
0221	Eastleigh No. 1 Up Goods	xx	
xx	Eastleigh Loco		
	Work No. 275		

All Fratton work (four sets) with Eastleigh P & D men preparing the 0045‖. Fratton men are on at 0200, 0915, 1645 and 2355.

Duty No. 275

4MT 4–6–0 BR Standard
OFF No. 274

	Eastleigh Loco	0430	‖
xx	Eastleigh E. Yard	0500	F
0536	Fareham	0640	F
0654	Hamble Road	0704	EBV
0735	Northam Yard	0800	F
1117	Fareham	1131	V
1155	Eastleigh Carr. Sdgs	xx	‖
xx	Eastleigh Loco	1415	‖
xx	Eastleigh E. Yard	1445	F
1525	Southampton E. Docks	xx	‖
xx	Southampton Term.		
	C. shunting 1630 to 1730		
	Southampton Term.	1817	F
1937	Bournemouth Ctl	xx	‖
xx	Bournemouth Loco		
	stable for No. 276		

Fratton men work the 0430‖ and work round to Eastleigh Loco. Eastleigh men work 1415‖ off shed and are relieved at 1937 at Bournemouth by Bournemouth men who dispose the loco.

Duty No. 276

4MT 4–6–0 BR Standard
OFF No. 275

	Bournemouth Loco (with 434)	0551	‖
0611	Bournemouth Loco	xx	‖
xx	Bournemouth West Sdgs	0648	E
0653	Branksome	0723	E
0731	Bournemouth Ctl	0737	P
0902	Eastleigh	0920	‖
0935	Southampton Term.	1012	P
1202	Bournemouth Ctl	1308	P
1427	Weymouth	xx	‖
xx	Weymouth Loco	1600	‖
xx	Weymouth	1647	P
1805	Bournemouth Ctl	1851	P
2159	Woking	2220	‖
2230	Guildford Loco		
	stable for No. 277		

Bournemouth men work round to 1202 when they are relieved by Weymouth men who work and dispose. Bournemouth men start the 1600‖ and work to Bournemouth Central where they are relieved at 1845 by Eastleigh men who work round to Basingstoke at 2110. Guildford men come onto the engine at 2110 at Basingstoke and complete the duty.

Duty No. 277

4MT 4–6–0 BR Standard
OFF No. 276

	Guildford Loco	0228	‖
0247	Woking	0318	V
0452	Portsmouth Hbr (propel)	0515	E
0525	Fratton Yard	xx	‖
xx	Fratton Loco	0625	‖
xx	Fratton Yard	0652	E
0713	Portsmouth & S.S.	0730	P
0815	Eastleigh	0830	‖
0835	Eastleigh E. Yard	0907	F
0958	Southampton E. Docks	1015	‖
1045	Eastleigh Loco	1400	‖
xx	Eastleigh	1427	E
1440	Southampton Term.		
	C. shunting 1445 to 1530		
	Southampton Term.	1612	P
1725	Bournemouth Ctl	1731	E
1739	Branksome	1747	‖
1800	Bournemouth Loco	2000	‖
2002	Bournemouth Ctl	2025	V
2157	Eastleigh	xx	‖
xx	Eastleigh Loco		
	Work No. 274		

Guildford men start the duty work round and prepare the 0625‖ at Fratton. Eastleigh men relieve at 0625 and work to Bournemouth. Bournemouth men get the 2000‖ ready and are relieved at Bournemouth Central at 2010 by Eastleigh men who complete the duty.

Duty No. 278 NOT USED

Duty No. 279
4MT 2-6-0 BR Standard
OFF No. 270

	Fratton Loco	0945	‖
xx	Fratton Yard (propel)	1015	E
1025	Portsmouth & S.S.	1115	P
1135	Fareham	1606	P
1630	Portsmouth & S.S. (propel)	1649	E
1659	Fratton	xx	‖
xx	Fratton Loco	1830	‖
1840	Portsmouth & S.S. ·	1906	V
2010	Eastleigh	2100	‖
2125	Northam Yard	2204	F
2222	Eastleigh East Yard	xx	‖
xx	Eastleigh	2251	V
2329	Basingstoke		
	C. shunting 2330 to 0020		
	Basingstoke	0020	‖
xx	Basingstoke Loco		
	stable for No. 280		

Fratton men work round to Eastleigh at 2010 (two sets) to be relieved by Eastleigh men who finish the duty (two sets). Presumably the engine stands at Fareham in the sidings from 1135 until 1606.

Duty Nos 280 & 281
280 off No. 279
both spare at Basingstoke Loco
281 work No. 282

Duty No. 282
4MT 2-6-0 BR Standard
OFF No. 281

	Basingstoke Loco	0830	‖
0835	Basingstoke		
	C. shunting 0835 to 0905		
	Basingstoke	0935	V
1115	Southampton Term.		
	C. shunting 1130 to 1300		
	Southampton Term.	1300	‖
1305	Northam Yard	1334	F
1437	Woolston	1445	F
1456	Northam Yard	1505	‖
1510	Southampton Term.		
	C. shunting 1615 to 1645		
	Southampton Term.	1645	‖
1655	Bevois Park	1731	F
1748	Eastleigh Yard	xx	‖
xx	Eastleigh Loco		

Basingstoke men prepare the 0830‖ and are relieved at 0930 by Eastleigh men who complete the duty. On Mondays and Thursdays only the engine works a 1520 vans from Southampton Terminus to East Docks.

Duty Nos 283 to 307 NOT USED

Duty No. 308
4MT 2-6-4T BR Standard

	Eastleigh Loco	0745	‖
0755	P.A. Depot		
	CCE shunting 0800 to 1600		
	P.A. Depot	1600	‖
1610	Eastleigh Loco	1740	‖
1815	Southampton West Docks O/R	1912	‖
1922	Millbrook	1924	V
2003	Salisbury	xx	‖
xx	Salisbury Loco	2130	‖
2230	Eastleigh Loco		

Eastleigh men have all the work which includes working at the permanent way assembly depot shunting for the civil engineer as ordered. (Two sets).

No. 34060 *25 Squadron* pulls away from Fareham with the diverted 11.30am Waterloo to Bournemouth on 4th November 1962. No. 34060 was an Eastleigh engine in the 1966 allocation. Duty No. 249 is shown for a 'West Country' class with Eastleigh men.

Duty No. 309
2MT 2-6-2T Ivatt

	Eastleigh Loco	0800	‖
0805	Eastleigh	0831	P
0848	Southampton Term.	0910	‖
0922	Woolston	0932	F
0941	Northam Yard	0955	F
1000	Southampton Term.	1010	‖
1020	Bevois Park		
	F. shunting 1030 to 1530		
	Bevois Park	1532	F
1537	St Denys	1620	F
1625	Bevois Park		
	F. shunting 1630 to 1730		
	CCE shunting 1730 to 1900		
	Bevois Park	1900	‖
1905	Southampton Term.	1945	V
2004	Eastleigh	xx	‖
xx	Eastleigh Loco		

Eastleigh men have all the work, an early turn set on at 0630 and a late turn set on at 1304.

Duty No. 310
2MT 2-6-2T Ivatt

	Eastleigh Loco	0352	‖
0415	Southampton Ctl	0537	F
0636	Millbrook		
	F. shunting 0640 to 0840		
	Millbrook	0845	‖
0858	Totton Yard		
	F. shunting 0900 to 0945		
	Totton Yard	0949	‖
0955	Redbridge Engineers Yd	1019	F
1121	Eastleigh Yard	xx	‖
xx	Eastleigh Loco	1345	‖
1255	Eastleigh E. Yard	1415	F
1451	Redbridge	1540	‖
xx	Totton Yard		
	F. shunting 1545 to 1635		
	Totton Yard	1640	F
1830	Eastleigh		
	C. shunting 1935 to 2115		
	Eastleigh	2115	‖
2120	Eastleigh Loco	2325	‖
2340	Southampton Term.		
	C. shunting 2345 to 0215		
	Southampton Term.	0220	‖
0241	Eastleigh Loco		

Eastleigh men (four sets) have all the work which includes working engineers' trains out of Redbridge Sleeper Depot. This is where the Region's sleepers were landed from abroad and processed on site.

Duty No. 311
4MT 2-6-4T BR Standard

	Eastleigh Loco	0745	‖
0750	Eastleigh		
	C. shunting 0800 to 0830		
	C. shunting 1000 to 1300		
	Eastleigh	1303	‖
1322	Southampton Term.	1330	V
1340	Southampton Docks	1410	‖
1425	Millbrook		
	F. shunting 1430 to 1915		
	Millbrook	1925	‖
xx	Southampton E. Docks	2020	V
2043	Eastleigh	xx	‖
xx	Eastleigh Loco	2305	‖
xx	Eastleigh	2335	V
0018	Southampton E. Docks	0030	‖
0045	Southampton Term.	0134	V
0148	Eastleigh	0300	F
0410	Southampton E. Docks	0506	‖
0536	Eastleigh Loco		

Eastleigh men (three sets) work local freight and van trains for almost 24 hrs. 1st set on at 0645, 2nd set on at 1230 and 3rd set on at 2205. One hour is allowed to prepare the loco.

Duty No. 312
4MT 2-6-4T BR Standard

	Eastleigh Loco	2355	‖
xx	Eastleigh	0025	V
0037	Southampton Term.		
	F. shunting and trips Southampton Term. to Ctl		
	Southampton Term.	1110	V
1122	Eastleigh	xx	‖
xx	Eastleigh Loco	1555	‖
xx	Eastleigh	1622	P
1637	Southampton Term.		
	C. shunting 1645 to 2040		
	Southampton Term.	2040	‖
xx	West Docks	2122	F
2200	Eastleigh Yard	xx	‖
xx	Eastleigh Loco		

Eastleigh men work local freights, shunting, and trips in Southampton but include a passenger train working (three sets). 2215, 0430, and 1415 are the signing on times.

Duty No. 313
4MT 2-6-4T BR Standard
OFF No. 313

	Basingstoke Loco	0500	‖
xx	Basingstoke	0530	F
0620	Andover		
	F. shunting 0625 to 1000		
	Andover	1005	F
1117	Ludgershall	1225	F
1252	Andover	1415	F
1505	Basingstoke Up Yard	xx	‖
xx	Basingstoke West Yard	1525	F
1550	Overton	1720	F
1738	Basingstoke Up Yard	xx	‖
xx	Basingstoke Loco		
	Work No. 313		

Basingstoke men start the duty at 0500‖ and are relieved at Andover at 1000 by Salisbury men who work the Ludgershall freight and a trip to Overton. Basingstoke men return at 1738 relieve and dispose the engine. The Andover Town branch is worked as required from Andover, the branch closed to all traffic on 18th September 1967. The loco is based at Basingstoke all week.

Duty No. 314
4MT 2-6-4T BR Standard

	Eastleigh Loco	0820	‖
0830	Eastleigh Yard	0850	F
0944	Brockenhurst	1107	F
1120	Lymington Pier	1129	P

(Continued)

1141	Brockenhurst		
	F. shunting 1150 to 1330		
	Brockenhurst	1415	F
1501	Bevois Park	xx	‖
xx	Eastleigh	1720	P
1805	Fratton	xx	‖
xx	Fratton Loco	2223	‖
xx	Fratton (propel)	2253	E
2303	Portsmouth & S.S.	2332	P
0011	Eastleigh	xx	‖
xx	Eastleigh Loco		

Eastleigh men work round to 1715 (two sets) including a passenger trip to Lymington (electrified in 1967) and a freight from Brockenhurst. Fratton men relieve at 1715 and complete the duty.

Duty Nos 315 to 324 NOT USED

Duty No. 325
3F USA class 0-6-0T
Eastleigh loco F. shunts 0730 to 1630

Eastleigh men work the loco coal shunts with two sets of shed engine men. 1st set is on at 0645, 2nd set is on at 1415.

Duty No. 326 NOT USED

Eastleigh Class 4 2-6-0s rambled all over Hampshire. They replaced the ageing LSWR T9s in the 1960s and worked cross country and freight trains. Here, No. 76028 pauses at Wimborne on the old main line from Broadstone to Brockenhurst on 18th May 1963. The line was closed on 4th May 1964.

Ivatt Class 2 2-6-2 tank No. 41243 from the Somerset & Dorset runs into Creekmoor Halt on 18th May 1963. Both Eastleigh and Bournemouth had an allocation of this class. Creekmoor Halt opened on 19th June 1933 to serve a nearby factory but closed to passengers on 7th March 1966. It was situated between Broadstone and Poole.

Bournemouth had their fair share of inter-regional trains. Here is No. 73080 *Merlin* roaring along near Worting Junction with the 08.29 Sheffield to Bournemouth on 19th June 1965 with a summer Saturday duty.

Banbury had Class 5 4-6-0s which replaced the GWR 'Halls'. The "Black 5s" worked through to Portsmouth and Bournemouth on a regular basis. No. 45046 speeds past Worting Junction on 19th June 1965 with the 08.30 Leeds to Portsmouth summer Saturdays working.

Bournemouth had plenty of steam main line work to the very end of steam and duties 381–399 are shown for Bulleid Pacifics. No. 35008 *Orient Line* passes under the gantry at Worting Junction on 25th July 1964.

Duty No. 327
3F USA class 0-6-0T

	Eastleigh Loco	0715	‖
xx	Loco Works		
	shunting 0730 to 1530		
	shunting 1700 to 1800		
	Loco Works	1800	‖
xx	Eastleigh Loco		

The works shunter handled by two sets of Eastleigh men. 1st set on duty at 0630, 2nd set on duty at 1330. Trips of ex works engines are also delivered to the running shed.

Duty No. 328 NOT USED

Duty No. 329
3F USA class 0-6-0T

	Eastleigh Loco	0715	‖
xx	Carriage works		
	C. shunting 0730 to 1730		
	Carriage works	1730	‖
xx	Eastleigh Loco		

The carriage works shunter worked by two sets of Eastleigh men. 1st set on duty at 0630, 2nd set on duty at 1300.

Duty Nos 330 to 381
Diesel rosters.

BOURNEMOUTH

Duty No. 381
8P MN class
OFF No. 384

	Bournemouth Loco (with 412)	0618	‖
0620	Bournemouth Ctl	0623	‖
0630	Branksome	0643	E
0653	Bournemouth Ctl	0656	P
0934	Waterloo	1042	E
1054	Clapham Junction	1125	‖
1140	Nine Elms Loco		
	Work No. 382		

Bournemouth men prepare the 0618‖ but are relieved by Nine Elms men at 0656 who work the rest of the duty.

Duty No. 382
OFF No. 381
spare at Nine Elms
Work No. 383

Duty No. 383
8P MN class
OFF No. 382

	Nine Elms Loco	0959	‖
1012	Waterloo	1030	P
1345	Weymouth	xx	‖
xx	Weymouth Loco	1650	‖
xx	Weymouth	1730	P
2051	Waterloo	2125	‖
2140	Nine Elms Loco		
	Work No. 384		

Nine Elms men work down, Bournemouth men relieve at 1245, work to Weymouth and dispose. Weymouth men work the 1650‖ and are relieved at Southampton at 1914. Eastleigh men work to Waterloo to be relieved by Nine Elms men at 2051 who work and dispose the loco.

Duty No. 384
8P MN class
OFF No. 383

	Nine Elms Loco	0758	‖
0812	Waterloo	0830	P
1045	Bournemouth Ctl	xx	‖
xx	Bournemouth Loco	1550	‖
	(with 411)		
xx	Bournemouth Ctl	1555	‖

(Continued)

1602	Branksome	1620	E
1633	Bournemouth Ctl	1637	P
1853	Waterloo	1913	‖
1928	Nine Elms Loco	2051	‖
2106	Waterloo	2120	P
0007	Bournemouth Ctl	0023	E
0031	Branksome	0039	‖
0052	Bournemouth Loco		
	Work No. 381		

Nine Elms men work to Bournemouth. Bournemouth men relieve at 1045 and work the engine until disposal at 0052 (three sets, 1025, 1618, and 2348).

Duty No. 385
8P MN class

	Bournemouth Loco	0736	‖
	(with 413)		
0738	Bournemouth Ctl	0741	E
0749	Branksome	0813	E
0821	Bournemouth Ctl	0920	P
1022	Weymouth	xx	‖
xx	Weymouth Loco	1245	‖
xx	Weymouth	1325	P
1652	Waterloo	1741	‖
1755	Nine Elms Loco	1855	‖
1911	Waterloo	1930	P
2241	Bournemouth Ctl	2246	E
2254	Branksome	2302	‖
2315	Bournemouth Loco		

Bournemouth men start the 0736‖ and work the engine until 1430 at Bournemouth Central. Nine Elms men relieve at 1430 and work the engine until 1710 at Waterloo. Bournemouth men relieve at Waterloo at 1920 work, and dispose.

Duty Nos 386 to 392 NOT USED

Duty No. 393
7P/6F WC class

	Bournemouth Loco	0552	‖
0555	Bournemouth Ctl	0622	P
1022	Waterloo	1044	‖
1055	Nine Elms Loco (with 436)	1457	‖
1512	Waterloo	1535	P
1852	Bournemouth Ctl	1857	E
1905	Branksome	1912	‖
1925	Bournemouth Loco		

Eastleigh men start the engine with the 0552‖ and work round to Basingstoke at 0900 where Nine Elms men take over and dispose. Nine Elms men work the 1457‖ off shed and are relieved at Eastleigh at 1732 by Basingstoke men who work to Bournemouth at 1852. Bournemouth men relieve at 1852 and complete the duty.

Duty Nos 394 to 398 NOT USED

Duty No. 399
7P/6F WC class

	Bournemouth Loco	0645	‖
0100	Christchurch	0808	P
0837	Brockenhurst	0915	‖
1000	Bournemouth Loco	1031	F
1038	Bournemouth Ctl Goods	1057	F
1102	Bournemouth Loco	1125	‖
1135	Bournemouth Ctl Goods	1202	F
1240	Poole	1250	‖
1308	Bournemouth Loco	1500	‖
1535	Brockenhurst	1603	P
1637	Christchurch	1700	‖
1710	Bournemouth Ctl	1808	P
1926	Weymouth	xx	‖
xx	Weymouth Loco	2130	‖
xx	Weymouth	2213	P
2328	Bournemouth Ctl	xx	‖
xx	Bournemouth Loco		

Bournemouth men work the morning trains and on Wednesdays work a 0900 Brockenhurst to Eastleigh empty stock train in lieu of the Central Goods working. Eastleigh men work the return empty stock on Wednesdays but Bournemouth men have the rest of the work (three sets).

Waterloo, with a much lamented 'Lord Nelson' class 4-6-0, No. 30865 *Sir John Hawkins*. The class dominated the Bournemouth line until replaced by Bulleid Pacifics in 1962. Duty No. 393 had a WC class rostered in the 1966 diagrams. Note the 4COR unit in the background.

P. J. Winding

Duty No. 400
4MT 2-6-4T BR Standard

	Bournemouth Loco	0615	||
0617	Bournemouth Ctl	0640	P
0715	Brockenhurst	0800	E
	work the Lymington branch until		
1829	Brockenhurst		
	F. shunting 1855 to 1955		
	Brockenhurst	2022	||
2108	Eastleigh Loco	2253	||
xx	Eastleigh	2323	V
0052	Bournemouth Ctl	xx	||
xx	Bournemouth Loco		

Bournemouth men start the duty and are relieved at 0750 at Brockenhurst by Lymington men who work the branch passenger train until 1830 when Bournemouth men take over and finish the duty. Two sets of Lymington men are involved.

Duty No. 401
4MT 2-6-4T BR Standard

	Bournemouth Loco	0645	||
0647	Bournemouth Ctl	0708	P
0835	Weymouth	xx	||
xx	Weymouth Loco	1140	||
xx	Weymouth	1210	P
1505	Southampton Term.	1710	P
1828	Bournemouth Ctl	xx	||
xx	Bournemouth Loco		

Bournemouth men (two sets) have all the work on local passenger trains. 1st set is on duty at 0600, 2nd set is on duty at 1330.

Duty No. 402
4MT 2-6-4T BR Standard

	Bournemouth Loco	0800	||
xx	Bournemouth Ctl Goods	0838	F
0851	Christchurch	0935	F
1055	Bournemouth Ctl Goods	xx	||
xx	Bournemouth Loco	1719	||
1745	Hamworthy Junction O/R	(bank) 1802	E
1818	Branksome	1821	||
1833	Hamworthy Junction	1914	E
1940	Bournemouth West (propel)	1945	E
1950	Bournemouth West Sdgs	2003	||
2018	Poole (bank)	2050	F
2102	Branksome	2108	||
2114	Poole (bank)	2150	F
2205	Bournemouth Ctl Goods	xx	||
xx	Bournemouth Loco		

Two sets of Bournemouth men have all the work which includes banking 'on rear' from Hamworthy Junction to Branksome.

Heading for Bournemouth Bulleid Pacific No. 34085 *501 Squadron* makes plenty of clag as the 08.30 Newcastle to Bournemouth passes the flying junction with the West of England line on 19th June 1965. Southern engines worked through from Oxford.

BR Standard No. 73085 *Melisande* works the 2.20pm Bournemouth to Waterloo near Basingstoke on 25th July 1964. Twenty of the BR Class 5 4-6-0s were named after scrapped 'King Arthurs'.

Maunsell's U class 2-6-0s were used on passenger trains as well as freight. They differed from the N class in that they had larger driving wheels. U class No. 31791 started life as a 'River' class 2-6-4 tank in 1925. Built as No. A791 *River Adur* in 1925, the engine was converted to a 2-6-0 tender locomotive in 1928 and withdrawn in 1966. It is seen with a Bulleid set about to depart from Havant with an LCGB special commemorating the closure of the Hayling Island branch on 3rd November 1963.

Duty No. 403
4MT 2-6-4T BR Standard

	Bournemouth Loco	1405	‖
xx	Bournemouth Ctl Goods	1420	E
1425	Bournemouth Ctl	xx	‖
xx	Bournemouth Loco	1758	‖
1755	Bournemouth Ctl		
	C. shunting 1755 to 2000		
	Bournemouth Ctl	2000	‖
xx	Bournemouth Loco		

Bournemouth men work local trips and shunts. One set signs on at 1320 works the 1405‖ and disposes the engine on Bournemouth Loco.

Duty No. 404
2MT 2-6-2T Ivatt

	Lymington Loco	0545	‖
0547	Lymington Town	0602	P
0617	Brockenhurst	0704	P
0721	Lymington Pier	0730	P
0744	Brockenhurst	0756	P
0832	Bournemouth Ctl	0838	E
0846	Branksome O/R	0851	E
0901	Bournemouth West	xx	‖
xx	Sidings	0955	E
1000	Branksome	1008	‖
1023	Poole (bank)	1030	P
1049	Bournemouth Ctl	1058	‖
1100	Bournemouth Loco	1323	‖
1350	Bournemouth West Goods	1425	F 'Q'
1435	Branksome Yard		
	F. shunting 1435 to 1550		
	Branksome Yard	1623	F
1633	Poole Yard	1635	‖
1648	Bournemouth Loco	1752	‖
1824	Brockenhurst	1838	P
1902	Lymington Pier	1948	P
2004	Brockenhurst	2050	P
2102	Lymington Town	xx	‖
xx	Lymington Loco		

Lymington men start the 0545 and work the branch until relieved by Bournemouth men at 0750. Bournemouth men work the rest of the duty until 1830 when Lymington resume work and dispose.

Duty No. 405
2MT 2-6-2T Ivatt

	Bournemouth Loco	0535	‖
0622	Wareham	0635	E
0657	Swanage		
	work Swanage branch until		
1726	Wareham	1745	P
1812	Dorchester South	1822	E
1901	Poole	1933	‖
1944	Branksome	2008	E
2018	Bournemouth West	2023	E
2033	Sidings	2120	‖
2125	Bournemouth West	2155	F
2200	Branksome O/R	2205	E
2213	Bournemouth Ctl	xx	‖
xx	Bournemouth Loco		

Bournemouth men start the turn for which they book on at 0450 to prepare. Swanage men take over at 1155 at Wareham and work the branch until 1737 when they are relieved by Bournemouth men who complete the duty.

Duty No. 406
2MT 2-6-2T Ivatt

	Bournemouth Loco	0438	‖
0508	Bournemouth West Sdgs		
	C. shunting 0510 to 2140		
	Bournemouth West Sdgs	2140	E
2142	Bournemouth West	2214	‖
	(with 426 D/L)		
xx	Bournemouth Loco		

Bournemouth men (three sets) cover the Bournemouth West pilot with C. shunting and empty stock working.

196

Wareham, with a Weymouth train arriving behind Class 5 4-6-0 No. 73017, and the Swanage branch train with M7 class No. 30129 waiting in the platform, on 18th May 1963. The Swanage branch was later operated with Class 2 and 4 Standard tanks which replaced the aged M7s. The branch was worked by Bournemouth as well as Swanage men (duties 405-408) and closed on 3rd January 1972.

Lymington Town had its own shed which opened in 1858 with the line, and housed the branch engine which, in 1966 was a Class 2 2-6-2T. The line was the last steam worked passenger branch on the Region, and No. 41224 was one of the last locomotives to be in steam on the night of 9th July 1967. Lymington had its own men (duty No. 404).

M. Wilkins

Southampton Docks was the haunt of the USA class 0-6-0 side tanks, known in the USA as switchers. The Southern purchased 15 of these standard US Army Transportation Corp engines in 1946 (including one for spares), and put them to work in the docks. Some later found their way into preservation and can be seen today. No. 69, in plain Southern black, is seen at work in 1947. Duties Nos 325-329 at Eastleigh refer.

Frank Moss

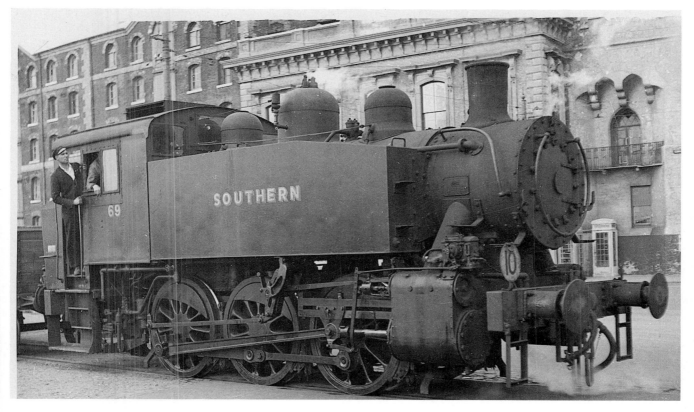

Duty No. 407

4MT 2-6-4T BR Standard

	Bournemouth Loco	0545	‖
xx	Bournemouth	0600	V
0605	Bournemouth Ctl Goods	xx	‖
xx	Bournemouth Loco	0820	‖
xx	Bournemouth Ctl O/R	0838	E
0846	Branksome	0851	E
0901	Bournemouth West (propel)	0906	E
0916	West Sidings	0930	‖
0945	Poole Yard	1010	F
1030	Wareham		
	F. shunting 1030 to 1145		
	Wareham	1155	F
1207	Furzebrook Sidings	1307	F
1313	Wareham	1325	P
	work Swanage branch passenger until		
2007	Swanage	2010	‖
xx	Bournemouth Loco		

Bournemouth men work until 1130 when they are relieved by a Swanage driver who works with a Bournemouth fireman until relieved by a Bournemouth set at 1700 who work and dispose.

Duty No. 408

4MT 2-6-4T BR Standard

	Bournemouth Loco	0100	‖
0120	Bournemouth Ctl		
	C. shunting 0120 to 0445		
	Bournemouth Ctl	0655	‖
0715	Poole	0735	F
0813	Blandford Forum	1003	F
1050	Poole	1110	‖
1130	Bournemouth Loco	1630	‖
xx	Bournemouth Ctl	1702	P
1800	Swanage	1817	P
1839	Wareham	1852	P
1914	Swanage	2025	P
2047	Wareham	2127	P
2149	Swanage	xx	‖
xx	Swanage Loco		
	stable for No. 409		

Weymouth men work the 0100‖ off shed and are relieved at 0205 by Bournemouth men who have the rest of the work (four sets) until 1737 when Swanage men take over at Wareham and complete the duty. The morning freight runs to Blandford on the former Somerset & Dorset which closed on 6th January 1969.

Duty No. 409

4MT 2-6-4T BR Standard

OFF No. 408

	Swanage Loco	0715	‖
xx	Swanage	0740	P
	work branch passenger until		
1247	Wareham	1330	F
1405	Poole	1427	‖
1446	Bournemouth Loco	1730	‖
xx	Bournemouth Ctl	1750	EBV 'Q'
1830	Bailey Gate	1903	F
1945	Bournemouth Ctl	2105	F
2113	Branksome	2259	E
2309	Bournemouth West (propel)	2315	E
xx	Sidings	2346	‖
xx	Branksome	0036	E
0046	Bournemouth West (propel)	0051	E
xx	Sidings	0103	‖
xx	Bournemouth Loco		

Swanage men start the 0715‖ work the branch until 1125 when they are relieved by Bournemouth men at Wareham. Bournemouth men work the duty and do a freight trip to Bailey Gate or Wool as required before completing the duty. Bailey Gate was on the Somerset & Dorset and closed on 6th January 1969.

Southampton Docks, before the USA tanks arrived, was the preserve of the LSWR B4 class 0-4-0 tanks, built in 1891 for shunting. Southampton shed with three of the class visible can be seen here on 26th July 1947. Two members of this class have survived into preservation.

Lens of Sutton

Duty No. 411
4MT 2-6-4T BR Standard

	Bournemouth Loco	0515	‖
XX	Bournemouth Ctl	0544	P
0706	Eastleigh	XX	‖
XX	Eastleigh Loco	0810	‖
XX	Eastleigh	0838	P
1005	Bournemouth Ctl	1056	E
1104	Branksome	1204	E
1212	Bournemouth Ctl	1256	E
1304	Branksome	1403	E
1411	Bournemouth Ctl	XX	‖
XX	Bournemouth Loco (with 384)	1550	‖
1620	Branksome	1653	E
1703	Bournemouth West (propel)	1708	E
1713	West Sdgs	1759	E
1804	Branksome	1838	E
1848	Bournemouth West (propel)	1853	E
1858	West Sdgs	1931	‖
1936	Branksome	1940	E
1950	Bournemouth West (propel)	1955	E
2000	West Sdgs	2028	‖
2033	Branksome	2050	E
2100	Bournemouth West (propel)	2105	E
2110	West Sdgs	2120	‖
2125	Branksome	2205	E
2213	Bournemouth Ctl	XX	‖
XX	Bournemouth Loco		

Bournemouth men (three sets) work empty stock between Bournemouth and Branksome after an early morning trip to Eastleigh and back.

Duty No. 412
2MT 2-6-2T Ivatt

	Bournemouth Loco (with 381)	0618	‖
	(via Branksome)		
0652	Bournemouth West Sdgs		
	work empty stock to Branksome and shunting until		
1930	Bournemouth West Sdgs	2030	‖
2051	Bournemouth Loco		

Bournemouth men work local empty stock and carriage shunting with a Class 2 2-6-2T nicknamed "Mickey Mouses" by the engine men. Two Bournemouth sets one on duty at 0528 the other on duty at 1500.

Duty No. 413
4MT 2-6-4T BR Standard

	Bournemouth Loco (with 385 to Ctl)	0736	‖
	(via Branksome)		
0802	Bournemouth West		
	work empty stock to Branksome and shunting until		
2155	Bournemouth West	2214	‖
XX	Bournemouth Loco		

Bournemouth men (two sets) work local empty stock and shunting. The passenger service from Bournemouth West was withdrawn on 6th September 1965. The site is now occupied by a road scheme.

Swanage station in BR days with M7 No. 30129 and Maunsell two-set of which there were 20 formed in 1960–61. The scene has changed little today although closed on 3rd January 1972 by BR. Two M7s are preserved, Nos 30053 and 30245, the former having been purchased from Steamtown USA and repatriated to the UK.

Lymington Town station had an overall roof and the trains were worked by M7 class 0-4-4Ts until replaced by Class 2 2-6-2s of the Ivatt design. The Ivatt 2-6-2s worked the branch until electrification in 1967. M7 No. 30029 as seen there on 6th July 1962.

Duty Nos 414 to 419 NOT USED

Duty Nos 420 to 429
Diesel rosters.

WEYMOUTH

Duty No. 430
8P MN class (large tender)

	Weymouth Loco	0645	‖
XX	Weymouth	0730	P
1102	Waterloo	1133	‖
1146	Nine Elms Loco	1558	‖
1613	Waterloo	1635	P
2015	Weymouth	2030	‖
2035	Weymouth Loco		

Weymouth men have some main line work as far as Bournemouth Central where they are relieved at 0830. Bournemouth men work to Waterloo where they are relieved by Nine Elms men at 1102. Nine Elms men work back to Bournemouth Central where Weymouth men relieve at 1909 and finish the duty.

Duty No. 431
8P MN class
OFF No. 434

	Weymouth Loco	0835	‖
XX	Weymouth	0921	P
1303	Waterloo	1332	‖
1343	Nine Elms Loco	1658	‖
1712	Waterloo	1730	P
2028	Bournemouth Ctl	2037	E
2045	Branksome	2057	‖
2107	Bournemouth Loco	2310	‖

(Continued)

2312	Bournemouth Ctl	2337	P
0034	Southampton Ctl	0037	‖
0042	Southampton Term.	0121	P
0411	Waterloo	0458	‖
0510	Nine Elms Loco		

Bournemouth men work to 1021 at Bournemouth Central when Nine Elms men step onto the footplate and work round to 1912 when they in turn are relieved by Eastleigh men who work to Bournemouth Central at 2028. Bournemouth men take over at 2028 and work until 0132 when they are relieved by Nine Elms men who complete the duty.

Duty No. 432
OFF No. 431
spare at Nine Elms Loco
Work No. 433

Duty No. 433
8P MN class
OFF No. 432

	Nine Elms Loco	1257	‖
1312	Waterloo	1330	P
1752	Weymouth	xx	‖
xx	Weymouth Loco	1945	‖
xx	Weymouth	2015	P
2119	Bournemouth Ctl	xx	‖
xx	Bournemouth Loco		

Nine Elms men work to Waterloo where Bournemouth men take over at 1320 and work on the engine until the end of the duty. Weymouth men prepare the 1945‖.

Duty No. 434
8P MN class
OFF No. 433

	Bournemouth Loco	0551	‖
	(with 276)		
0616	Bournemouth West Sdgs	0633	E
0638	Branksome	0658	E
0706	Bournemouth Ctl	0724	P
1009	Waterloo	1041	‖
1054	Nine Elms Loco	1155	‖
1210	Waterloo	1230	P
1445	Bournemouth Ctl	1449	E
1457	Branksome	1504	‖
1517	Bournemouth Loco	2100	‖
2102	Bournemouth Ctl	2126	P
2245	Eastleigh	2250	‖
2255	East Yard	2325	F
2345	Northam Yard	2355	‖
0007	Southampton Ctl	0042	P
0047	Southampton Term. (2235 Wloo)	0127	P
0346	Weymouth	xx	‖
xx	Weymouth Loco		
	Work No. 431		

Bournemouth men take the 0551‖ off shed to Bournemouth West bring the empties in for the 0724 and work to Waterloo. Nine Elms men relieve at Waterloo at 1009 and prepare the engine for the 1230 being relieved at Waterloo at 1220 by Bournemouth men who work the engine and dispose at 1517. Eastleigh men work the 2100‖ and are relieved at 0223 by Weymouth men who take the engine home.

Bulleid Pacific No. 34042 *Dorchester* heads a Waterloo–Weymouth train near Poole; a Bournemouth duty for a Bournemouth engine.

Victor Hand

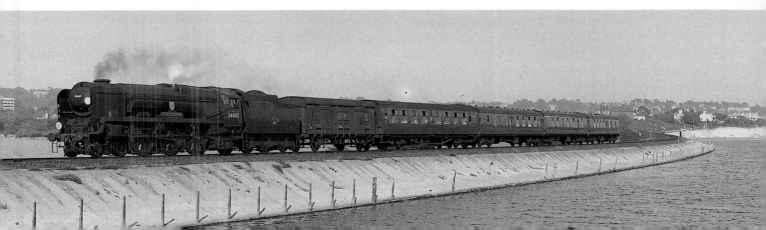

Duty No. 435
8P MN class

	Weymouth Loco	1050	‖
1055	Weymouth	1125	P
1451	Waterloo	1512	‖
1525	Nine Elms Loco	1757	‖
1812	Waterloo	1830	P
2158	Weymouth	xx	‖
xx	Weymouth Loco		

Weymouth men are relieved at Bournemouth at 1229. Bournemouth men take over at 1229 and have the engine until 2052 when they are relieved by Weymouth men who work and dispose.

Duty No. 436
8P MN class

	Weymouth Loco	0615	‖
xx	Weymouth	0643	P
0806	Bournemouth Ctl	0825	‖
0833	Branksome	0910	E
0918	Bournemouth Ctl	0924	P
1157	Waterloo	1222	‖
1234	Nine Elms Loco (with 393)	1457	‖
1512	Waterloo	1530	P
1926	Weymouth	xx	‖
xx	Weymouth Loco		

Weymouth men start the duty and are relieved at Bournemouth Central at 0920. Bournemouth men work to Waterloo and back and work round to Weymouth where they are relieved by Weymouth men who dispose the loco.

Duty Nos 437 to 439 NOT USED

Duty No. 440
5MT 4-6-0 BR Standard

	Weymouth Loco	0745	‖
xx	Weymouth	0815	P
0834	Dorchester West	0920	‖
0937	Weymouth	1015	P
1139	Bournemouth Ctl	1150	‖
1152	Bournemouth Loco	1400	‖
1402	Bournemouth Ctl		
	C. shunting and steam heating		
	Bournemouth Ctl	1501	P
1630	Weymouth	xx	‖
xx	Weymouth Loco		

Weymouth men start the duty but Bournemouth men take over and work from 0937 until 1152. Weymouth men work the 1400‖ and complete the duty.

Duty No. 441
5MT 4-6-0 BR Standard
OFF No. 442

	Weymouth Loco	0640	‖
xx	Weymouth	0710	E
0728	Dorchester South	0740	P
0755	Weymouth	xx	‖
xx	Weymouth Loco	1020	‖
xx	Weymouth	1055	F
1110	Dorchester South		
	F. shunting 1215 to 1300		
	Dorchester South	1315	F
1338	Weymouth	xx	‖
xx	Weymouth Loco	1545	‖
xx	Weymouth Junction (bank)	1623	P
1630	Bincombe	1635	‖
1645	Weymouth	1741	P
1900	Bournemouth Ctl	xx	‖
xx	Bournemouth Loco		
	stable for No. 442		

Weymouth men have all the work which includes banking the 1623 passenger up to Bincombe. Three sets are utilised.

Duty No. 442
5MT 4-6-0 BR Standard
stabled off No. 441

	Location		
	Bournemouth Loco	0445	‖
xx	Bournemouth Ctl	0515	V
0650	Weymouth	xx	‖
xx	Weymouth Loco	0755	‖
xx	Weymouth	0827	P
0945	Bournemouth Ctl	xx	‖
xx	Bournemouth Loco	1530	‖
xx	Bournemouth Ctl	1552	P
1721	Eastleigh	1925	P
2131	Bournemouth Ctl	2258	P
0009	Weymouth	xx	‖
xx	Weymouth Loco		
	Work No. 441		

Bournemouth men have an early start at 0345 and are relieved at Weymouth Loco. Weymouth men work the 0755‖ and dispose on Bournemouth Loco. Bournemouth men start the 1530‖ and are relieved at Southampton Central at 2000 by Weymouth men who complete the duty.

Duty No. 443
5MT 4-6-0 BR Standard

	Location		
	Weymouth Loco	0715	‖
xx	Weymouth	0749	P
0859	Bournemouth	0913	E
0921	Branksome	0929	‖
0940	Bournemouth Loco	1030	‖
1032	Bournemouth Ctl	1051	P
	(0930 Wloo)		
1147	Weymouth	xx	‖
xx	Weymouth Loco		

One set of Weymouth men on at 0615 have this nice little turn.

Duty Nos 444 to 451 & 453 to 460 NOT USED

Duty No. 452
2MT 2-6-2T Ivatt

	Location		
	Weymouth Loco	1330	‖
xx	Dorchester West		
	C. shunting 1400 to 1530		
	Dorchester West	xx	‖
xx	Dorchester South	1750	P
1805	Weymouth (bank)	1825	P
1840	Bincombe	1850	‖
1900	Weymouth Loco		

Weymouth men have a local trips and shunts turn including banking to Bincombe.

No. 35022 *Holland America Line* heads uphill from Weymouth with a light train of Bulleid stock bound for Bournemouth and Waterloo. The engine was withdrawn in 1966 but is now at Swanage awaiting restoration.
Victor Hand

'Merchant Navy' class No. 35026 *Lamport & Holt Line* approaches Bincombe Tunnel with an up Weymouth to Waterloo train. The Bulleid Pacifics worked these trains until electrification from Waterloo to Bournemouth in 1967. The Weymouth portions were worked from Bournemouth by detachable TC units which were diesel hauled from July 1967. The engine was withdrawn in March 1967.

Victor Hand

Duty Nos 456 to 460 Diesel rosters.

SALISBURY

Duty No. 461
7P/6F WC class
OFF No. 463

	Salisbury Loco	0600	‖
xx	West Sdgs	0625	E
xx	Salisbury	0649	P
0916	Waterloo	1002	E
1012	Clapham Junction	1040	‖
1055	Nine Elms Loco (with 161)	1732	‖
1747	Waterloo	1800	P
1952	Salisbury	xx	‖
xx	Salisbury Loco		

Salisbury men work the 0600‖ and are relieved at 0930 at Waterloo. Nine Elms men take over at 0930 work and dispose. A late turn set prepare the 1732‖ and are relieved at Waterloo at 1750 by Salisbury men who finish the duty.

Duty No. 462
7P/6F WC class

	Salisbury Loco	1805	‖
xx	Salisbury	1835	P
2029	Waterloo	2053	‖
2105	Nine Elms Loco		
	stable for No. 463		

Salisbury men prepare the 1805‖ for Basingstoke men who relieve at 1830 and work to Basingstoke at 1925. Nine Elms men take over at 1925 and complete the duty.

Duty No. 463
7P/6F WC class
OFF No. 462

	Nine Elms Loco	0500	‖
0515	Waterloo	0530	P
0910	Bournemouth Ctl	0925	‖
xx	Bournemouth Loco	1205	‖
xx	Bournemouth Ctl	1259	P
1609	Waterloo	1627	‖
1640	Nine Elms Loco	1827	‖
1842	Waterloo	1854	P
2144	Salisbury	xx	‖
xx	Salisbury Loco		
	Work No. 461		

Nine Elms men have all the work but Bournemouth men prepare the 1205 at Bournemouth Loco and Salisbury men take the engine home after relieving at Waterloo at 1844.

Duty No. 464
7P/6F WC class

	Location	Time	
	Salisbury Loco	0710	‖
xx	West Sidings	0730	E
xx	Salisbury	0746	P
0939	Waterloo	1012	‖
1024	Nine Elms Loco	1121	‖
1136	Waterloo	1154	V
1348	Basingstoke	xx	‖
xx	Basingstoke Loco	1600	‖
xx	Basingstoke	1651	P
1803	Salisbury	xx	‖
xx	Salisbury Loco		

Salisbury men are relieved at 1348 at Basingstoke by Basingstoke men who work on the engine until 1803. A second set of Salisbury men relieve at 1803 and dispose the engine.

Duty No. 465
4MT 2-6-4T BR Standard

	Location	Time	
	Salisbury Loco	0730	‖
xx	Salisbury		
	C. shunting 0735 to 0935		
	Salisbury	0935	‖
xx	Salisbury Loco	1050	‖
xx	Salisbury	1119	V
	Southampton Term. (turn)	1256	V
1430	Fratton	1435	‖
1440	Fratton Loco	1700	‖
1710	Portsmouth & S'Sea	1745	V
1938	Salisbury	xx	‖
xx	Salisbury Loco		

Salisbury men have all the work including turning the engine at Southampton Terminus Loco sidings. Two sets of Salisbury men work the engine.

Duty Nos 466 to 500 NOT USED

Salisbury had an allocation of Class 4 2-6-4 tanks which could be seen on main line work. No. 80145 heads the 07.18 Waterloo to Salisbury near Pirbright Junction on 10th June 1967, on a Saturday only working.

Salisbury station at the north end in July 1962 with No. 34056 *Croydon* on an up West of England train consisting of a Bulleid coach leading followed by an LNER Thompson vehicle. The Exmouth Junction engine worked through but Exmouth Junction men were relieved at Salisbury.

The 18.54 Waterloo to Salisbury was a regular steam working in the last year of steam on the Region. Here, No. 34021 *Dartmoor* passes Earlsfield on 13th June 1967. Nine Elms men have the work on duty No. 463. The 4-6-2s had been rostered away from Nine Elms by 1966 as part of the run down of the depot.

The Salisbury pilot was an M7 until replaced by a Class 4 Standard tank. No. 30033 is seen here with horseboxes and a Bulleid coach which was detached from the down "Atlantic Coast Express" and put on to an all-stations down train.

The Isle of Wight was steam worked until 31st December 1966 but the engine workings were published separately from those on the mainland. The locomotives were all O2 class 0-4-4 tanks of ex-LSWR Adams vintage dating from the 19th century. Here, No. 24 *Calbourne*, now the sole survivor, is seen at Newport taking water.

A general view of Ventnor with an O2 running round the train for Ryde. The station layout here was of interest as the island platform was isolated and had to be reached by a 'draw-bridge' at the country end. Ventnor closed to all traffic on 31st December 1966 and the site is an industrial estate with the caves still in use for storage.

Depot Workings Featured

South Eastern Division – London East District

Ashford	68
Bricklayers Arms	20
Dover	83
Faversham	50
Folkestone Junction	82
Foreign engine workings	101
Gillingham	46
Hither Green	33
Ramsgate	91
St Leonards	78
Stewarts Lane	7
Tonbridge	57

Central Division

Bricklayers Arms	107
Brighton	144
Electric loco duties	161
Foreign engine workings	164
Norwood Junction	113
Redhill	119
Stewarts Lane	102
Three Bridges	135
Tunbridge Wells West	125

South Western Division

Bournemouth	192
Eastleigh	177
Guildford	171
Nine Elms	165
Salisbury	204
Weymouth	200

The last days of the Bluebell line in BR ownership. A Class 4 tank leaves Newick & Chailey for Sheffield Park, 15th March 1958.

Erratum The caption for the top picture on the back of the jacket should read: An Ivatt Class 2 2-6-2T works an empty stock train into Clapham Yard on 14th January 1967.